The Raven's Quill

INDRODUCTION

Disclaimer: Trying to be uber efficient I sorted the titles in the table of contents alphabetically. After doing so, I realized that meant that there would be no chorological order to this book. Aarg. I am not typing them all again so be it. My book shall be eclectic as I am.

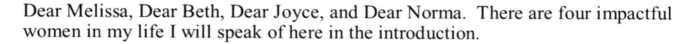

I will never discount the encouragement of my life partner, my one true love, my best friend, my husband, Don. He gets a whole chapter. Our son Josh is making our lives so much easier and is always encouraging too. There are so many other encouragers... but I have to mention our good friends Art and Larry. Monday mornings we all get together and solve all the world's problems. Fridays are like that too with our art family.

Dear Melissa, Dear Beth, Dear Joyce, and Dear Norma. There are four impactful women in my life I will speak of here in the introduction.

"Dear Melissa, How I cherish that we text each other nearly daily and often many times in a day." Just last week I whined... "I used to be wash and wear; now it takes me a long time to get ready for the day. I have morning medications, special shampoo for my scalp, hypoallergenic sunblock for my face, nasal spray for my allergies, drops for my dry eyes, denture adhesive for my partials..." (Cleaning my teeth is a whole process in its self. For the sake of good taste we will stop right there and not proceed to discuss preparations below the chin.) She promptly replied, "Try 8 hours of dialysis, every night, for a year, in a cabin in Alaska." Reality! Melissa is my dear sister and great friend. We have been friends since she was born and have shared amazing adventures throughout our lives. Our lives are busy, mine here in the Blue Ridge Mountains and hers on an island in the middle of nowhere Alaska. Living on an Alaskan island, surviving the winters in a cabin with a wood stove, and living a subsistence life is never a picnic. It is hard work day in and day out. I admire her and her husband Vern greatly, especially that they do this with such thought, grace, purpose and enthusiasm.

Don and I lived in that cabin for a summer while we built our own cabin. I picture in my mind the half inch wide cracks in the floor caused by moving the cabin back after the island sank in the 1964 Earthquake. No picnic!

When we were there those cracks had been filling for half a decade. Seriously, no amount of sweeping was going to make a bit of difference. Intense sweeping at one point made me realize that actually the dirt packed in those cracks was creating a packing, calking, insulation of sorts. Year-round Alaska can gift you with cold breezes when you are half dressed in the morning. I had to tell myself, "Walk away from the cracks, Phoebe!!"

I mention this because in order to perform home dialysis, strict sterilization rules must be employed. Dialysis liquid, delivered to the beach monthly by the mail boat had to be carefully prevented from freezing. Her husband is an amazing can-do-it all kind of guy. His son had a liver transplant so he has experience. Between the two of them my sister endured not a single infection in that year.

Alaska has stunningly beautiful scenery and the summer months are primo weather. We have seen it snow in September and in May, so June, July and August are the months to do things outside, to grow produce, and to enjoy the beauty you work to live in. You might think that produce can't grow in three months, but you can in Alaska. Summer months there experience very little darkness, the opposite of winter. Winter there are only a few hours of dusky, but not dark, night. Summer light and the peat mossy soil make cabbages grow to the size of a small car. Summer months are planting and tending the garden, gathering and canning the food for the winter months, and this means working out the storage so none of it freezes over the winter in a cabin with a wood stove. They love the solitude and the isolation. They love living companionably with nature through the seasons and for them, every bit of work is worth it all when they live in one of the most beautiful spots on earth. Photos by Melissa with the exception of the top photo of the two of us as children.
Thank you Melissa.

'Dear Beth, I love how our sharing makes both our lives richer."

Beth is our niece and she came to live with us in Alaska for a summer. That summer she became more of a daughter than a niece (photos top two right).

Later she would live with us for 6 months when she started her life over (photos second down). Once we moved to North Carolina she filled my grandmother heart by sharing her daughters, as did her sister Tiffany. Those daughters, those girls and I had magnificent times together for over a decade of my life. (third photo down)Now they are grown up. One of them, and grandmother Beth, are sharing the next generation with me.

I taught Beth to Quill; she taught me to make good Southern biscuits. After I punctured my hand trying to get an avocado pit out, she got me the best avocado tool ever and it won't cut your hand. We sew together, make art together and garden and clean together.

Her life has in many ways been a mirror of mine. Similar troubles endured, harsh enough trials that you think you cannot go on, and grand adventures dared. These small things have cemented a relationship begun in her youth.

Now she comes and gardens with me. She helps me with hard work I can no longer do. She brings her grandson and shares an evening with us once a week and I so look forward to that.

Thank you Beth, for being in my life.

"Dear Joyce, I hope this letter finds you well." Joyce and I served together in the headquarters of the Alaska Air National Guard. She was an amazing woman I am proud to have called a friend. A degreed psychologist, she was the first person to write a terrorist profile for Interpol. In the Air Force she was tasked to go to bases where there had been an airframe loss to help the survivors deal with the trauma. She saw so much and was one of the movers and shakers that helped make national programs to help first responders long before we hit the year 2000. A 30-year Air Force Veteran, we became friends when she joined the Alaska Air National Guard. We worked together in the Headquarters on Fort Richardson in Anchorage. She joined our family 'Friday Night' gatherings in Anchorage getting to know us as a family, to know my mother, my siblings and our kids. Over all the years  we kept emailing, calling and writing. I very much enjoyed making her long letters with lots of pictures telling her about our lives. She told me she loved getting them and read them more than once. She was also a kind supporter of our art school. Sadly she passed in September 2023 before I got this book done. Thank you Joyce for your friendship, I sure miss you!

"Dear Norma, thank you so for your continued loving encouragement." Norma was once an art student of my husband, although I sometimes wonder if she didn't just attend his classes for the fellowship. She is an excellent artist who was juried into the permanent display at NCCCA in Raleigh [North Carolina Community College Association]. She joins us for our Open Studio Sessions and has become a dear friend. I don't remember how it started but at her encouragement I began printing off my weekly writings and giving them to her to read. She told  me she loved reading them and with her difficult life, it was the joy she saved for her one free day a week, Thursdays. She also told me I have to write a novel about my military service, so Norma, I'm trying. I will name it 'A Novel Approach' and it has now gone beyond the military years. Thank you Norma for encouraging me.

These are just some of the encouragers in my life but there is one more, my mother, she gets a whole chapter.

Onward and upward we go!

A week ago, I brazenly stated in Open Studio that I was writing a novel. Several people, my husband being the primary proofer, have read chapters as I have written them. When I announced that, several said, "No you are writing an autobiography." I didn't want to write an autobiography, I wanted to write a novel. I delved into definitions and found that an autobiographical novel (as defined by writers.com) is any work of fiction that is based on the real-life events of the author.

Hello, let me introduce myself. I am an alien as far as being able to understand human social mores of the society in which I live. In my mind I imagine I am a Selkie. After all it explains my love of the water. Something terrible must have happened to me when I was young and the trauma of that event has so far prevented me from transforming and returning to the sea.

I can almost talk to animals; I talk to our dog and he understands. When I say, "School" he turns left exiting the house and goes directly to our school. This is just a pinch of the skill I think I once possessed. I used to be able to talk more to animals. My first pet was a hamster I got when I was 4 years old. He was a handsome and smart hamster. He would stand on his hind legs, put his front paws on the top of my hand, look into my eyes, and we would talk. We would share simple love thoughts and both felt better after. I promised him I would be the best pet owner a pet could want.

My older sister got a pet that day too. She got a rat. If I have any prejudice' it would be against rats. Rats are harmful to humans. The carry diseases. They bite and share those diseases. They poop out contaminated poop and bring nasty stuff into places they live which hopefully is not where you live too. They can chew though nearly anything. That night that rat chewed through his enclosure and into my hamster's enclosure. Then he ate him. I do not like rats. I had failed miserably in being the best pet owner. Once I regain the ability to transform and can return to the sea, I will be able to talk to anything living in the sea or on land. I bet if I then stuck my head up out of the water and spoke to a sneaky rat on a ship it would confirm my thoughts. I would find truly that they are not nice creatures; they are selfish and as mean as mean gets.

I remember vaguely one Selkie journey with my beloved grandmother. She was kind and gentle and loved me very much. She took me on an adventure to visit with whales. Whales are the seers of the ocean. They are scholars of the finest order. They are genius deep thinkers. They are also kind and have the most amazing sense of humor. They are simply wonderful story tellers. You know I love to laugh, and to talk, and to listen, and since we did all that, it was one amazing adventure. I will share that tale in a future chapter.

As an alien I have had difficulty understanding life. Some say that we create our own destiny. I have to ardently refute this because that would mean I chose to have all the sad, bad and crazy stuff that happened to me in my life so far. That is what eventually brought me around to the solid belief in God. I had a solid belief as a child. As things piled up on me in life so heavy, I could hardly breathe, I doubted. I would say to myself, "Surely God would not want me to endure this thing!" I cried myself to sleep a time or two and other times went to sleep so flaming mad that I smelled a burn smell in the morning.

Finally, I come to recognize several facts about myself. First, I have by necessity learned an overly developed sense of self-defense. I lost the use of it for a while when I stopped believing in myself. Second, I can be stubborn. (I hear my husband making rude noises. I see his noise and raise: "that is the pot calling the kettle black." He too vies for the title of World's Most Stubborn—what a pair we are. Maybe I did indeed create some things in my life by how I reacted. Perhaps because of my stubbornness and rigid self-defense, God figured I needed more or longer lessons in life. One day I will know the truth.

My life was a series of storms and adventures and more storms, often with no time between storms, until I was quite weary. Then God sent me Don. The things he has done for my boys have freed my heart. He had no part in birthing Nicholas, but I know for a fact he loved him as though he had. We sorrowed deep and together upon his passing.

Now my life is a tropical garden with no bugs or snakes. This Alaskan girl cannot come to grips with snakes being acceptable and bugs being necessary. Sure, I understand that the many good bugs are absolutely necessary—intellectually—or God would not have created them, but do there really have to be so many? I wonder, do Southerners just become immune to bugs sharing their living spaces? Or, is there some secret hormone that they exude that prevents the bugs from coming too near them?

My one true love and I have built a life filled with joy and love and fun. We have the best friends and great times together. We have family close and share times that fill our hearts. We have a mission to use our talents for God's glory and we are pursuing it with all we have. The flowers that are blooming in this tropical garden of ours are unlike any that ever bloomed on earth. They are so beautiful they bring tears to my eyes and great joy to my heart and to the hearts of others. This tropical garden is a sanctuary that is changing lives for the better.

What is fiction and what is fact? You have to decide which is which in this eclectic autobiographical novel.

TABLE OF CONTENTS

1 - Copyright Page
2 - Introduction
3 - Table of Contents
4 - All About Don
5 - Amazing Children Part 1 Andrew
6 - Amazing Children Part 2 Nicholas
7 - Amazing Children Part 3 Christopher
8 - Amazing Children Part 4 James
9 - Amazing Children Part 5 Joshua
10 - Amazing Children Part 6 Jennifer
11 - Amazing Children Part 7 Elizabeth
12 - Bathroom Tiles
13 - Childhood Memories
14 - Different Childhood
15 - Ever so Long Ago
16 - Everything I Could Want
17 - Falling In Love
18 - Family Stories
19 - Freedom and Liberty
20 - I Guess You Might be Wondering About
     Phoebe
21 - Lost Loves
22 - Mary Engelbreit's Art
23 - Military Honors
24 - Military Part 1 - Basic Training
25 - Military Part 2 - Technical School
26 - Military Part 3 - Spangdahlem AB, Germany
27 - Military Part 4 - Altus AFB, Oklahoma
28 - Military Part 5 - Elmendorf AFB, Alaska
29 - Military Part 6 - Alaska Air National Guard
30 - Military Part 7 - Things Wrong
31 - My Mom
32 - Phee Stories
33 - Philosophies of Life and Random Thoughts
34 - Poems
35 - Random Thoughts of Worry
36 - Raven Affairs
37 - Renovation of Doris
38 - See No Evil
39—September
40 - The Quill
41 - Under Aunt Phoebe's Table
42 - Vienna Virginia
43 - ZZ The Finale

ALL ABOUT DON

I married an exceptional man. He creates art that touches people deeply. He does not set out to impress, he sets out to put down what is right, what is in his heart, what has inspired him. Here are some of the stories that are why I love him so.

The story of Laura Lindemuth. Laura Lindemuth won the lottery in the marriage deal too. She and her husband, Paul Lindemuth, were in love with each other from the moment they met. Together sharing great adventures, rearing amazing children, and having a wonderful life. Then suddenly he was struck down in the prime of that life. That has to be the hardest thing one can endure, watching your love be decimated before your eyes and completely unable to do a thing about it. Brigadier General Lindemuth, our base commander, died of Lou Gehrig's disease. After his passing the new operations building at Kulis Air Guard Base was finished and it was decided to dedicate it to him. They asked Don to do a portrait that would hang in the center rotunda. He chose colored pencil and captured the face of a man who was dedicated, handsome, rugged, honest, and patriotic proud! Don asked Laura to view it before the ceremony and she was eager to do so. When she saw it, she cried; she told Don how the disease had eaten away at the man she loved in a horrible manner, changing his very looks. How at the end she could hardly recognize the man she married so wasted from the disease was he; her heart broke with it. She said Don had captured the man that he was and she would be forever grateful for that image of her one true love. Okay maybe she didn't say one true love, my romantic bend took a side trip…but everyone knew they were! They overflowed with enthusiasm from that love and she still sorely missed him. It was a moment.

The story of She Carves. Well actually to do the story of She Carves I first have to tell the story of Coconut Joe, these then are the Hawaii Stories. The first in Don's words: "My wife and I decided to buy some property on the Big Island of Hawaii. In 2000 we took a vacation to the island with our kids to look at that land. On a side trip to Hilo, we went to Rainbow Falls Park. We saw a man sitting in the side door of his van splitting palm fronds with his pocket knife. He would then weave those palm fronds into baskets, hats, and creatures like fish and birds which he then gave to the children visiting the park. Our son Chris was fascinated by him and stood and watched him for a long time. Coconut Joe wove

him a number of creatures. This allowed me time to take great pictures. After asking permission to use his likeness to do some art work, we started asking questions. He told us his name is Coconut Joe and that he traveled to schools all over the Islands of Hawaii to teach the children about their heritage of weaving palm fronds."

Coconut Joe passed from medical issues before we could find him to give him a copy of this print Don did.

The story of She Carves, this time for real. At that same visit in 2000 to Rainbow Falls, on the other side of the parking lot was a woman carving. When we moved to Hawaii in 2003 Don completed first the portrait of Coconut Joe and then the portrait of her. We were clearing our land to build a home, landscaping and working days and although we had gone to the Rainbow Falls and other places in Hilo, we had been unable to ever find her or Coconut Joe again. Hawaii was not for us and in February of 2004 Don left for North Carolina, to find us a house. I stayed in Hawaii with our youngest son to see the completion of our house in Hawaii and sell it. On the last weekend we were there, late in June, I took the artists proofs and set out to find the models of "She Carves" and "Coconut Joe". At Rainbow Falls Park there happened to be workers repairing something near the parking lot so I showed them the prints and I asked them if they knew these two individuals. They explained that Coconut Joe had gotten very ill and had been taken to the mainland for treatment. No one knew if he would ever return. As for the woman who was carving, sure enough they knew her and said she was supposed to be in the Hilo Market that day selling her carvings. I went to the market. It is huge! Over 200 local farmers and crafters sell gift items, tropical flowers, plants, crafts and of course, produce. Under tents it is a festive outdoor atmosphere and is the largest and most popular farmers market on the Big Island of Hawaii and located in the historic downtown Hilo area.

I started at one end showing the print and asking if they knew her. I kept getting sent further and further into the market. It seemed that as soon as I showed the print to the person at the front table that the word passed quicker than I could walk. Whispers, pointing, and people followed me through the market. When I got close enough to see her there was still a table between us. The noise of the crowd whispering, or some intuition, had her turn toward me. I made eye contact and said, "Did you know that you are famous?" "No..." she responded. "Well, you are..." I said, then held up the print. People had crowded in behind me and it seems as if everyone in the market stopped in their tracks to watch. There was an audible gasp from both Leilani (yes, I think that is her name) and others nearby as the impact of Don's print hit everyone. His work carries such great emotion and is so accurate in the portrayal of the person. Leilani put her hands to her cheeks and tears came into her eyes. I rounded the table into her small area and spread the print out on the table for her to see. Everyone was crowded around jostling to see the print and I could hear comments about how it looked just like her.

Once she had had a chance to really look at the print, she looked up at me, tears now freely flowing, and she grabbed me in a hug and told me that I had Blessed her day. I explained that my husband was the artist and had recently completed this portrait. I told her how Don likes to give the model an artist proof and I had brought two prints for her. She hugged me again and then she told me her story.

Right after we had taken her photo at Rainbow Falls, Leilani became deathly ill and was unable to even get up to do any art work for a long time. Just in the last months she had finally recovered enough to carve again. This was her first venture out to sell her work since that day four years earlier. She had been very apprehensive that morning and seriously considered not going. Anxious and feeling as though something were going to happen, and sure she would not be able to handle it, she had come to the market. She had children to support and no money. She kept looking back at the portrait and shaking her head as if she could not believe it. She told me that this had changed the quality of her day, blessing that day, and perhaps even her whole life. By now the crowd was dispersing but people were sharing the story with those not close enough to have heard. As they moved away from us, they chattered… Hawaiians do love a good story. I gave her one last hug and there were still tears in her eyes as I turned to leave. As I walked back out of the market, I tried to record in my memory all the sights, the sounds and feelings of that amazing event to share with Don. All the time I was wishing he could have been there with me to experience the impact he had on this woman's life. It was such a moving moment that I still am overcome with emotion telling the story.

The story of Kit's grandson. This story is a sweet one… A friend of ours, an Air Force Chief Master Sergeant named Christopher 'Kit' Frey, was retiring from the Air Force. In true military style there would be a big woopty-doo ceremony. Don picked out a set of his wildlife prints to send to Kit as a retirement gift. We sent the prints and a few days later Kit sent us a photo of his grandson (right). This two year old child was fascinated by the pen and ink 'Mama's Boy' (left) that

Don had done and spent hours in front of it, staring at the mother and child in wonder. (photo right) He loved it so much, they give it to him .

During his time in the military, Don produced a tremendous number of pieces of art. His dinner dance prints funded the whole event each year. His retirement pieces were very sought after and even used as a gift from the Alaska Air National Guard to the retiring General head of the National Guard Bureau.

We were the first unit to do an exercise on Russian soil. Don was asked to do a commemorative print of this first monumental SAREX (Search and Rescue Exercise) in 1993 (right). The exercise was military units from Alaska, Canada and Russia working together. While we had an existing relationship with Canada, who even had an office near the Alaska Command on Elmendorf Air Force Base, working with the Russians was a whole new thing. Don chose to do a portrait of James Delong. His was an interesting story. His ship got caught in the ice pack off Russia. He split his crew into three groups and each set out in a different direction to find help. Two groups were successful in finding a Native village that helped them. His group was not and they were found frozen to death. James Delong was frozen with his arm straight up in the air and a Bible in his hand.

Tiksi is located approximately here

The place in Russia that we were doing the exercise with was a city called Tiksi. It sits at the top of Russia. Neither Don or I were able to go on the exercise but at the event afterward, General Ralston, the Alaska Commander, told Don that he had changed the entire atmosphere of the exercise. Crossing his arms the General explained how the Russians had heard about these Americans and were standoffish at best. Recrossing his arms the General explained how the Americans and Canadians had heard about the Russian communists and were assuming the same stance. Then they brought out the original of Don's SAREX print and announced that they were donating it to the Tiksi Museum. This totally broke the ice, the vodka flowed, and the exercise was a huge success. Letter size prints had been made of the piece as well and all the profit from their sale was used to buy art materials for the children of Tiksi. This cemented the relationships. Right are the other two SAREX posters Don did. In 1994 it featured Ben Eielson, a man who had much to do with the aviation field in Alaska and after whom Eielson Air Force Base in Fairbanks is named. He died crashing his plane in Siberia. The last SAREX

print in 1997 was three horses for the three countries of Russia, America and Canada, pulling a Russian Troika. Since the Russian group in Tiksi had adopted the 210th Rescue's motto, "That other's may live" Don added their mascot, the rescue angel, driving the troika.

Another interesting thing is that the 1997 SAREX was based on Yukon Island in Kachemak Bay, Alaska where my parents originally made their homestead. Photo right is the three generals (left to right: American, Russian, the translator, and the Canadian) Next to my parents homestead land was a parcel of land that my grandmother purchased. It was once a

Russian fox farm. When my sister and her husband began building on the island they found a huge Russian cross. When we retired in 2000 all the SAREX prints hung in the Pentagon.

One last story here…. The last dinner dance poster that Don did was Victory "WWII V-Dance 1995". All the models were Alaska National Guard related… five Alaska Air National Guardsmen, one son of one of those Guardsmen, one woman who was our SATO ticket clerk, and one Army Guardsman dressed as an Eskimo Scout.

One day, more than a decade after doing this print, Don got a text from a woman named Violet. Once she verified Don was the artist she was looking for, she explained that her husband, Sean, was the Army Guardsman who modeled as the Eskimo Scout (upper left corner of the print). He had since passed away. She wondered if she could buy some copies of the poster for her children. Don explained that the large posters were for an event and long gone. Then he decided that he could actually have some copies made on smaller paper. He got those done and mailed them to her. She wrote back a wonderful and very emotional letter about how she had given what Don sent to her children and their reactions of wonder on receiving the print with their father featured.

Don is a man who stands for what is right. He might have been wild in his youth (well who wasn't) but when it came time to acting, he did the right thing. He was proud to serve his country and extra proud to be part of the Pararescue Team. If he would have been younger when he discovered the Pararescue career field, screws in his legs or not, he would have passed that course. It has been my distinct honor to serve with Don.

Not only to serve with him, but to be his mate. It does something special to your heart when you hear a person confess that you saved their life. I have heard many people say that to Don. He gives them the gift of creating. He gives them encouragement. He gives them a place to share their love of art and create. He loves art in all its forms so very much that others just get caught up in his enthusiasm. He genuinely feels such delight in seeing something one of his students has done, that he positively beams. Then he tells them how proud he is and they beam too. It is a beautiful thing to see. It is a magical thing that can heal hearts and patch up souls thereby saving their life. Our school is the perfect outlet for that gift. The school is also a community growing and changing with friends who have become family. The time together inspires one and all.

AMAZING CHILDREN PART 1 FIRST BORN

I have had the blessing of amazing children. Just like my military career was never a dull moment, neither was life with my children.

When I hear the song by Harry Chapin, "Cat's in the Cradle" I think of my first born son, Andrew. His birth was one of the most profound moments in my life. He was so perfect, so beautiful, and such a gift. I was hooked from the start. We toured Germany with my mother just days after he was born. He amazed people everywhere we went. The most common question as they oohed and ahhed was, "Wie Alt?" (How Old?) When I lived in Germany you rarely saw children out in public until they were old enough "to conduct themselves." To have a 7 pound, 5 day old baby, out traveling was astonishing to them. He was so good, so sweet, so pretty everyone wanted to look at him. We waited for the Glockenspiel in Munich and were late for lunch and he started fussing. Some German's thought I should just sit down and breast feed him right there in down town. We went for lunch to a beer garden, I went in the stall to breast feed him and one woman screeched at me for doing that out of my home. I took hundreds of pictures of this miracle in my life.

My mother came to Germany when Andy made his appearance. Actually my mother decided to not come until the baby was born and consequently I was just out of labor when my husband-to-be, armed with her photo, went to the Luxemburg International Airport to pick her up. I had done extensive babysitting in my high school years but the enormous solo responsibility of him gripped me. A friend came to visit who happened to have Native American blood. He and my   mother hit if off right away, and sensing my worry, plotted to tease me. I was told that Native American babies are also born with long black hair like my son; that sometimes the hair falls out, wraps around their little toes, and cuts off the circulation. Sure enough, I had him laid on the bed checking his little toes for hairs when I heard the two of them chortling in the doorway watching me. Because I was a female overseas, I had to have a passport for Andy. He was 10 days old when this photo was taken.

We visited a sister in Sweden journeying on the train through Denmark when he was just a few months old. Part way through Germany these two men really became enamored with him, moving in to sit beside me, wanting to hold him, and it made me very uncomfortable. In my rush to get away from them I left my expensive, brand new, goose down coat on the train as I traveled north. My husband was furious about that.

In Germany I found the best diaper rash cream. There are words to describe Germans in general: effective, inventive, concise, and engineered. I bought a large tin of this cream before leaving Germany. When I left Germany I travelled home to my mom. This entailed the following legs of our journey: Spangdahlem to Frankfort, Frankfort to New York, New York to Chicago, Chicago to Seattle and Seattle to Anchorage with a 7-month old baby.

The last thing I had to do before leaving Germany was clean us out of the house we had rented off base in the small town of Preist, Germany. I needed the vacuum cleaner to do that adequately. I was not thinking about the fact that my household goods shipment and hold baggage shipment were both gone.

Also the vacuum was pretty new and I could not afford to throw it out or give it away. I did not think about the many things I still had to carry with me. This wound up being more than I thought. I got a box from the base that was about two feet wide, 4 feet long and 8 inches deep. The floor portion of this vacuum folded flat for easy storage. I laid that vacuum down in the box and then packed around it all of the baby's and my clothes. Of course the box wasn't long enough so the handle stuck out of the top of the box. That was actually a bonus as it gave a handle for dragging the box. I filled that box to absolute capacity including one special bottle of Germany Mosel wine for my mother. I used an entire roll of duct tape on that box because I knew it would be a mess if it came apart.

I had my military issue duffle bag with the rest of the clothes, diapers and things to be used in the first week, plus jackets for Alaska. The military issue duffle bag (top right) is 21 inches by 21 inches square and 36 inches tall. It carried a lot and I packed it to capacity. I also had the diaper bag with the usual array of baby needs including milk and snacks and my military issue black purse (second photo down on the right).

At this time the baby had a special 'must have to sleep' blanket as most babies do. This blanket, a gift from our good friends, was a 4 foot by 5 foot fleece blanket from Spain. (Photo third down on the right— blanket has now lost its yarn edging and belongs to his younger brother.) Also this child went **nowhere** with out his buddy Ernie. Ernie of Sesame Street was approximately a nine inch tall stuffed doll (photo bottom right.)

Using the back pack straps, I put the duffle bag on my back. I held the vacuum box with my left hand and slung the diaper bag over my left shoulder. I slung my purse over my right shoulder and with my right arm held my son, his Ernie, and his blanket. I made it though five airports, with lay-overs, on a 26 hour journey without losing anything. Obviously I was exhausted when I arrived.

My mom had an extra bedroom and I just put my son in bed with me and we slept hard. Perhaps only I slept hard. When I woke up I felt something sticky on my cheek. My son had woken up early, gotten into the diaper bag, opened that tin of almost waterproof diaper cream and spread it everywhere. It was in my hair (which had to have 4 total washes before it was all out.) It was on our pajamas and all over the sheets and blankets of the bed clothes. This required 7 washes with heavy duty tide detergent. Ernie somehow escaped being creamed, but the walls of the bedroom did not.

I had time with him by myself, before getting married when he was two, and before added a little brother when he was four and another when he was seven. This time was precious and I found he was an extremely bright, wonderful, normal kid. For this reason there are not as many stories of him as of the others. He never seemed to get hurt, he rarely got in any trouble and through his junior year in High School was an Honor Roll student. In the whole of his childhood he only really did three naughty things:

1) (the diaper rash crème at 7 months, and 2) poking at his little brother's head the day they met, and 3) flushing a case of cups down the toilet at 4 years old. The poking at his brother's head startled me. Andy was 4 years old when I had my second child, I assume he liked being an only child. When we came home from the hospital I put the baby in a play pen. I went to make a bottle and came back out to find Andrew hanging on the railing of the playpen poking his baby brother's head all over muttering, "Where's that soft spot." He was jealous and didn't realize what he was doing.

Of course it is always easier when you only have one child to deal with. If Andy started a fit over having a toy in the store, I just put the cart back, left and shopped later. When you have two children, your time is so limited you might not be able to afford to do that. When Andy had his first kicking screaming temper tantrum, I picked him up and held him under a cold shower, clothes and all. Once he was done gasping in amazement, he was over being mad and realized there was a price to pay for temper tantrums. That was that, and he never did it again. When I tried this with Nicholas, he was delighted! A natural water baby he threw his hands in the air, laughed at my face, and danced in delight. Truthfully, having my second child was like being a first time mother again. Anything I had learned that worked on my first, did not work on the second. I did discover that Andy honed my deductive skills. He was never the one caught holding the bag, but nine times out of ten he encouraged his little brother into the act, or handed off the evidence just moments before I appeared on the scene.

Nicholas broke all the rules. He crawled at 2-weeks old and was running through the house like a destructor tornado at 6-months old. Andy would strategically stick out a tripping foot when his little brother charged past. They were at war from day one. This was particularly hard on Andy who never broke a toy in his life, who carefully saved all the special little pieces to a set, knew where and when he got the toy, and was quiet and well behaved. His little brother was like a small tornado, even as an infant breaking toys advertised to stand up to children. He did in See-N-Says, Tonka Toys, Fisher Price and even wooden toys. He would get into his older brother's things, removing all the special small parts, chewing them apart, flushing them down the toilet, putting them into the garbage disposal and other devious methods of destruction.

On my parents Alaskan homestead, away from toys and television, was the only place the two of them actually played together well. I must say that somehow, through all the fighting, they did establish a relationship and by the time little brother outgrew some of the destructiveness in his teen years, they became quite good friends.

When Andy was five we moved from Oklahoma to Alaska. This move is explained in more depth in Military Part 4 Altus. Once in Anchorage, Alaska we moved three times. The first place on M Street (just down from my mother's in what is known as Bootleggers Cove) and was actually a sublet in the basement. Google photo top right. Across the street from this apartment is Elderberry Park. My boys would always associate that park with my mother, even calling it "Grandmother's Park". The man who sublet the apartment to me had just built a duplex and offered to rent to me so we moved to the Spenard area of Anchorage on Iowa Street (Google photo second from top). When I got pregnant with my third son we had to find a place with more bedrooms because there was no way the two boys could survive sharing a room and I didn't dare put a baby in with either

of them. We then rented on Telequana Street in the Turnagain area. (Google photo third down.) It was near the elementary school where Andy was enrolled. The last move was to Doris Place. It is now renamed Outta Place. I suppose it was confusing to have Doris Street and Doris Place next to each other as it was when we lived there. This put us back in the Spenard area about 8 blocks from the place we lived on Iowa Street. Bottom left photo is Andy and Nicholas on the porch at the Iowa Street Place. Bottom right photo is me, very pregnant, with the boys in front of the Telequana house.

Andy's kindergarten was blissfully uneventful. He met this girl and they became best friends. In first grade they were again in the same class but in second grade they got put in different classes and we

began having problems. His teacher maintained that it was be-cause "he was an Air Force brat". I maintained that he was missing his buddy, he was bored and the battle was on. The little girls father was a Colonel in the Air Force and had the school change his daughter to Andy's class and things settled some. When his first CAT Scores came in and he rated in the 99 percentile I won the battle and things went fine from there. Because he was so good all the time, because he had no major

medical needs, because he got such good grades almost without any help, because he was always my best helper with his brothers, I always felt I did not spend as much time on Andrew after Nicholas was born. I guess you just do what you can.

Photo right taken at Telequana is me and my three sons in a hammock.

When Nicholas started Kindergarten, Andrew was in 4th grade. I had them both enrolled in the Camp Fire After School Program as I worked full time in the military. I told Andy when school was out he was to go to the hall where the kindergarten classes were, collect his little brother and then go across the grounds to the building where Camp Fire was. Andy was a very dependable kid and I knew it would work. What I didn't know was that there was a boy, Brad, that had been harassing Andrew for over a year. They wound up in the same class again in 4th Grade. As directed Andrew proceeded to the kindergarten area, collected his little brother, and was just opening the door to go across the school yard to the Camp Fire building when this bully spotted him. Brad was taller and slammed Andrew in the back hard enough that Andy fell, his jean knees ripped, and his knees were bleeding. Nicholas never hesitated. He launched himself on to this bully boys back, gripped his strong little fingers in that boys hair and held on for dear life. No swinging or screaming or reaching dislodged him. Once the teachers entered the fray they managed to calm the bully boy down enough that the whole caravan could be escorted to the principals office. Nothing the adults said made Nicholas release his hold in that boys hair. They called me at work, "Can you please ask your son to let go of this boy's hair?" they pled. I talked Nicholas finally into letting go and the bully boy never again bothered Andy. I think this solidified my two sons friendship's with each other.

Andrew was enrolled in a program called PACT (Program for Accelerated Children Teaching or some variation there of) in the second grade on Elmendorf. At first he was excited about this program and they bussed the kids to one school where the classroom was set up with interesting stations to excite an exceptional child. Unfortunately, when he entered 3rd grade it was a new PACT teacher who thought the answer was just to add lots of homework. Andrew lasted one year and then declined to further participate. When we moved him to Turnagain his 4th grade teacher was the same way—more homework for smarter kids. I remember one report he had to do. He chose Michealangelo to report on. The requirement was a 30 page report complete with Title Page, Biography, Reference Page, and Photos. This was high school level education given to a 4th grader! Complaints to the principal had no effect, but I will have to note here that they were at this time coping with his brother, Nicholas.

Whatever test kids take in the seventh grade Andy just about aced. His math skills were noticed and he was offered a spot in the John Hopkins Talented Youth Program. This required him going across America by himself to the John Hopkins University in Maryland for a summer in residence experience. There is no way we could afford it but I was well on my way to getting funding commitments when he announced he was not going. Andy was usually very good, very kind, and very compliant. Not this time, this time he absolutely refused to be swayed into going away.

As I have mentioned Andy was great with adults and loved to talk to people in general. His 5th grade teacher mentioned that he was so devoted he asked to stay in at recess and work on school work. The teacher gave him extra projects. His 6th grade teacher stated that in his opinion he was so searching for adult male approval, getting none from my ex-husband, that he didn't even want to go to recess.

I had to go to Juneau for a few days for my work and asked Don, who didn't yet live with us, if he would babysit. All went well for him until bedtime. They were watching a show and begged to stay up until it ended. He agreed to that stipulating that then there would be no further negotiating and all would go nicely to bed. The show ended and in coordination they all refused to go to bed. Just giving a mad look sent Chris off to comply. Nicholas wiggled a bit but Don laid down the law verbally and said he could give him a spanking if he needed, and he was off to bed. Andrew, arms crossed across his chest, watched all this carefully. When Don turned to him, he announced sassily that he was too old to spank and ask what Don was going to do about him. Don responded by saying he would have no problem "punching his lights out" if he wanted to go there. Andy looked in his eyes and saw it was not a threat but a promise and he was off to bed.

Once Don came into our lives I saw Andy's issues with getting male approval radically change. Don was encouraging and a great listener. He was wise in the ways of boys and began teaching them how to be good people. Once Don came around the corner and found the two oldest had me backed into a corner demanding something in an abusive manner. He grabbed each boy by the neck, steered them into another room, and had a talk about respecting their mother. Andy led the way at first in challenging Don at every turn and it was three against one. Don asked me to marry him, but I wanted to delay until I could see if the poor man could survive.

Andy had really excelled in math in junior high school and his 8th grade math teacher raved about his exceptional abilities. In his freshman year of high school he had heavy math and science but the math teacher was average and the science teacher exceptional. For a lesson on germs the teacher sent the students around the school to get swabs that they analyzed for germs. At his parent teacher conference we were told that he would run down the hall when the exam grades were posted to look and see the grades, always hoping his was the highest.

Andy took gifted education and honors classes (like AP Chemistry) all the way through school - well, except his Senior year in high school. He participated in wrestling and swimming in High School, had a natural athletic ability, and was a great looking and well-liked kid. Near the end of his junior year in High School he stopped with the heavy partici-pation. Our lives changed and he finally had some freedom to join sports and participate in other things outside our house. His teenage hormones were madly popping and he discovered girls. Handsome, debonair, smart—even the coolest, richest girls were glad to date him. He was just what a parent wanted their daughter to date and was welcomed. He could entertain and hold his own in conversations with adults, a product of our lifestyle and my mother's Friday Night gatherings. We had the Air Force Academy recruiter checking in routinely to recruit this honors   student for the Air Force. Suddenly his grades in his senior year were barely passing. He dropped all the honors classes and the scholarship offers dried up and blew away. At his graduation he handed over the folder they give graduates while he posed for a picture, and Don and I were frankly relieved to see a diploma inside.

Don retired from the military and began really devoting time to our business, Raven's Wing Studios. We moved all the rooms around giving Andy the 1st floor to himself and established an art studio space on the third floor for Don. Andy would get home from school and immediately head for the studio. He spend hours and hours with Don and it changed his worry about adult male approval. When I really saw this was with the boat. When we got all our bills paid off we purchased a boat. We were getting out of Anchorage and going to the island every chance we got. Having our own transportation across the bay would eliminated asking a sister for a ride or paying water taxi fees. Wa-

ter taxi fees were then $60 per person for a round trip and we were a five person family, it adds up quickly. Owning a boat had been a lifelong dream of Don's and the boys shared his enthusiasm, particularly Andrew. It came with its own trailer and they helped Don pick out all the safety gear we needed so it was a fully equipped vessel and we all were invested. We named it *The Kudzu* (photo right) and spent many wonderful hours with her. We knew it was a good sign when the first time we ran the truck with

the boat and trailer through the weigh station. The combined weight 3313 was the exact house number of our current address.

The maiden voyage of the Kudzu was remarkable in many ways. The first way was the trip down. There is a saying my brother loved. "If you live on a homestead in Alaska you need one of everything in the Sears catalog." When you live on an island everything must be transported first down the Homer over 200 miles away and then by boat to the island. Since the sister with the boat had provided the transporting for years alone, she was glad to see another boat in the family. Being a real people pleaser I magnanimously offered to transport things they might have, "Since we were going with a nearly empty boat!" I am not a good packer, I am an exceptional packer. As the sisters brought things they wanted on the island, I packed them in the large bow space. I don't think Don really even knew what all got packed in that space. Traditionally, we stop in Soldotna because it is just over half way. We would gas up, get something to eat at McDonalds, run to the stores behind for any last minute forgotten items, and give everyone a chance to stretch their legs. While Don was gassing up the truck this man wandered over and was looking at the front of the boat. Don began talking to him, proud of his new boat and willing to show it off. Then the man pointed out the weight in the bow of the boat had actually bent the steel tongue of the trailer. "I don't think I have ever seen that!" Don was totally astonished at what had happened to the trailer. He later hired someone to straighten it back out and weld extra braces on to the tongue. I felt so bad I never asked the sisters if they had stuff to transport again.

The second way that was remarkable was when we returned to Homer after our time across the Bay. Don had let the boys steer the boat on the way over which Andrew really liked. Don took over again for the voyage through the Homer Boat Harbor as it is a busy place and there are rules of boating in the harbor and fines if they are not followed. We motored down to the very end of the harbor where the boat launching ramp was. Nicholas, the good deck hand, jumped out and grabbed the ropes to hold the boat by the dock. Don turned to Andrew and told him he was going to get the truck and trailer, all he had to do was drive the boat up on the trailer, and Don said he knew Andy could do it. He clapped him on the shoulder, nodded and left.

Although Andy was nervous he performed admirably. Don backed the trailer down and Andy pulled the boat on perfectly. Don hooked up the winch and trailered the boat. When he was done he went to Andy, shook his hand like he was a man, and told him no one could have done it better. I could see Andy change. He put his shoulders back and stood tall. I was so proud and thankful I cried. He joined the wrestling team and the swim team and did well. For the first time I saw in Andrew real self esteem and confidence.

Teaching this son to drive was almost more than I could handle, it frankly scared me to death. I never had driven much myself and was not a relaxed competent driver so this added to the problem. One of my sisters took him out for some lessons and then my husband, Don, took over and taught him the fundamentals, the dangers, and the rules of good handling. He managed to pass his driving test the first time out. After he had had his license for about 6 months, we bought a new van and I sold him my Subaru. The first night he drove "his own car" to work he had an accident. Originally, he told Don that he just pulled into the parking lot at his work, going only about 20 miles per hour, and slipped on the ice. When the car was not capable of being driven home, Don and my nephew went down to his work to check it out. The damage was so extensive - the fender bent into the tire, the tire was bent over, and the tie rod to the wheel was broken off. The true story was that he was excited to be driving his own car, he was most likely running a little late, he was going too fast, and was tried to "pull a Brodie" in a four-wheel drive car.

Andy then proceeded to get one hefty speeding ticket and then have another accident. Two weeks into ownership, he and his younger brother were supposed to take their SAT Tests. Although his brother was only 13, he was taking it at the request of John Hopkins for their Talent Search Program, tagged for his exceptional math skills just like his older brother. Andy was running a little late, as always, and was going too fast, also as always. He hit the ice not 10 blocks from our house, slid into the snow berm on one side, bounced to the snow berm on the other side and proceeded to take the car airborne. He rolled completely over and back down on the wheels. Both boys were exceptionally lucky to escape with no injuries, particularly since neither was seat belted. In his normal style, Andrew never said a word. The next morning Don noticed his car was backed in under the porch.

Never one to take an extra minute if he didn't have to, Andy *never* backed his car into the space. Now suspicious, we walked to the other window and looked down at the car. There was a significant dent in the side we could see from that vantage point. When he woke up I asked him about it and he said he had hit a snow berm. Later that day we were at my sisters for a birthday party and he arrived late in his own car. As Don and I were talking we looked out and noticed that it also had a dent in the roof (which the porch had hidden at home). The car being parked the other direction we then noticed a scrape dent in the other side from the side we had seen the dent in the morning. That's when we finally got the whole story.

Andy began dating and had very nice girls he escorted around. For his prom photo we cautiously loaned him our new van and he looked like James Bond all decked out in black standing by the van with a beautiful girl on his arm.

Right after graduation Andrew's girl friend was off to college in Seattle. First they were to share an apartment over the summer but at the last minute she backed out and Andy had to shoulder the whole cost for the six month lease. Broke and discouraged we let him move back home with us. Then in the fall she was off to Seattle. He said they had an agreement that he move in with her and he packed all his stuff into two duffle bags and bought a ticket to Seattle. A week later he was back, it didn't work out after all, and between that and the apartment he blew all the money he had earned crabbing.

Andy did graduate from High School and at 19 was deeply regretting having ruined his own chances to go on to college with financial help. To earn money he signed on with his cousin as a crewman on a crabber in the Bering Sea. You might remember a show called "The Deadliest Catch." Andrew was the youngest in the fleet his initial trip. We only agreed to let him go on the first trip because our more experienced nephew was the first mate and we knew would watch out for him. That nephew lived 5 houses down the street and was really more like an older brother to my boys. He saw Andy's foot on the rope coil and kicked his foot off, probably saving his life. Andy did crab fishing two seasons. If I have my percentage and figures right they get a percentage of the catch based on their position. I think the Captain got 5%, First Mate 3% and Deck Hands 1% of the total earned, the rest belonged to the boat owner. They go out for several days at a time, they don't really sleep, just nap standing up somewhere, and it is very hard work in dangerous conditions. But, Andy earned thousands the first trip out which was only 5 days. It was hard to convince him not to go a second time. I was ever grateful that he didn't decide to pursue this as a career.

When we began renovating the house, floor by floor, we moved all three boys downstairs. We built a new hall leaving to Chris's room and Andy and Nick shared what was once two bedrooms but had the wall between knocked out. They never did learn to put things away and never minded living like pigs. Photo right is the dirty dishes collected from one trip down to the boys room.

Andrew now has four boys of his own and he is a wonderful father. He works one week on, one week off at a job in Valdez, Alaska, just under 300 miles away from his home. He lives (according to google) 4,238 miles from us; and like in the song I referenced at the beginning of this chapter, I don't see him much.

I must add a few stories about renovating the house on Doris Place. It really did cost blood, sweat and tears. When we first moved into the house my ex bought a disposal and a dishwasher and installed both himself. Long after he was gone we found out why folks should not install their own appliances. The boys were messing around as usual, with my nephew in the mix as well. The nephew threw a butter knife from the dining room aiming for the sink in the kitchen. The knife hit dead center, and dropped into the disposal. It then produced an electrical arch out of the disposal that we all saw in horror. I told him to get a pair of dykes and cut the electricity to that thing. Once that was done he found the knife standing still in the disposal and pulled it out. One half inch was gone off the end.

We had a flood in the kitchen because someone left the water running in the sink. Andy and I were on hands and knees sopping up the water with towels. Andy took a break, sat back on his heels, and said, "I hate this zapping feeling we get sometimes." I told him I did too. When we began renovating, the first appliance Don bought was a dishwasher. Because he is a smart man he insisted on having it professionally installed. When the man pulled the old dishwasher out he found that my ex had not understood all the wires and had left two bare wires laying on a 2x4 board at the back. The installer shook his head and told Don, "It's a wonder no one was electrocuted.

I know that Nicholas was the most like me and I always had trouble turning down a dare. Andy knew this and often dared his younger brother. Nicholas would always be the one holding the bag, but investigation would prove that often Andy cooked up the scheme.

The house next door to us had stayed empty, mostly because they had to install a new city water line. We had to cut off their water line because it was illegal for it to run under our house. When people did move in, to our kids disappointment it was a yuppie couple who did not like kids. One day I heard giggling and investigated. They were on the neighbors side of the house, two were look outs and one had our remote control and when the man turned his head they changed his tv channel. They lost their boomerang in one of the neighbors trees and when they asked to climb the tree to get it, the neighbor refused and war was declared. Our dog, Gabe, felt this. The neighbors built a greenhouse right on the lot line. Since our porch hung over toward that line it was only two feet from the edge of the porch to their greenhouse door. Gabe would wait in the house until the woman came out to go in her greenhouse. When he heard her he would race out, madly barking, right to the edge of the porch, two feet from her. He was an exceptionally large golden retriever. He felt her scream each time was a glad reward.

Above is a photos at a party at my sisters house. She had big open beams above her living room. The older two were happy to hang out there until they got bored. At one particular party when I wasn't paying attention they coached their little brother out on to the beam too. He had to be rescued.

Andrew

Family Pictures

Top right: Andy in red; Nick in green and red sweater; Chris in blue overalls.

Bottom right: Family photo—Back row left to right—Andy, Me, Don, Josh. Front left to right—Nicholas and Chris.

Sledding party 1999 Arctic Valley, Alaska. It was so much fun doing things all together. I went down the first time, hit a mogul and squealed. Our dog, Gabe, ran down the hill and pulled me off the sled. It was a 20 min run so we had two cars to ferry everyone back and forth. First Born came down the hill on his cell phone!! First Born in red snowsuit with sun glasses. Second Born in blue snow-suit. Third born in blue sweat pants and white shirt. Second Add in tan pants, white shirt and red hat. Don in black snowsuit.

Mom, Becky & Jeremy came over....

and we built a luge run off the

porch. They never tired of it, never got too cold to quit...

...of course that gave them the expertise to....

build one on Doris St that started from the 2nd floor, went down the

stairs across the yard... over the 5 ft fence and 15-20 feet into the air....

vaulting Doris Place.

Homer AK boat harbor—Andy, Nicholas, Chris and cousin Justin.

AMAZING CHILDREN PART 2 SECOND BORN

Nicholas was a surprise all around. My first clue about the determination of this child was when I did not go into labor at 9 months. He always did things his way in his time. We lived in Altus, Oklahoma, and August September are hot months there. If I remember correctly for 90 days of my last trimester, it never went below 90 even at night! I went from my air conditioned house, to my air conditioned car, to my airconditioned work and back. I was hot and bothered. I tried every old wives tale of starting labor… I drank a bottle of castor oil and had horrible diarrhea and no labor. I walked around the house like it was an Olympic track—no labor. I went down a 50 foot water slide. The water was wonderful, I got a horrible sunburn, and no labor. I begged my doctor to induce labor… But, NO!…. Air Force regulations stipulate that labor shall not be induced until the mother is documented to be at 10 months. I feel sure that was not written by anyone who ever carried a baby late term in a hot place.

I kept Nicholas in my room at the hospital in the wheeled crib provided. He had jaundice and we had to stay an extra week in the hospital. By then I was helping clear their administrative backlog . I had to go to the bathroom and wheeled him into the nurses station so they could watch him for me while I went. I came back and they were all grouped around him and he was, at 4 or 5 days old, making faces at the nurses. He was playing to an audience like an experienced thespian, and those nurses were in hysterics.

Nicholas crawled at two weeks old and I was in no way ready for that! At his two week appointment I told the doctor that. He pooh-poohed that idea so I told him to put a piece of paper down on the floor, put the baby down and he quickly crawled over and ate the paper. The doctor was apologetic. I complained that the child was afraid of nothing. The doctor did a test where you hold the baby about 3-4 feet above the floor and you flip them over. Most babies will be startled and begin to cry. Nicholas squealed his joy. They did more tests and discovered two things. He had no noticeable fear factor. He did not feel pain as you and I might. They told me if he lived long enough to be a professional athlete he would be excellent at it.

Nicholas was a tornado let loose. My ex-husband had no patience. He worked a whole Saturday installing child guards to all the doors, closets and cabinets in the kitchen because this boy could make a mess with absolutely anything. Home Depot has them, yes you can still get them and they still work for most kids. Cabinet doors are not all that thick and cannot take a long screw for greater holding power, add to that Nicholas being a 10-month baby who was walking at six months and very strong, and you know it didn't work even once. He strutted into the kitchen when we called him. We invited him to open a cabinet door, something he knew usually caused a fuss. He looked at us like "Is this a trick?" Deciding it was okay this time, he strutted to the first cabinet and attempted to open it. It opened only an inch or so. He paused for just seconds, then placed one hand on the top corner of the opening, one hand on the side at the top corner and yanked. The screws came right out and he swung the door open and turned and grinned at us. My ex roared in anger and left the house. The only relief from the heat besides air conditioning was the base pool. This was also the only truly entertaining family thing that was free. My oldest son and Nicholas were true water babies and loved the

The cabinet child proofing my ex pur-chased for our kitchen cabinets were like these in the photo from Home Depot.

pool but Nicholas scared me. He liked to put his head under the water and just stay there… it was as if he were saying if I do this enough sooner or later I will be able to breathe under water. No, you will not. I was actually relieved to be moving to Alaska where there was not a base pool.

Nicholas, red-headed, was born with many allergies. He also had ear infections one after another. The first time they gave me penicillin for an ear infection he was only a few months old. He turned slightly blue but went back to his normal color pretty quickly. I called the base and they just said to watch carefully with the next dosage. The second time he turned blue and it didn't go away so I rushed him to the Altus hospital. By the time I got there he was having breathing troubles. They gave him epinephrine and as they watched these small explosions began happening under his skin and you could watch the bruise being formed. This is called HSP or Henoch-Schoenlein Purpura. They had to do two more shots before it all quit and had called most of the doctors in the hospital over to see this rare reaction. They were worried about if this had caused any damage to his bones so once they had him stable told me to take him to the x-ray department. I was in fear for my child's life and as they worked and nothing helped I began crying and praying. I arrive at the x-ray department with Nicholas just covered in bruises as if someone had taken a stick and hit him all over his body. It was Halloween and the x-ray department was full of Trick-or-treaters getting their candy x-ray for razor blades and the like. As I was hustled to the front of the line people looked at the baby, and then at me with judgement of child abuse in their eyes.

My ex was not relieved to be leaving Oklahoma, in fact he was downright angry about being assigned in Alaska. I arrived in the fall and my car from Oklahoma, a 1971 Challenger, experienced its first Alaska winter. I came out to go to work and as always scraped the windows clear of snow and ice. The back window had shattered overnight and was cracked into pieces about one half an inch square. Since my ex was still in Oklahoma he was able to get a back windshield, there certainly were not any in Anchorage. I didn't pick this car, I got talked into it. First it was olive drab green, which aside from orange might be my least favorite color. Once I added a third child the car was not large enough to seat the whole family comfortably unless there were no backpack, diaper bags, purses or other necessities requiring space as well. The trunk was small enough that I could not fit a whole grocery run of bags in it at once. This meant I could not take both boys and their stuff when I did the grocery run. I paid dearly every time "my lack of planning" created a situation where he had to watch the kids for a time. Next problem with a Challenger in Alaska is the traction on icy Alaskan roads. I was headed to the base hospital for an appointment for one of the boys. As I began to turn left on to the hospital road, this jerk entered the base at the Boniface Gate, floored it, and was set to hit me broadside.

I floored it...wrong move. We did go forward enough that the jerk did not hit us but then I tapped the brake and we did two full 360 degree spins before being stopped by the edge of the road. I was glad my heart was still beating and wanted a second of silence to recover. But No! (Best said as John Belushi did.) From the back seat I got a son cheering, and a son chanting, "Again, Again, Again..." over and over.

When we arrived in Anchorage Nicholas was 7 months old. I had told my mom she needed to babyproof her house because I knew she had an L shaped planter box in her living room. It had plants with artifacts among them in her combined kitchen, dining, living room area. She was thrilled to find that he actually had red hair, just as her father did and that was all she could talk about. In the 1940's her mother had offered $100 to anyone giving her a red-haired grandchild. None did. However, my cousin, a strawberry blonde, and I, with auburn hair, both had one. By then my grandmother had passed and besides they were great -grandchildren. We set Nicholas down as we entered the house. She had a bar separating her kitchen area and dining area. One bar stool was blocking passage. He grabbed it by the leg, slammed it on to the floor and headed straight for the artifacts in her living room. She went to her shop and got a roll of 4 foot high corrugated cardboard and stapled it to her living room planter boxes. She didn't baby proof her kitchen either and one Friday night he drank a small bottle of miracle grow. I learned early about Ipecac.

Once we were in Alaska Nicholas's ear infections became more frequent and we got one cured when another set in, no more than two months between. He had tubes twice and they came out both times. I wrote what I thought was a really nice letter to the Chief of the Pediatric Clinic asking for help. I asked that one doctor be assigned until we could get him to the point of no ear infections because I had concerns that we could be looking at permanent ear damage. They assigned me to the head pediatrician and when I had my first appointment it was quite obvious he had not taken the letter in the light I intended. Nicholas was very empathetic and could feel and see that this man was angry. He responded by going nuts... he spit, hissed, hit, squirmed and never stopped moving for the entire appointment. He flat out would not allow that doctor to get near him. At that point the doctor told me that this child needed to be on Ritalin and until I agreed to give him the drug we were not welcome back in the pediatric clinic. I really didn't want to get sucked into the drug the child routine. I knew that most of the issues with my boys were created from boredom and I could relate. Three miserable months later that doctor was reassigned and a wonderful civilian woman took his place. We then went through the process of adenoids and tonsils being removed at different times and the doctors having issues Nicholas as a patient.

To do the first operation they needed the prep work which included getting a blood sample. Nicholas was a brat about this. He would wait until they just put the needle in and jerk his little arm so the needle exited the vein. They tried five of them holding him down, but that didn't work so one tech went off and found a hospital papoose (A Pediatric Immobilizer). This was the only way they succeeded in getting a blood sample. The routine is to be placed in the recovery room for a time after the operation and before being put in a room. I was advised he was out of the operating room and in recovery. Ten minutes later they came and got me. There were comments positive and negative mumblings when they handed him off to me to take to his room.

While we were staying in that small two bedroom apartment there was a great shortage of space and our household goods, still in their packing boxes, formed a wall in our bedroom behind the head of our bed. Shortly after my ex arrived we experienced an earthquake. I think it was like a 5 point but fairly long. As it rippled across Knik Arm toward us in Anchorage it snapped the ice that had formed and it was like a sonic boom going off. Both of us sat up in bed and then the shaking began. We both froze in place. My ex seemed mesmerized by the swinging light fixture in our room. I was noticing the box wall swaying and wondering if we would be buried in boxes. When it ceased, he jumped from the bed and began pacing saying "No!" in different intonations for quite some time. It was good we were not there very long.

This might be a repetition but we moved from the sublet apartment by my mom in Bootleggers Cove, to a brand new nice two bedroom duplex in Spenard. It was difficult having the first two share a room. There was virtually no yard to speak of for playing outside. Nicholas continually scared us by throwing himself down the long uncarpeted stairs to the garage with its ten foot ceilings and I was pregnant again. We moved to a three bedroom place in Turnagain where we added our third child. The last move was back to Spenard.

Nicholas was not one who waited well. He disdained walking down stairs and would throw himself at the top of the stairs and like a surfer on a wave ride on down to the bottom. In the Spenard duplex, the stairs from the bedrooms on the second floor to the first floor were carpeted and I didn't worry much. The stairs to the garage however, were bare wood, steeper than usual, and long because of the high ceilings in the garage. Also they ended in a cement floor. My ex forgot that he did this and left his tool box at the bottom of the stairs and we had new stitches in Nicholas's head.

Nicholas had been given one of those horses on springs they called Rocking Riders or Wonder Horses or something. He loved this thing and would ride it for longer than any other thing he did. It reminded me of my sister and I on the island atop the saw horse riding to adventure. His older brother came over and asked, "Want to go higher?" Nicholas was delighted to say yes. His brother bounced him so well that he was propelled over the front of the horse and hit a stereo speaker requiring stitches in his head.

One night I heard a "Thunk! Thunk!" sound and leapt from bed and down the stairs to the kitchen. The refrigerator door was open and there were oranges all over. There was Nicholas, sitting in the middle of the kitchen floor. Two handed he held the biggest knife we owned and using it like a vanquishing sword was chopping the oranges. The "Thunk" was the sound of the knife hitting the floor.

Nicholas put a whole peanut butter and jelly sandwich into our VCR Player once when we lived in Turnagain. Remember that my ex had very little sense of humor and complete ignorance of the term "Sh_t Happens!" Another time Nicholas destroyed the VCR and the television in once fell swoop. I was helping my older son with his homework in the dining room and Nicholas, now 4 years old, stated he was hungry. I moved a chair to the kitchen, sliced some celery sticks for him, and putting him on the chair, showed him how to put the peanut butter in the celery stick with his small "made for kids" little knife. I then went back to helping with homework. It wasn't long before Nicholas created trouble. He explained to me the whole sequence of events in a fascinating manner. First he said he wanted to watch tv in the other room so he put all the celery sticks in his hand (the right hand) and the jar of peanut butter in the other. Without even falling he hopped down and went to the living room. [Evidence proved that preferring the faster method of using his fingers to spread the peanut butter, he discarded most of the celery sticks soon after.] He went on to explain that the only way he could hold the jar of peanut butter with one hand was with his thumb inside the jar. He said after he reached the living room he only then thought of possible repercussions of having his finger in the family jar of peanut butter. He further reckoned that since he was already guilty of the finger in the jar, and had forgotten the knife in the kitchen, he would just use his finger to put the peanut butter in the celery sticks. Then he reckoned he didn't even care for celery that much and just went for plain peanut butter. The first hand print he didn't even know he did, but had put one hand on the control to change the channel and the other hand on the picture tube to keep his balance. These peanut butter leavings were easy to see. After changing the channel he sat back down and saw the smear on the tv. Using both hands he tried to wipe it off so he could see. Soon enough the peanut butter was all over the television screen. He then laid down in front of the tv to watch and absentmindedly placed one little foot on the left hand corner and one little foot on the right hand corner of the picture tube. He never admitted to me that there might have been some finger painting, or rather foot painting with peanut butter going on once he was laying on the floor, but I could see patterns on the poor picture tube. While he lay there watching, a scary person appeared on the screen and it startled him. He pushed back with his feet to get away from the television. His strong little legs broke the brackets holding the picture tube into the console. About that time my ex-husband arrived home and as usual made a bee line for the couch and the tv. Here was me on the floor beside the peanut butter boy who still had his hand in the peanut butter jar, and smears of peanut butter all over him and his clothes and everything within 4 feet. The sad VCR lay on the floor and never did work again. Nicholas was still explaining what happened to me. Then my ex saw that the console was empty, and that the picture tube lay dark on the floor unusable and exploded in anger.

I picked up Nicholas and put him in the bathtub leaving the door open so I could hear him and monitor the filling of the tub. We had finally convinced him that he would never be able to breathe under water naturally and except for overflowing the tub was good to be left for a short time. I had well developed "mom hearing." I could tell the difference in the flow of water into the tub, I could hear the sound of a small foot hitting the floor and could wake from a dead sleep at the sound of a child out of bed at night. I got cleaning supplies and cleaned the console and the decorated picture tube sadly laying there on the floor. There was quite a bit of peanut butter in the rug and that took extra time to get out. His clothes had to be rinsed out or the whole wash would be peanut buttered. I had to look in on my other son doing homework to see that he was still on track.

When I returned to the bathroom, Nicholas had silently gotten out of the bathtub and with his sticky peanut butter hands had managed to paint two walls in the bathroom. After making, serving and cleaning up dinner, finishing helping with homework, getting all three kids into bed, and cleaning the peanut buttered bathroom I was exhausted. The next morning I was dressed for work in my dress blues. While the boys were eating breakfast I needed to use the restroom. I shut the door, went to the bathroom, washed, then reached for the doorknob to go out and found my hand covered in peanut butter. There was no peanut butter on that wall or anywhere else on the door, just on the doorknob and I had missed it.

Nicholas waltzed, he didn't walk. He waltzed, he strutted often, and he danced with joy through life, well most of his life. When he passed at 24 years old the dancing stopped, and my heart broke. He liked to sing and would get the tune right but not necessarily the words. One friend told me he heard Nicholas singing the 60's hit song *Soul Man* as he walked up the beach. Instead of singing "I'm a Soul Man" he was singing "I'm a So Mad." Recently I mentioned that incident and his older brother said he felt sure Nicholas knew exactly what the words were and chose to say that instead.

I put the two boys into the Elmendorf Day Care Center. They picked up the oldest from his school not far from there for after school care, and accepted Nicholas at 7 months old for the whole day. Things were fine for awhile until Nicholas got used to being there. He then would climb up the drawer handles on to the counter that ran down one wall. He timed it so the workers would be on the other side of the room. He would look them in the eye, grin big, and leap attempting to land on a table a few feet away. When he started talking he would add an enthusiastic, "Superman!" Most times he did landed on a near by table. A few times he misjudged and we had to get stitches in his head. The third time I took him to Elmendorf Emergency Room for stitches, the Major, doctor, informed me that he would have to turn me in for child abuse due to the frequency. I said that's fine, I just picked him up from the base day care center. No charges were filed.

Soon Nicholas tired of the leaping game as he called it. The next adventure was jumping up on to the half door (photo top right) of the day care room. These were what is called a Dutch door. The top and bottom of the door could be opened without the other half. The bottom half had a shelf on the top of it like in this picture from House Beautiful. The door knob on the inside had a child proof handle. During operating hours at the day care the top second of the door was kept open. Nicholas would take a little running start and leap up on to the shelf of the bottom door, reach the door handle on the outside which was not child proof, open the door and escape. To his credit he never let another child out. For some months he was happy just heading down the hall to the kitchen where the chef he called "Cooker" wore a puffy white hat and never minded the visit. Nicholas especially enjoyed the part where a breathless worker would appear at a run and say, "There you are!" (Photo center right is a photo taken at Elmendorf Day Care.)

1986 Elmendorf Day Care

Photo bottom right: Nicholas wanted to *ride* that horse they put him on for the photo and was annoyed when prevented from doing so. You can clearly see that in his expression.

Needing a new adventure Nicholas soon discovered that he was shorter than the front counter desk. Just beyond the kitchen he could walk past the front desk unnoticed and right out the door. They would call me in a panic saying he was gone and I would leave work, cross the base to the day care center and then down the road and there he would be heading for the playground.

He was barely three years old when he racked up his 19th escape. They informed me that they could no longer keep him. " You need a one-on-one babysitter for that child!"

Nicholas liked to climb slides from the bottom up. One day he slipped and slammed his face into the steel slide. He hit hard enough that one tooth shattered and was lost and his other front tooth jammed up into his gums and had to be surgically corrected with stitches to boot. Neither affected his permanent teeth which came in nice and straight. He didn't smile as big for the school picture that year because he was embarrassed about the gap. (Photo right.)

We had been renting a house in the Turnagain Arm area of Anchorage. I found a huge house for sale pretty cheap. My older sister offered to purchase it since we couldn't qualify with the foreclosure in Oklahoma. The house had lots of problems and had been on the HUD extended listing for years. The price was only $75,000 for a three story, just under 3000 square feet, house. A realtor friend of ours said she could help us with the problems that had it on the extended listing, so we bought it.

I found a nice woman in Base Housing that could take my boys and the one I was expecting as well. The youngest had health complications from birth, and she dealt with them in stride. Meanwhile, on the home front we were moving again from Turnagain back to Spenard and from renting to buying. First there was all the extra time and effort of getting the water line under the house that serviced the neighbors fixed. Next there was the process of getting grandfather rights for our porch that was too close to the road for the current property laws. If I remember correctly we also had a base wide exercise and 12-hour shifts in the middle of all this. When Nicholas was 4 we moved across town and there were new things to get used to. I should first tell you about the moving event.

Before we could move we had to fix up and clean the rental house we had been in. Nicholas had done a lot of damage. Through out the house the metal top of the registers had been removed because he liked the feeling of walking on the vanes and when efficiency was low we had to bend the vanes back into shape. One particular dawn morning he climbed up the kitchen drawers to the counter. Then he stacked up the flour and sugar containers to get up to the top of the refrigerator. There he got my haircutting kit. I did my ex-husband and boys haircuts and had clippers and very sharp little pointed scissors. He used those sharp little scissors to cut a hole in the middle of the kitchen floor that was a one piece linoleum affair. Luckily my ex found a substance that melded linoleum together. He cut a circle piece out from under the refrigerator and the same size circle where Nicholas had cut the piece out and melted it in. You would never know it was there.

In the basement there were three areas that took us a long time to fix. The laundry room had an accordion door. Nicholas had removed the screws anchoring it to the door frame so he could swing on the door. Next to that was the bathroom and using a screw driver he had managed to remove most of the 1 inch tiles covering the vanity. We could not match the tiles so had to remove them all and my mother taught me how to install tile and grout. The third room in the basement was the rec room. The room was about 20 x 30 feet. One 30 foot wall was wall to wall cabinets, except the doorway. There was no exit from this room and it made a great place for the kids to play. Nicholas had swung on, stepped on or ripped out over half the cabinet doors. At one end was a work bench with a long two part accordion door that could be shut so it was out of view. Both these two parts were no longer anchored to the walls. The last thing was the ceiling tiles. It was a drop ceiling with 2 foot by 4 foot ceiling tiles. They were made from foam with a painted coating. Nicholas knocked one down somehow. He pinched the coating and pulled and ripped a piece down the center of the tile. He found this a pleasing sound and activity and by piling toys and furniture up so he could reach had stripped a good number of these tiles. Twice this piling up resulted in stitches in that boy's very hard head.

Back to moving across town… Nicholas loved to take things apart and our new house had issues. I walked into the bathroom and he was standing in the toilet tank with the parts in his hands. He held up the parts and told me, "I can fix it!"

Another time he came to me while I was beginning the process of making dinner and demanded to have a popsicle. I told him he couldn't as it was too close to dinner and would spoil his appetite. He marched away and soon marched back in and declared that he had put Lego's in to the wall and would only get them out if he got a popsicle. I investigated and found he had pushed the Legos down in the crack between two pieces of sheet rock in the bathroom closet. I told him that he better get them out or he was going to get a spanking and no popsicle.

It wasn't long before he came back with the seven or eight small Lego pieces and dumped them on the kitchen counter where I was working and stomped off. When I had time to investigate I found that in getting those Lego's out he had removed the whole piece of sheet rock that was the bottom of the closet and the ceiling of the stairs to the basement. The sheet rock had slipped down exposing the 2x4 structure. I believe that after he got the Lego's out he just stomped on that sheet rock in spite!

Four years old was a year for Nicholas. He had his real naughty moments. He put a shirt and other miscellaneous items in the upstairs toilet and flushed it at the Babysitter's house. He said he was wondering what would happen. The Babysitter shrieked when this caused water to come out of her light fixture in the kitchen below. Civil Engineering (CE) was involved in solving this event and that took some time and being noticed on base.

Being noticed on base when you live in base housing is almost always a negative thing. After all, issues with your housing could impact your job and even your status in the Air Force. When living in base housing they control certain things you are allowed to do in your home, babysitting for instance (which required a base license). They performed inspections for various reasons and anything from dirty dishes to an unmowed lawn could cause you problems. It is for this primary reason that I never lived in base housing once I had children.

By the time CE was done, the Babysitter had tired of watching Nicholas's every move and grew lax. Having been entertained by the ruckus of his first toilet episode he did it again and it was definitely on purpose. When his younger brother heard these last two sentences he laughed and said, "Lulled into a false sense of security, then strike!" Well, you can imagine the consequences—they took away her babysitting license. She had two other children besides mine and years later I would be stationed with their father. My husband spent his last 11 years in the military on the Alaska PJ Team and their father was a PJ I met when he transferred into the team.

The Search for Day Care should be a whole book because it certainly was a whole learning experience for me. The first questions when placing a child who is obviously not a newborn is often "Where was he before this?" and "Why is he not there still?" That's the cake right there and if they know you are military, the frosting is, "Why not put him in the base day care?"

I found out that there was a special dispensation in the Anchorage School District where a child who is not at the correct age to enter kindergarten, can be enrolled if they past this test that they would give Nicholas.

I took a day of leave from work, I made sure we had a good nights sleep and a great breakfast ... We were raring to go! I had coached Nicholas relentlessly in my desperation. "You want to go to school like your big brother don't you? You have to pass this test and you can!" After signing in and waiting just minutes a woman approached and after identifying our selves led Nicholas off to testing. Some time later she walked him back out, told me he had done wonderfully so far, and announced there would be a break and then another test. He folded his little arms over his chest and said, "My mommy said *one* test!" He flat refused to take the other part of the test so they disqualified him from the program. He scored as a third grader on the first part.

The first day of kindergarten for Nicholas, in the family tradition my parents started with my youngest sister, I presented the teacher with a bottle of aspirin. This was received with confusion on her part but then she was one of the tallest women I ever met and brooked no nonsense in her class.

You remember how the school called me when Nicholas had his fingers in the bully's hair and wouldn't let go? Shortly after that they called me at work and started with, "We want you to know your son was very brave through this incident." "What Now?" Nicholas was skinny and fast moving. He had this attitude that anything he could get his head through, his body would fit. I guess that is what happened because he got stuck between the wood and metal of the playground equipment. First the playground monitors attempted to free him but could not. They tried pouring hot water on the metal part thinking he was stuck to the cold metal. Finally the principal got involved and with the janitor tried all her ideas. Nothing worked so they called the fire department. The school had a playground in the front for the kindergarten and first graders, and a playground in the back for the second through sixth graders to have recess. Since the front of the school was close to the busy Northern Lights Boulevard the fire department pulled their trucks in the back of the school and proceeded through the playground, and around the school to the front. The teachers kept the older kids from following and there was much speculation on what was happening. One child said, "I heard that red-headed kid cut his head off." Nicholas's brother heard that and responded, "That's my brother!" Nicholas was the only red head in the school. I believe Nicholas still holds the record as "the only child removed from playground equipment with the jaws of life in the Anchorage School District." I was fortunate to always have good bosses at work. I was also fortunate in how I did my job. I was organized and efficient and able to accomplish a lot quickly so I was always ahead in my work. I was also good at picking up where I left off after an hour break running across town. Turnagain Elementary School enjoyed frequent visits throughout the entire time Nicholas and his younger brother attended there.

Once we retired in 2000 Don picked up this job and it seemed like there was not a single week that didn't involve trips to the school for one reason or another.

I believe it was Christmas 1992 that my youngest son received a Big Wheel like the one in this photo. Nicholas took it to the top of the stairs and rode it down smashing into the wall at the bottom of the stairs and creating a front wheel sized hole in the sheet rock there. The Big Wheel did not survive the impact though Nicholas did. When I ran to see what the noise was he looked up at me sheepishly and said, "I thought the wall would be stronger than that."

One day I returned from a break to find a frantic call from his third grade teacher. Actually it was hard to tell from the call if she was frantic or so mad she sounded frantic. Nicholas loved to be the clown of the class. When the teacher stepped out, he could act out. One time he took all the clothes pins she used to hang art work and clipped them on this lips, eyelids, nose and hair and danced around the class. When I returned the teachers call she wasn't mad anymore. She proudly told me that he had told her she had the most well developed sense of humor of any adult he had ever met. I thought to my self as she went on and on… "Hook, line and sinker, Lady!"

In the corner of our dining room was a small table with a television that hooked to a Nintendo, where the kids played video games. In survival mode you do not have the fortune of considering how good or bad video games are for your child, especially when they are so popular with all the other kids. I did gratefully accept the fact that this was the one thing that kept Nicholas busy for any amount of time. I am not sure how this happened, or actually whether it happened with only Nicholas involved or if there was help along the way. Regardless the story I got was that Nicholas was excited with the game and reared back in his chair to celebrate a particularly good move (which after the fact was explained in far too much detail for me… "TMI, TMI!!") When he reared back he apparently began to lose his balance, threw himself forward and smacked his forehead flat on the table splitting his forehead and needing stitches. (Photo bottom right.)

This is in the wrong order but I want to put here the story of the most stitches. I think Nicholas had accumulated 200 stitches from his chin up before he was 9 years old. Those were many different incidents. The following story was the most stitches in one setting.

My ex said he was going to fix the unstable railings on the porch that surrounded two sides of our newly purchased house. He tore off half the railings on the second and all the railings on the third floor. The third floor was the flat roof of the second floor and even had a door access on the third floor. He never got around to doing any more than that. I was always too broke to ever do it myself and had long since banned the kids from these two

---

TMI stands for Too Much Information.

Dangerous places. When Don moved in, he put up all new railings fixed loose and rotten boards and we enjoyed the second floor porch very much. (See photo of Nicholas and I on that porch much later),

Back on track… My ex bought some steaks to barbeque. The barbeque which was located on a three foot wide walk way portion of the porch with no railings. The two older boys were not supposed to be out there but they were. I was told Nicholas forgot where he was and took a step backward right off the porch and straight down to an asphalt driveway. His brother yelled for me and I knew by the tone of his voice it was bad. I rushed to the porch, looked down and there lay Nicholas with blood coming from his head. I jumped off the porch on to a junk car parked outside the first floor and from there to my son. I yelled at his brother to get my purse and meet me at the car. I picked Nicholas up and carried him up the stairs to the car in the second floor driveway. He was bleeding from his chin, his forehead and his eyes were already beginning to change color. It was a horrifying moment for me. He was usually so quick on his feet and now lay in my arms with his eyes shut.

At the ER they sewed an amazing amount of stitches to close his chin which had split up his jaw toward ears. Although they figure he put his hands out to stop his fall his velocity was such that his chin hitting second, hit very hard. He had two black eyes, a broken nose and a broken wrist. My sister was a nurse and often asked for Nicholas to act as a moulage victim in disaster drills. He was a great little actor and loved the makeup. He scared me more than once walking up to me with the makeup still on! Also with all the accidents and mishaps we pretty much knew all the ER doctors by first name at this point. So, as he lay there on the gurney, the doctor recognized him and quipped, "Why you look just like when we moulage you!" I think this was the first time Nicholas had actually experienced real pain and had lost his sense of humor. He responded rudely, "Just get on with it!" The next day when some of the swelling had gone down we were able to determine that his other wrist was sprained as well. When he would tell the tale of this adventure he ended it with a sad face saying, "But I never got to see my mom jump off the porch!"

Below is a photo of one of the ramps in the Homer Boat harbor. The area has 30 foot tides so the access ramps are designed to rise and fall with the tide. It's a very clever system. They are steel grids designed to prevent slipping even when feet are wet or covered in fish slime. My sister had a Russian visitor she was taking down to the island. He had a son the same age as Nicholas. She asked to borrow him as a companion. As usual Nicholas was messing around. He was either going to fast on the ramp, clowning around and lost his footing or he actually had an accidental slip. He face planted on that ramp (see photo).

Photos left and center by Janet Kotwas found at Alaska dot org

So many times he got stitches I have forgotten all the details. I do know that one large stitching in his head was above his right eye and when he had his head shaved in this picture you could see it real well going up his head. Initially it was a quite impressive three inch plus cut. When the doctor was ready to stitch it up he wouldn't let them start until he got a mirror saying he wanted to watch the stitches go in.

I wasn't present for the "no stitches in the leg" event at my sister's house. The two older boys were downstairs out of her sight and having a ball jumping on one of the beds there. She had bent over nails on the wall near the windows to hold the curtains open. Apparently Second Born jumped right on it and the nail head split his leg open a couple inches. She "Steri-stripped" it, figuring after all it would be under his clothes for most of the time.

Friday Nights at Mom's were a whole thing. There is one boy and five girls in my family and all of who were in town would show up at Mom's after work on Friday's. We took turns brining dinners and often brought friends. When Nicholas climbed up the toilet, on to the ledge of the shower enclosure and batted and broke her nice globe light shade in her bathroom we moved Friday Nights to our house to limit the destruction at hers.

The house in Spenard still stands and is a three story house built on or into a hill. It had once been a tri-plex with all three floors rented separately. The bottom floor (first floor—photo third from the top courtesy of Google) has an entrance under the second floor porch where two cars can be parked. When we moved in, this first floor was a two bedroom, two bath, living room and kitchen area layout. The kitchen was trashed. The appliances there were too old, abused, and far too neglected to save. Electrical wiring hung down from the ceiling in the kitchen where part of the ceiling itself was missing. I did not even want the boys down in that mess so my ex took the liberty of filling this entire 1300 square feet with car parts (four parted out Mopar's) and tools further trashing it.

The second or middle floor was in the best shape. 1300 feet as well, with a big living room, hall kitchen, large dining room, two bathrooms, and two bedrooms. One we made a playroom for the boys close enough I could keep track of them. That playroom stayed sometimes inches deep in Lego's, except when I went in to pick them all up—see photo bottom right. I painted a Mario Brothers theme in the playroom (blue skies and white clouds with Mario Brother wall stickers. The other bedroom on the second floor we used as a library and office.

My mother helped me build shelves down one wall for the larger books with a computer desk at the end. We then built rows coming out from that base for all our VCR tapes. The second floor had a front door with an arctic entrance that allowed for individual access to that floor and stairs to the third floor. An artic entrance is a small entry room with an outer and inner door. This allows entry into the house without allowing the weather into the living space. You enter, shut the outer door, take off your coat and only then open the inner door. That door opened to a parking place in front that could hold three or even four smaller cars. The back door and the sliding glass door in the kitchen opened to the porch that wrapped around two sides of the house. The top or third floor had a kitchen area marked with linoleum but was not in the bad shape of the first floor. The boys used this area for a play room later. It had a large living room area we used as a bedroom when my ex was still there and two more rooms the boys shared down the hall with a bathroom at the end.

Much later when Don moved in we began fixing up the house. First we had to clean out the first floor of car parts—it was a massive undertaking. My ex had parted out four Mopar cars and stored all this here. There were four high speed transmissions, and four motors—one was a 440 and another a 383. There was four cars worth of doors, mirrors, seats… actually everything in a car except the tires. It looked just like a junk yard. Between all these stacks of car parts were boxes of little things. One box may have all the old greasy gaskets he replaced in his car and below that a set of tools he used to do it. Another box held door handles and such and another set of tools. At some point my ex decided he would only use Snap-On brand tools. This floor was filled with discarded Craftsman brand mechanic tools. Don bought two tool boxes and filled them with a complete set of tools, giving one each to the older boys.

We had the two younger boys take the two bedrooms on the third floor. Don painted a really cool mural of Dead Pool in Nicholas's room. We let our oldest move to the now car part free first floor and he fixed up the room and bathroom almost completely by himself. The living room on the third floor became Don's art studio, and mine also when I began painting silk. We converted the second floor playroom into our bedroom and fixed up the porch. Photo right is Nicholas holding Lady with his younger brother behind him. The photo was taken before the porch renovation.

I give you this house description so you can imagine the following events. We had a dog named Lady and the boys loved that dog. Nicholas was always an animal person and loved hugging her gently and playing with her nicely. Nicholas also liked to jump off the second floor porch and practice rolling upon landing. When he jumped off with Lady her leg was hurt and he couldn't understand why she got hurt when he never did.

I bought them a plastic pool, the biggest they had, which was just over 4 foot across. Filled completely, it reached just a tad over 12 inches deep. Don was in the living room cleaning when he heard the noise of a boy running wildly through the house followed by a yelled "Wa-Hoo!" He investigated immediately and found

Nicholas beginning at the front door on the second floor, running through the house to the back door and leaping off the porch into the one foot wading pool.

The photo bottom right, again thank you Google, you can see it is a corner lot, and you can see the fence and the distance was 6-10 feet in different places between the yard level and the road below.

The five foot tall fence was a gift from my family. They all came and it was a bit like a barn raising. It was the first thing done when we moved in. Everyone agreed we had to try to keep the boys contained some- how. Photo center is Nicholas, Andy, and Jamie.

My family had helped me make a sled run (we called it a Luge Run) in the back yard in Turnagain and the older two boys remembered it fondly. When we had good snow in the Spenard house they packed the snow on to the railing free stair that ran from the second floor porch to the back yard on level with the first floor. Packed hard and smoothed down this made an ideal launching ramp. They then banked snow across the yard to keep the sled on track and then created a ramp up the back fence. With a good run they were up and over the back fence. Their logic as explained to me was that there was no danger from cars because they were up and over at a good ten feet above street level. Nicholas tried it first and they had not allowed for the fence on the other side of the road. Head stitches of course.

I mentioned before about Nicholas being loaned to my sis- ter. He stayed a few days down on the island after her visi- tors left. One day the PJ's were doing water work near the island and Nicholas was watching them from the beach. They had an hours long break between parts of the training and thought they would go halibut fishing. They knew Nich- olas from the base as one of the guys, Mike, had two sons around the same age and we were a tight knit community. They stopped and asked if Nicholas could go with them. This would be Nicholas's first halibut fishing experience. Mike said he would bait the hooks. They are a massive steel hook almost as big as a persons hand. The first fish Nicholas caught was small for a halibut—its called a chick- en. Mike encouraged him to throw it back in the ocean, alive of course. He was hav- ing none of that. It was his first fish ever. The second one he caught you can see in the photo right, was twice that size. It still qualified as a chicken but Mike didn't encourage him to throw that one back. He said, "That's a big one. Why it's so big I bet you could reach in and get my hook back." He was kidding of course, knowing his boys would look at him like he was crazy and not attempt the taunt. Mike told me later that when Nicholas retrieved his hook and bait from that fish, he decided he would never dare one of my boys again.

I quote a friend who said, "Abbott's are easily entertained." In the bottom right photo the entertainment of the day was when we found a big old front end loader tire. Nicholas and another boy would climb into the tire and at low tide we would roll it down the beach toward the water, some 3-400 feet. If you look at the photo on the previous page with Nicholas and the halibut you can see that at low tide, from the beach head to the water is almost the length of a football field and has at least a 10 degree slope. Their goal was to balance well enough that the tire did not fall over until they wanted it to, that being just before entering the water. From the beach head we all were loudly cheering them on which was their reward. It moved pretty fast.

Living on an island in nowhere Alaska has lots of challenges, and lots of dangers. When we were kids these dangers never worried us, but we rarely told our mom about them either. Like the time we were playing in the big cave and the tide came in and we had no where to go, surrounded by cliffs on all sides. My brother threw down a rope and hauled us up. This one my mother did find out about. The ocean in Kachemak Bay ranges in temperature from mid thirties to even as high as 55 in the heat of the summer. Summer back then was usually 60 and 70s. Now temps are higher, a few years ago they had unheard of 90 degree weather in Anchorage. This is not blazing hot weather where you are thirsting for a cold dip. This is nicely warm weather and the water cold enough to give you brain freeze like eating ice cream too fast. Photo top right is Nicholas leading another boy out of a "caught by the tide" adventure. The white on the rocks is barnacles and is not the most comfortable thing to use as a handhold.

Nicholas was never afraid and the older he got the more that scared me. When we had our first ever family vacation and went to Hawaii he loved swimming there. He would fill his swim suit pockets with frozen peas or crushed potato chips, swim out and empty his pockets. Fish would immediately surround him to eat, sometimes even nipping him in their frenzy. At Hanauma Bay on Oahu two Asian tourists saw this and began clicking off pictures and pointing. "Fish Boy" they said with delight.

My sister built a house on the island and the ceilings are around 26 feet high. The first summer of building she hired my oldest as a helper to the builders. He was a great helper, often anticipating needs before being asked and happy to be building with them and of course, thirsty for their approval. The second summer of building he had a job so she hired Nicholas. The main builder came to her and said that Nicholas really scared him. He would look up and see him hopping or running across the beams all the way up there like he is strolling on a side walk. Thinking of him being only 14 this qualified for him as a heart check.

When we were on the Big Island of Hawaii we took the kids to a place called Kapoho. Here the tide pools were enormous, some 20 feet deep, and safe from currents and things. These pools were made of A'a lava. Hawaii has more than one kind of lava flow formations. One is called Pahoehoe lava and is a solidified form that is "smooth, billowy, or ropy" but is comfortable to walk on. Another type is called A'a lava. A'a lava is rough, has sharp edges and can easily cut you if you try walking on it. For places with A'a lava you have to wear water shoes to avoid being cut. We watched in horror as Nicholas ran, with fins on, from one pool to another. If he had fallen he could have been cut up badly. (I imagined the Hawaiian word coming from someone walking on A'a lava and saying, "Ah!" "Ah!" with each step.)

When Nicholas was 16 we began clearing land on the island to build a cabin. Some of the trees on our spot were 100 foot tall spruce trees. Don had cut one really tall one and as it fell it caught on several other standing trees on the edge of the clearing. Without thought for safety, Nicholas ran across the clearing yelling, "I'll get it!" He ran right up that massive tree and began jumping until it broke loose—a dangerous act to be sure. Then like an expert surfer he rode it to the ground without falling.

There is much more to the story of Nicholas but it is sad because of drugs. He wound up being arrested and had a probation officer. In his Freshman year of high school he stopped participating in school. We gave him three choices: Go back to high school until he finished; attend the Alaska Military Academy for six months and get a GED; Or sign up and take the GED test then go to work and pay rent. He chose the

Academy and graduated with an award in fitness. The moment he graduated he was back into drugs. He knew where to get them in Anchorage. When we moved to the island to build the cabin he refused to go with us and became a runaway.

At the end of that summer he turned 18 and told us in no uncertain terms that he was done with our rules and did not want our assistance with

anything. In October 2002 when we moved to
Hawaii we begged him to come with us but he was
not interested. In the next 8 years he would onset
Bi-Polar Disorder (although some medical opinions
named it Schizophrenia) and choose to live on the
streets. He had several times of being locked down
in the Anchorage Psychiatric Institute and would
inhabit a group home for a time after. Finally, the
State of Alaska assigned him a case worker and
placed him in an apartment. In 2010 on Mother's
Day weekend, he was found dead from hanging in
downtown Anchorage. Police named it suicide but
there were many indicators that it was actually a

homicide. He had been a real pain to the police and no further investigation was done.
Additionally he was trading his prescribed meds for illegal drugs from thugs and has
already had one ER visit after being beat up. We will never know for sure which it was.
It was the most   horrible thing to ever happen to me and I will never be over it. Such
potential, such charisma, such an amazing human… gone. He is buried on the island in
Alaska and my beloved younger sister and her husband lovingly tend his grave.

A few more photo of Nicholas. Top
right photo is him at Goose Lake
burying his head in the sand. Below
that is all three boys asleep (and not
fighting for once) on a drive back to
Anchorage from Homer, Alaska.
Bottom row, left to right: The last
time we saw Nicholas when we gifted
him a ticket to come stay with us in
North Carolina; Freshman year school
photo— you can see the anger; First
day of school, kindergarten, in 1991.

Nicholas

AMAGING CHILDREN PART 4 NICHOLAS AND ME. Nicholas was the most like me in personality (nature and animal lover), and the one that looked the most like me. He could push my buttons like no one else.

I could easily have wound up dying young as he did if not for joining the Air Force and getting out of Hawaii.

Give Him Rest

Precious Jesus, hear my request
Take my son, Nick, to your breast
End his pain and give him rest
His heart has been too long distressed.

P. Blackwell 9 May 2010.

Joy

Hope

my hair was not wonderfully red — but auburn.

I look into your precious face
And see myself reflected there.
Your teeth, your eyes, your freckles
And your wonderful red hair!

P. Blackwell 10 May 2010

AMAZING CHILDREN PART 3 THIRD BORN

I guess I was not destined to have run of the mill labors. With Andrew it was fairly usual (9 months) barring having appendix removed and carrying him traverse lie (vertically). With Nicholas it was full documented 10 months. I documented in desperation trying to get them to induce labor. Air Force regulations require 10 months for inducing if there are no health risks to mother or baby. I carried him traverse lie too and there was the state of my face. Christopher broke all his brother's records. My ex had an eye doctor appointment off base for his rare eye disease. He had to have a driver so I drove. While waiting I had one single contraction but it lasted 20 minutes, I timed it. This is where God intervened. I might have gone abruptual right then and there for that is where it began. My sister knew the advanced age doctor and later when she told him the story he blanched and said I would have died in his waiting room. A few days later my mother carefully cut out a bit in the newspaper about there being five incidents of Placental Abruption in Anchorage in that five year period. In four incidences both mother and baby perished. I don't always like to bother people so I just sat and waited for my husband's appointment to end. Eventually it did. I told him that we needed to go to the base hospital. I think he saw something in my eyes because for the first time ever he didn't argue. We arrived at the base and went directly to labor and delivery. There was a young lieutenant on duty. He examined me and told me I was fine and should go home. A few weeks earlier a female colonel had told me that she saw something odd. She told me it was like the placenta and baby were aging at different rates. She got me eyeball to eyeball and said, "You have delivered two children already. You know how it goes. If anything different occurs come directly here." Based on that I told the Lieutenant no I was not going home. I tried to explain but he was not used to being thwarted by an enlisted person, particularly one of only Staff Sergeant (E-5) rank. Then this doctor walked in the door. They told me later that there were nine OB/GYN docs assigned at Elmendorf and only three of them would have known what this was. He was one of those. He said he just wanted to check something on some slides he had gotten that day. The lieutenant pointed at me indignantly and said, "She won't go home." He walked over and put his hand on my knee and kindly asked what was up. At that moment I experienced a Placental Abruption. When this happens the Placenta and Uterus rip apart. The mother begins to bleed to death from this unnatural event and the baby is instantly denied oxygen. An event such as this (according to March of Dimes) can cause problems for the baby including growth issues, preterm birth or stillbirth. This doctor never hesitated for one second. He grabbed betadine solution and threw it on my belly and cut. I was so in the moment I could only watch and pray for my baby's life. Just at the 4 minute mark he had Chris in his hands and he wasn't breathing. 4 minutes of oxygen denial can begin brain damage. He held him up and patted his bottom and Chris took his first breath. There was a bit of time while they cleaned the baby up, finished my delivery, and gave me the baby while they sewed me up. I looked at him with a prayer of thanks to God. I knew the baby was safe, then I went into shock. My ex ran out of the room, down to the appointment area and scheduled a vasectomy.

Chris was a "Preemie" and had certain health issues. He didn't make eye contact, I was afraid he was blind. He had Esophageal Atresia meaning his esophagus was not all the way developed and any food he ingested was projectile vomited back up. He was only 5 pounds at birth and lost a pound with this problem. At 4 pounds he was this tiny thing that

that I could almost hold in one hand. He was just a little bean of a fellow so that became his nickname, Bean or Beaner. This photo is Chris during our Christmas photo session having gained enough to get a hospital discharge. They gave me medicine to stop the vomiting, Ranitidine, for this esophageal condition and explained how it had to be administered. Three times a day you do this; 30 minutes prior to feeding administer the medicine and wait; once the 30 minutes is achieved he can eat for no more than 30 minutes. It was quite the routine. If the medicine worked as they hoped it would stop the vomiting while the tube grew the rest of the way. I asked, "How will I know when it has grown?" "Oh, you will know!" the doctor assured me. I genuinely wish he had taken the time to explain exactly how I would know. The answer is when my baby goes into full convulsions for almost a minute. Like any place there are good doctors and bad doctors. When my ex brought Andrew and Nicholas to the hospital they were suddenly just huge children. A time alone with this tiny baby made it startling to see. When they both jumped up on the hospital bed and added a few bounces I yelled something like stop you huge things!

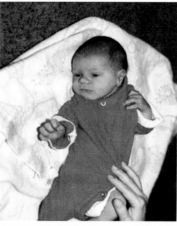

Next came the eye issues. I mentioned in the military pages about my friend Beverly and how she was the first person Chris made eye contact with at two months old. When I took him for a check up and explained about the no eye contact the doctor did some extra eye exams and then told me, "He's not blind, it's just an enormous capacity to ignore." "What?" I am yelling to myself. Then I am asking God questions. "Seriously, Sir!" "I have three children with no help and that is three against one. I have a full time job in the military and am under contract. My second born son is a disaster waiting to happen each and every day. Now you tell me this baby has an enormous capacity to ignore?"

I had a necessary method of communication I used with Nicholas. I would get down face to face with him and then gently take his chin in my hand and pull him in close until we had achieved an eyeball to eyeball confrontation. Only then was I able to assure that he had gotten the message. This was absolutely necessary if I wanted any compliance at all and only barely worked with Chris. I sighed and was thinking it was so easy with Andrew, what has happened here?

First there were three eye operations. The first was horrifying because the anesthesiologist recognized the odd last name and remembered Nicholas jumping on the bed in recovery so he gave him more than he should have and Chris slept for 26 hours straight. They finally got his eyes fixed so he didn't have a lazy eye. There was a pause in the eye checks and they kept putting me off for making the follow-up appointment. I finally went to the clinic to ask and it turned out that the doctor had PCS'd (Permanent Change of Station) and there would be no replacement until six months later. To this day Chris has trouble with his depth perception. There is always a silver lining. Because of this delay, Chris did not have his eyes working normally at first so he developed much better hearing than the average child.

Always sensitive to loud noises, but he enjoyed music a lot. Once he was sitting in front of the television watching 'Little Mermaid'. He was hardly talking yet but sang with "Ah's" along with Ariel. He had perfect pitch I was told.

Chris was small. In fact he was so under weight that the school allowed me to bring a box of fruit and protein snacks and store them in the school principals office. Twice a day (between arrival and lunch, and between lunch and end of school) he was allowed to go to the office for a snack to try to get his weight up.

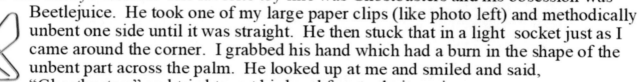

I had stupidly thought that having another baby would help in my marriage, but it only made it worse. We argued over everything. He said he hated how I followed a family tradition of giving the boys a family last name as their middle name as my parents had done with us. He finally agreed when I said I wanted it to be his mother's maiden name. Chris's middle name is Hanson. When he met his kindergarten teacher he proudly told her his full name was Christopher Handsome Czikra.

Chris was always curious. His favorite toy line was Ghostbusters and his obsession was Beetlejuice. He took one of my large paper clips (like photo left) and methodically unbent one side until it was straight. He then stuck that in a light socket just as I came around the corner. I grabbed his hand which had a burn in the shape of the unbent part across the palm. He looked up at me and smiled and said, "Ghostbusters" and tried to get his hand free to do it again.

During this time was when I lost the baby sitter on base and my ex changed to night shift so we did not have to pay for baby sitting. He was not a happy camper *at all* having to do this. We moved from the rental to the purchased house and it needed lots of fixing up. I left the Air Force and moved to the Alaska Air Guard. He retired from the Air Force and took a job in a civilian air transport company run by two retired Air Force colonels I had worked with. He began his last and longest affair and had the audacity to bring "his friend" to Friday night with my family. He also took the boys to see her son play baseball and such, even though he would not allow any of our three to participate in sports, have sleep overs, or even leave the confines of our house and yard without one of us. He also had four heart attacks during this time.

He was a completely non compliant patient and didn't change a thing after having a heart attack. It was only months before he had his second, and he was always very angry at all this. We were in the ER and he was on the gurney. His heart doctor had been called in from off duty and had obviously been hiking with his hiking boots and wool socks and shorts. He grabbed my ex by the shirt yanking him up face to face and said, "Was that last cigarette worth it?" and let him drop back down on to the gurney. They showed us a movie that showed the veins around the heart and the person took a drag off the cigarette and the veins actually contracted. I get lost in the order but after one heart attack they did some cybernetic complicated thing but it did not do much so he had another one. They finally decided to do open heart surgery with his fourth. You have to know that his heart doctor postponed his surgery because he was such an awful patient, terrible to the hospital staff, and he insisted it be done when he was off vacation and could run blocker at the hospital.

As always I bought the boys to visit him after his open heart surgery. He lay in his hospital bed with all these wires connected to him for monitors and the big old staples going down his bare chest. Chris took one look from the door and planted his heels and would not go in the cubicle. This angered the ex who began yelling over and over, "Then he is not my son!" and setting off all the bells and whistles, so we had to leave. It was really more like fleeing.

One night Nicholas woke me up and said "Beaner's on the roof." Apparently he had crawled out his third floor window on to the roof which by then had no railings because my ex had torn them all down. It was a two story drop. There he was, in his little sleeper, knocking on the window. I did wonder later about Nicholas being awake to witness or perhaps assist in this event, but he assured me the knocking had woken him up.

When my ex had recovered enough to go back to babysitting we were grateful it was only Chris he had to watch. He didn't cook or fix food so to feed Chris he would drive to the grocery store and buy something at the deli. Chris particularly loved the teriyaki chicken on a stick. The deli person commented on the fact that they, regulars, had been gone for a while. I found out later he replied, "Yeah, my kid gave me a heart attack."

Chris was very particular about food and basically only wanted to eat baloney and cheese and macaroni and cheese. Fresh fruit is very expensive in Alaska and was outside our budget but he had words for each kind of canned fruit. "Pears taste like they have sand in them. Peaches are like slimy slugs. Mandarin oranges are like a squirt of juice in a cellophane bag."

We had a wonderful, female, civilian pediatric doctor at the base. She was smart, observant and kind. When I took Chris in for a checkup he solemnly asked, "Are you gonna take all my clothes off and put me on the table?" I freaked. This seemed to me an obvious indicator of sexual abuse. But this doctor was smart. She leaned down to his level and asked him why he wanted her to do that. Chris replied, "So you can check my heart is still beating."

At any rate this was the beginning of the end. I took the boys all to counselling at the base because the atmosphere was violent and difficult. It was a big deal to have to leave work, pick up the kids from the off-base schools, take them to the base hospital for counseling, and wait while they all three had their appointments. The oldest two did not survive more than a month before I called it quits. Andy passed the one on one sessions quickly and was put in group. There, he told me, he was the only one who got A's; he was the only one who had never been arrested, he was the only one who had not been to jail… I got the point and didn't make him go again. Nicholas convinced the psychologist that I was just a poor mom experiencing the grief of going through a divorce. She deemed him fine and moved him to group. I asked her, "Then why does he bang his head against the wall in anger?" Nicholas said they had races with the wheeled chairs in group. I was mad! I asked what the adult in the room was doing and he replied that she was keeping score. I didn't take him back either. Chris on the other hand needed the assistance of this kind psychologist and told her many things. When my ex followed me to the clinic she got right in his face and told him he was never to come back there or she would get her cattle prod out and use it on him. They requested that I get restraining orders against him for all the doctors in the clinic. Once he was really violent and I took shelter at the base. Kulis Air Guard Base was a small community and being a social butterfly I knew most everyone on base. The gate guard recognized me and waved me through on to the base, but stopped the ex in his car as he had caught up to us.

He jumped out of the car and began berating the security police so they planted him facedown in the dirt until he calmed down. I eventually wound up at the Anchorage Women's Shelter and I have to say some of their classes were very beneficial to me. The last straw was when we were arguing and Andrew tried to step between us, I knew it had to end.

Before school began each year I made an appointment with the principal. We found it essential to confer and choose the best teachers for my boys in hopes of lessening problems. For Chris, I chose the kindergarten teacher who had been doing it for 27 years. She decided to quit after that year with Chris and he was given a complimentary pass having not completed the normal tasks for kindergarten.

First they told me he could not pay attention at all and was disrupting all the other children. They put him at the back of the room to lessen the impact of this and it happened to be right where the class pencil sharpener was. I arrived to pick him up for a doctors appointment and they said I had to wait until he finished cleaning the pencil sharpener. The noise was irritating him so he extracted the peanut butter from his peanut butter cracker snack, opened the pencil sharpener and proceeded to "Oil It" which did stop the grating noise but also covered the pencil in peanut butter. I thought it was pretty smart. He stopped up the toilet so many times he became buddies with the janitor. They then insisted he be medicated or they wouldn't let him stay. We tried Ritalin and it was not a good fit. He told my friend (later niece) that he felt like there were bugs crawling all over his skin. In class he shoved his desk across the room from the windows because he told the teacher the plants on the window sill were touching him.

Next we tried Dexedrine. This worked pretty well for school but caused problems at home. He no longer slept at night and could get into all kinds of mischief. They added a medication to help him sleep at night. Later they added one because this made him gain weight so fast. Regardless of what was added when, when Don moved in with us I had a chart on the wall listing all the adult psychiatric medications and when they were to be given. They were still treating him for ADHD (Attention-Deficit / Hyperactivity Disorder) and OCD (Obsessive-Compulsive Disorder) and had decided that he also had Bi-Polar Disorder.

I had a collection of Madame Alexander dolls. Chris was fascinated and could not keep his hands off. Soon Jamaica's sandal was in two pieces; Captain Hook permanently lost his hook; Tinkerbell's hair was trashed and the tiara missing; and Peter Pan lost his hat feather. These were collector dolls and right now on eBay, on sale at a discounted price, in pristine condition in the box, Peter Pan and Tinkerbell cost $72.47 and Captain Hook $44.99. My mother built me a doll house for them. I packed them up and put them away again. Then he removed all the cool barnacles from my Japanese Glass Balls (like the ones on the photo from Pinterest but my barnacles were huge, two inches at the base.)

I had a lace fan that my grandmother had received from Japan on her world tour, he shredded it.

Chris destroyed the portable VCR we had by reaching in the slot for the cassette and ripping out a piece of the playing mechanism. He claimed that he didn't think it looked like it belonged in there. I never did discover what happened to VCR number four. He took the toaster apart to put it back together. He did not like going outside in the winter months. The frozen ground really creeped him out and his brother complained he took five times as long to cross the school yard to Camp Fire because of placing his feet like he was going through a land mine field in order to not step on any earth that crunched.

Like me he is a social butterfly and his older brother complained to me. "He knows everyone's name in the whole school, including every girl in my class. It's embarrassing!"

My mother gave Andy skating lessons and Chris wanted to skate too, but hated being out in the winter. Nearly every school had an outdoor rink but he also did not like the cold. So he buttered the kitchen floor to have an indoor skating rink. I heard the phone ring and entered the kitchen to answer it. As you can see in the photo on the right, the kitchen was just a hallway about 10 feet long between the living room and the dining room with a sliding glass door at the end that opened onto the porch. I was slipping and sliding and trying to get my footing to answer the phone. Now, it having rung long enough, Andrew came tearing in to get it and his speed had him slide right through the kitchen and up against the sliding glass door, luckily it did not break.

One event in kindergarten was their annual Christmas Concert. The school presented a program for the parents. Each grade performed several songs. The lunch room was full of standing parents and the children brought in grade by grade and performed standing on some bleachers at the front of the room. Although I arrived before it started, I was too late to get a seat up front and was in the standing room only at the back of the sea of parents. The teacher had put him on the front corner right next to her. When he started acting up I didn't know what to do. First he was tugging on the music the children near him were holding. Then he began swaying and pushing and some of the children who almost fell. His teacher's face was getting redder and redder. I exited the room, went down the hall filled with children waiting to perform and into the door nearest the bleachers. I stood next to the wall there and caught his attention pointing my finger at him so he knew I was saying to behave. He grinned ear to ear when he saw me and instead of facing forward like the rest of the children, he turned sideways so he was facing me directly. He began making sweeping gestures with the music like he was performing a great play for me. I could hear whispers in the crowd. "He is so cute." I wanted to say, "That is why he is still alive."

In first grade he got an exceptional teacher who was delighted with his amazing brain. She was writing a book about him she told me. I was in the kitchen and he was in the bath tub 8 feet away when he yelled to me, "I figured out life, Mom. Its like the bath, the longer you stay, the more wrinkled you get." He thought completely out of the box.

When they had a part in class about ethnicity and were discussing hair colors, skin colors, and eye shapes. He had a friend named Kenny who was of Japanese decent. The teacher asked the class, how can we tell Kenny is Japanese. Chris frantically waved his had to be called on and she finally did, delaying it because she was afraid what he might say, he said, "Lift up Kenny's shirt and see if it says 'Made in Japan'." When we had pizza one night he took the  small white plastic piece used to prevent the pizza from getting smashed. He balanced one on top of another and put some Italian sausage on both. He then asked me if I knew what it was. I said I had no idea, and he responded, "My table of contents."

We were very fortunate with this first grade teacher. She worked with him and in the first months he had conquered all the kindergarten curriculum. At the end of the year she chose to move to teaching second grade so she could have him again and he was very successful in school for those two years.

Then came third grade. In the first months of school he went through the three assigned third grade teachers. Two were regular and one was a class of two grades joined. They each felt they could not handle him and he wound up spending his days in a classroom with the extracurricular teacher one on one.

They decided they needed to test him and had a special group of tests. First he was observed leaving his classroom to go to the principals office where he would be picked up for the testing. They wrote it all down. He skipped out of his room, went down the hall reaching up and touching each piece of artwork that was hung in a row down in the hall. He arrived at a library cart left in the hall which he used for a short ride before returning it to where it was. He stopped three times to speak to someone passing by in the hall.

On the IQ test he scored off the charts. The tester took time to meet with me. He said he had been testing children for 25 years and Chris was the brightest child he had ever tested and he had actually quite enjoyed his time with him.

From very early Chris had an exceptional vocabulary and a curious nature. The night Don moved in with us he set his room on fire. He had gotten up after we went to bed, had collected various items from around the house including newspaper, my little metal egg cups (that have no handle because they go in a rack that fits in the pan), a candle, matches and more. First he was exploring the making of paper from some show he had seen on television. For this he had taken the newspapers and shredded them, they were all over the floor. Then he moved on to his second experiment which involved the lit candle and the little egg cups. As he heated the egg cup with the candle, it got hot and began to burn his hand so he dropped it right on the candle which in one whoosh lit all that newspaper on fire. Luckily Nicholas woke up immediately at the smell of smoke. He ran down and pounded on our door saying "Christopher's room is on fire!" We ran upstairs and by now the fire had engulfed the rug, a fabric covered chair in his room and the curtains. Don stopped in the doorway flabbergasted and frozen, making a funny sound. I leapt into action, ran right past his room, got the trashcan from the bathroom next door, and was carting water back and forth putting out the fire.

We wound up moving him to a different school for fourth grade hoping for a new start. He was assigned a male teacher and this really seemed to help a lot. We got another kind male teacher for 5th grade and hope for the future was born.

In the photo right his head was shaved because he went to bed with a big wad of gum in his mouth and it was so tangled in his hair it had to be shaved.

His room was a health hazard. Don swore there were little elves in his closet that came and shredded papers and put trash all over right after his room was cleaned. The older brothers were like locust and ate everything, especially when friends were over. They finished off a gallon of milk and a box of cereal each morning. We bought $500 worth of groceries at the commissary (much lower prices) every two weeks and it was all gone the day we went shopping. Chris would find something he liked, like a fried chicken drumstick and hide it in his room. We found sour gallons of milk hidden in his closet, chicken bones in his dresser drawers with his clothes. Don tired of seeing me cleaning his room and said he would teach him how to do it himself. First he went with Chris and they cleaned the whole room, putting toys in baskets and filling a number of large trash bags with trash. In no time at all it was a disaster again. Don explained that he had showed him how and now he needed to do it on his own. We coached him, "Start with the clothes on the floor…" but he gave up before making much progress at all. Don told him he would clean it but Chris would not like it. Chris just shrugged. Don put everything on the floor in trash bags, clothes, toys and all, and took it away. This happened twice and then the next time he cleaned his room himself.

Annually they held an all schools concert and Chris was to play his trumpet in this event. He was most pleased with the spit valve and likely to empty it often, regardless of where he was. He was concentrating on that valve, never the consequences. Don saw him blowing his spit on the floor and getting it on the girl next to him who tried to move away bumping the kid next to her and causing the disturbance to go down the row. Although he loved to play and had a   natural knack for music this first concert didn't go well and they removed him from the floor.

One of the real treats for Chris during this time was getting Sourdough Mike for a music teacher. They really hit it off and it completely solidified Christopher's love of music. Sourdough Mike McDonald was a bass singer with an amazing voice. He sang in the Anchorage Chorus and in the Whale Fat Follies at the Fly By Night Club. He was an Alaskan Icon.

Sixth grade was a royal disaster. I am not sure how this woman became a teacher or was even allowed around children. She was horrible. Chris told us all about how she went out of the classroom to her car and strangled the puppies in there that were barking. She harassed and made fun of Chris, particularly when he drifted off from concentrating. We asked him how this made him feel and he replied, "It's actually kind of refreshing because I am not singled out, she harasses all the kids in the class."

At the end of the year there was a dance party for the 6th graders at the school. Chris begged to go but we were apprehensive. Only chaperon parents were invited into the dance so we dropped him off. Before time to pick him up they called and asked us to come. Chris didn't have the best hygiene and was known to pick his nose, draw with his spit, and other things girls that age find disguising. Not one of them would dance with him. He found an office chair on wheels and was pushing himself up and down the hall ways cussing most creatively.

This was a rough year with his brother, Nicholas, who was now experimenting with drugs. Nicholas was angry and lashing out, particularly at his little brother. He would be playing a video game and Chris, not allowed to play, would stand and watch. He has some inner sense that allows him to see a video game almost as if he were in it himself. He would blurt out, "Go this way." Nicholas would yell, "Shut up!" "But I know that is how it is!" "Shut up or I will pound you." Soon enough he was afraid of his brother.

He entered seventh grade and the problems were immediate. There is not the concentrated attention of a teacher in a classroom in junior high when they move to six different classes and teachers every day.

One day he wasn't paying attention and didn't make the bus before it left. We lived not more than ten blocks from Romig Middle School (2002) but to get to our house you must cross busy Northern Lights Boulevard. Chris made it two blocks in the right direction but then was tired and did not want to walk home all the way. Seeing a school bus in the 5th lane over on Northern Lights, he walked out into traffic. All the honking alerted the driver and he turned on his flashers, put out his flag, and stopped traffic, getting Chris onto the bus and kindly brought him home.

A week later Chris got in an argument with another special needs kid in his class who had hurt him so he slammed the boy's arm in the desk. At this point Don and the head psychiatrist at Elmendorf worked to get him into a residential center for some help. This was the place we got the first correct diagnosis—Aspergers Syndrome or High Functioning Autism. We dispensed with all the unnecessary drugs and he has never taken any since.

Left—First family portrait with Don in our lives. Right—Chris driving 4-wheeler on Yukon Island some years later.

When we retired from the Air Force we both cashed out our Air Guard retirement bonuses. This was an Alaska bonus of $100 for every month spent in the Guard. I also had an inheritance from my Mom, and Don had a big sale of his artwork. All this combined allowed us to build a cabin on the island.

Chris was with us during the summer of building and we decided to homeschool him as we spent the year there. We enrolled him in the Alaska State correspondence course. I was handling the academic portions and Don with his boat master certification agreed to teach him the boating safety course. While he did well on the academic portion of this, the practical was a disaster. Don took him out in our boat. He explained all the controls and what it meant to get the boat up on step. He showed Chris that rain water had accumulated in the boat and they would need to get the boat up on step, pull the drain plug, and drain the water. Chris wanted nothing to do with sticking his hand down in the cold dirty water to pull the plug. Don instructed him on exactly how he would have to run the boat while Don pulled the plug. Don got him all set then laid down on the deck and pulled the plug. All of a sudden he heard yelling and cussing. Chris had kept the boat up on step, at the correct speed but had come close to side swiping a boat with fishermen in it. When Don popped up they were still shaking their fists. He got the boat turned around and showed Chris the Homer Spit in the distance and told him to aim for the Spit. Again Don laid on the deck, pulled the plug, and got the water all drained out. Job done he stood up only to find the boat headed for a cliff and the rocks below which would have destroyed the boat. Don declined to continue boating lessons as he feared it would better for both their health and would wait until Chris was older.

By October the cabin was livable. We had sanded all the interior walls, installed a bar sectioning off the kitchen area. We put in the stove, stove pipe, and kitchen cabinets. We had built a pantry and Don had begun staining the outside. Chris dug the outhouse, we planted a garden and Don and Chris carted load after load of gravel with the Bobcat up to make our road . You know how to make God laugh? Tell him your plans for your life. Plans changed and instead of staying a year in the cabin to finish it, and saving our money, we moved to Hawaii

One last Yukon Island story. Andy came down for a weekend on the island with us. He had some trouble and was mad about something. He threw his keys (car and house) down on the dock in Homer. They skipped across the dock and went 'plunk' into the water. Although he borrowed a magnet from the Harbor Master there was no finding them. Chris was given a harmonica by Don's father, Seagle Blackwell. He made up a clever song, accompanied with the harmonica, about the whole incident. "Lost my keys in Ke-che-mak Bay…."

We purchased land on the Big Island of Hawaii that I found online—a 3-acre spaghetti lot for $8000—some years before going to see it. Don's brother accused him of buying a 'pig in a poke' since we bought the land without seeing it. We took this photo to send to him. I am the pig in the poke and Don the cigar smoking land owner.

Hawaii turned out to be the wrong place for us. We poured our hearts into landscaping and building a home there. We thought that would be the dream: the three beautiful months of summer on the island in Alaska and the other nine months in paradise Hawaii. In the time span between when we purchased the land and arrived to build, people had been growing marijuana on our land and our arrival was most inconvenient. We did manage to get Chris through the school year homeschooling and he caught up all his math and sciences and maintained a high B average. We knew he could do it. He spent his sophomore year in public school in Hawaii, which was also not a good thing due to drugs.

We held an art party with all the new friends we had met. One lady said to us, "This is unique. I have never been to a party in Hawaii where there were no drugs."

We had to wait six months to get the contractor to bulldoze our land so we could begin building and landscaping. During this time we lived in a rental. I had avocado seeds suspended with toothpicks in a jar and our landlord asked what that was. He was a botanist. He said you know how you grow avocados in Hawaii? I said no. He threw the seed down and said, "That's how." It tuned out to be true. We would go visit friends and if we liked a plant they had, they would cut a piece off and we would soon have our own plant. We drove all over the island picking up palm tree seeds and soon had a whole nursery of palms growing. I nurtured fruit seeds and later planted the resulting plant on our land. Soon we had 27 different fruits growing. When we sold it we got an extra $30,000 in the assessment for "excellent landscaping".

A Science Experiment Day
May 2, 2003

As part of his Earth Science course we did a survey of the flora and fauna in a
thirty six inch square area. His science teacher in Alaska thought this was very
interesting since all the rest of his student surveys were done in Alaska.

We moved up to our land and stayed in a tent city (top photo and bottom left photo) we built from four Costco garage tents. It was quite a nice arrangement. We had our bedroom (2nd photo down) in one tent to the left. Chris had his own tent to the far right (3rd photo down). In between were two more tents, one was our kitchen (4th photo down), the other (5th photo down) held all our packed boxes. We grouped the tents facing each other in a arrangement where all the tent openings faced each other. We got an old radio tower to put in the center. This raised the big tarp over all the entrances, creating a nice lanai for living room and dining room. Most of the time it was really great, when there was bad weather, like the three near hurricanes we endured, it was not so great. We spent 154 days in this tent arrangement. It was windy most of the time on the Big Island and my every morning chore was sewing the tarp back together.

Building a house on raw land in Hawaii is no joke. Nothing can go underground because its all lava. We had to run electric, install a catchment tank for water, have a septic system installed. Don handled it all.

Once on our land we had troubles. Twice someone set our lot on fire trying to burn us out, they still wanted to grow there. Luckily both times the contractor was on the roof of the house in progress and saw the smoke, so we got it put out. When I was picking up Chris from school someone stole all of Don's tools and other easy to sell items. We would work on landscaping all day then the pigs from the neighbor would come root up all our work. It just was not for us.

Bottom right photo shows the morning tarp repair affair.

There were other creatures like these huge spiders, cane spiders, on our land. These creatures have a leg span of 3-5 inches and can jump straight up in the air 5 feet… un-natural I thought. Because of the wind we bought 2 x 12 planks to bolt to the tent legs that ran the length of each tent on both sides.

For added help we placed sand bags all the way down these planks. One storm I stayed up all night to try to keep the rain out and assure Chris. At the height of the storm the 2 x 12s and sandbags were being lifted over a foot off the ground.

There were also guy wires for the tents. Don was tying one when Chris spotted a cane spider running down the spine of the tent. "Dad…" he yelled. Before he got the rest of the sentence out it traversed the tent, ran down Don's back and was across the lot. Once one took up residence in our Porta-Potty, Chris refused to go in there anymore.

One night there was this huge praying mantis, a full six inches long, that would not leave our bedroom tent. I was sure if we left it alone it would drop on me in the night so I spent two hours coaching him out of our tent.

We made an orchard area and planted a lime tree, two kinds of lemon trees, two kinds of orange trees, four avocado (so they would produce in all seasons), two kinds of banana trees, about eight papaya trees (they told us they have a short life span), one star fruit plant, a purple and a yellow passion fruit plant, four pineapple plants grown from a pineapples we ate and planted the stem, a guava tree, a lychee nut tree, a coconut, dragon fruit, mango, and noni, yes we went a little crazy.

We made a lovely wandering trail with all the trees and plants we collected and called it the Odessey Trail. Don built a structure at the beginning of the trail (photo center right).

Chris volunteered at the local no kill shelter after school (photo top right). He would sit for hours in the cage with the cats patiently petting every one that came near. The cats loved it and so did the people. One night this cat moved in with us and Chris named her Dolly. Much to his delight she produced three kittens for his entertainment (photo bottom right).

Realizing that we did not belong here, Don went on to North Carolina to find us a home and Chris and I stayed until the house was built enough to sell, as I said, a total of 154 days in that tent city. We never lived in the house but had no trouble selling it.

North Carolina is where we were meant to be. I thought it was neat that here Chris would graduate from the same high school as his dad, some 30 years later. Here Chris would get his high school diploma; get his Massage Therapy license; learn to play the guitar and begin writing excellent songs and playing in public; take violin and voice lessons; get an associates degree in Computer Networking and come into his own.

Christopher

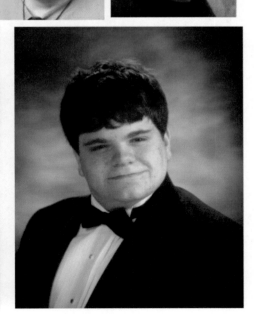

The beginning of our nursery business in Hawaii.

The plants below were Pheasant Wood Trees, the start of our nursery. They were supposed to be worth $30K when mature… maybe retirement too.

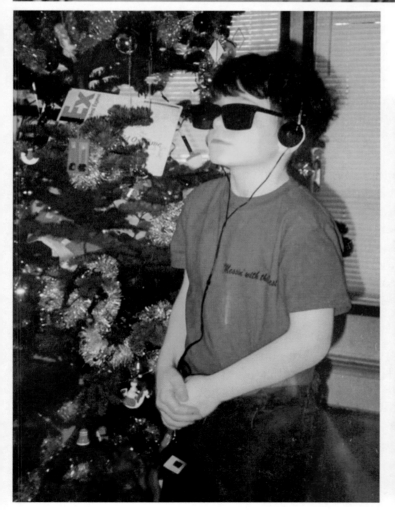

AMAZING CHILDREN THE STEPS

I cannot adequately tell you all the great blessings I have received from having step children. Jamie was my first step child and is the son of my ex-husband who has passed from this life. From first meeting him I felt bad for him because it was obvious, he was treated poorly compared to his younger half-brother. Seriously, his mother and father were brutal to each other and despite their vitriol towards one another face to face, it was most likely that they still loved each other to the day he died.

They were not high school sweethearts, although they could have been. Jamie's mother met his father in Ohio through her aunt that she was staying with. Jamie was told she had been sent away from New York for her behavior, and because her aunt (her mother's sister) was good with girls that were considered "behavioral problems". Oddly enough, this aunt never had any children of her own due to reproductive issues. At any rate her aunt was far and away more suited to be a mother than her own mother who was very narcissistic and self-centered. So they fell in love in Ohio.

His father, who was in the Air Force, got orders to South East Asia, (Thailand) during the Vietnam era. He left his wife and child stateside with practically nothing and no means to get around. His mother had never gotten her driver's license, and she had to bum rides from people for trips to the grocery store and laundry mat. When he managed a trip home, she finally convinced him to help her get her driver's license (and really, he relented only because she was threatening to start paying for taxi's and to report him to the base commander for abandonment.)

While they were married, she was working two jobs to support Jamie, at a club off base and at the base NCO club, as well as taking care of him as a single parent. Meanwhile, sending almost no money home they got pictures of him in Thailand "modeling" hand sewn, custom shirts and slacks. He told me how in Thailand they had a house maid who cleaned their house, made all their meals, polished their boots, pressed their uniforms, and "did anything they needed done". He loved being there with all that personal attention and even years later told me he wished he had never had to leave Thailand.

Home life for Jamie was not only sparce financially, but there were other factors – the brutal fighting. His mother's mother and his father despised one another (it was said, "they were two peas in a pod, both selfish, self-absorbed narcissistic personalities that could basically care less about others needs or feelings, as long as their own needs were fulfilled.) I feel certain Jamie's grandmother often pointed out the mistake his mother made in marrying his father. Additionally, there were hard feelings over him spending all his paycheck in Thailand and sending almost none home. Soon they were divorced. He told me that he had sent all these things to his son and they were either returned to sender or not acknowledged so he stopped sending them. I later came to doubt this was true.

Jamie's father married again to a woman in Louisiana. He claimed he married her just so she could get custody of her younger children. He had been stationed in Louisiana and actually dating one of her older daughters, who was still in her teens. He had shown me hateful letters from the daughter when he began divorce proceedings and told them about me. I really didn't want to know any more than that. Leaving Germany, I had orders to Altus AFB in Oklahoma, he had orders to Dyess AFB in Texas. We were not married so not eligible for the 'Join Spouse Program."

I was so dumb and naïve. We worked in the same area in Germany. He took me volksmarching in Luxembourg. Although I worked a later shift, he came on his own time and helped me learn avionic instrumentation. He was kind and funny. He convinced me that I had to be with him. He emphasized the difficulty of being a single parent. The baby needed a female and a male influence. Consider the cost of living for a single parent. We moved off base with another airman because I could not have a baby in the dorm. Somehow by the time we moved we were sharing a bedroom. He asked me to marry him. I held off, but then the baby was born. My mother met him and pled with me not to marry him, my sister met him and demanded I not marry him. He left Germany first and I had some months with no help. I had the nightmare of traveling with the baby and too much luggage.

I flew to Anchorage with Andy to be with my mom for a week. After my time there, I met up with Jamie's dad in Ohio where he was staying with his mother. I should have gotten a clue when he picked me up from the airport and we drove to his mother's house. His father was in the front yard and he walked right past him without acknowledging him, pulling me rudely along so I didn't address him either. He told me he had not spoken to him since he watched his father beat his mother bloody. While I was in Alaska, his second divorce was finalized and he insisted on getting married so we could get the same base of assignment.

One part of me believed him when he said I could not afford to raise a child on my own and I was concerned about taking good care of Andy. One part of me knew it was wrong to marry him. We were married by the Air Force Chaplain on Wright-Patterson AFB in Ohio. I was shaking so badly when the ceremony began that the chaplain asked his wife to hold Andrew (who was 7 months old or so) and took me in the other room. He commented on the shaking and asked if I was being coerced into marrying. I finally calmed down enough to stop shaking, and we resumed. For our honeymoon we went out and had banana-splits. Soon after we left to drive to Oklahoma.

As they say, "the days of wine and roses" were over once that marriage license was signed. Where before he could be charming, now he didn't bother. He began his first affair when we had been married only two months.

We drove from Ohio to Kentucky to Tennessee to Arkansas and as we crossed the border into Oklahoma, he told me his son lived there in Sulphur, Oklahoma, which was directly on the way to Altus, and he wanted to stop and see him. It was storming and pouring the rain when we got to Sulphur. He stopped at a phone booth and called to let them know he was coming. We arrived, soaked from the rain, Andy was sleepy and whiney, and from the moment we arrive the fighting began… "You can't just come unannounced!" "You haven't even been communicating with him so why come now?" On and on. By now she was remarried and had a child with her new husband.

Although the difference in treatment between the two brothers was startlingly obvious, I didn't really know what it was all about. Jamie told me, "As far as the situation with my younger brother, things were reasonably good when I was the only child, I didn't necessarily get everything that I ever wanted by any means, but in hindsight I received my fair share plus, but of course that changes when another comes into the picture, and initially things didn't change tremendously with the exception of the level of care that a newborn requires. I accepted this pretty easily as I realized in short

order that I certainly did not want that responsibility. 😂 However, as time went on, the duplicity of the household became over-whelming, and admittedly so, I was an overweight kid and my mother's method (or attempt) at my weight control was to strictly limit what I could and could not eat. This is a recipe for disaster because it only makes someone want it more or steers them to other avenues to satisfy any wanton cravings. So, of course, that's what happened, as well as creating a divide between my brother and myself. This was a terrible situation at that time for my brother as well, especially since he didn't have a clue as to what was happening because of her actions. It wasn't something he had any ability to make the connection between us for her actions. So needless to say, I hated life and everyone in it at that time. This created a situation that made me become fiercely independent, and it has been pretty much the same way ever since. Just get out of my way and I'll do it myself, I don't require any help. This also became the time where I withdrew from a lot of my family, as I was just of the opinion that if no one was going to make effort to reach out to me then I would reciprocate in kind."

When Jamie was 13 years old, he came to live with us. It was supposed to be a trial for the summer. He was smart, funny, always helpful and an all-around good kid. Since his father did not "do kids or women's work" and I had just had my second child it was a real boon to have a help-ful teenager. I insisted on being fair so although the two younger boys were my birth children and he was not, there would not been special foods he didn't get to share in, and certainly no special stock pile in a pantry he was not allowed to touch. There would be no privileges given them but not him. He had not experienced this and like a flower bloomed under this sun. He helped with his little step brothers, and he watched over them fiercely. He never had to be reminded of chores and often just hung around me to lend a hand if I needed one. We hit if off from the start and spent real quality time together that summer. It was a foundation solid and lasting.

But Jamie had to endure the nightly drill. His father would begin drinking and feeling better with every drink. He could not imagine how his ex could live without him. He would demand of his son details of what she did, what she and her husband did, what she liked, how she lived and every other question except any about him. This was sad for Jamie at first; later it became very burdensome. All summer the two parents fought hard over who he would live with next. Jamie remembered the different treatment he got from his brother if he lived with his mother. He thought of the badgering and indifference of his father. At least with his mother he had his friends and would be going back to school with them. In the end he chose to go back to Sulphur.

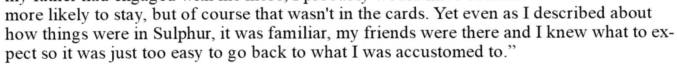

Jamie later told me, "The time spent in Altus was so different from pretty much anything that I had experienced up to that time. First, living in a new town with no friends was a bit daunting, but fortunately you made it far less frightening that it could have been. Your willingness to engage with me and trying to make me as comfortable as possible was absolutely a difference maker. Up to that point in my life, I had met only one other person like you that was seeing me for me and not just some kid that was in the way or something to have to find a way to deal with until I could be refocused so you could do whatever you needed or wanted to do. Like my best friend's mom, who was originally my den mother when I was a Cub Scout, you made it feel like what I had to say actually mattered. No matter how ridiculous or out of this world the idea that came out of my mouth, you still were willing to entertain it for at least a moment and even if it was for just a moment, that moment meant the world. Unfortunately, every effort that you made wasn't enough to keep me in Altus permanently. It was absolutely not your fault [that I left], quite the opposite. You were the one bright spot there was there, and honestly, if my father had engaged with me more, I probably would have been far more likely to stay, but of course that wasn't in the cards. Yet even as I described about how things were in Sulphur, it was familiar, my friends were there and I knew what to expect so it was just too easy to go back to what I was accustomed to."

I didn't see him again until we attended his wedding. He got through high school and was marrying his long-time girlfriend. It was suggested that he at least reach out to his father to let him know that his first born was going to be tying the knot. I was honored to be asked, thrilled for Jamie, and insisted we go. Of course, the two back together, the fight was on. It did not seem that the two had any regard for how it would affect everyone around them, much less how it would ruin what should have been a joyous occasion of marriage. I was terribly embarrassed by it all but also grateful to reconnect with Jamie.

He came to visit us in Alaska, and we reconnected like no time had passed. I was so glad for my mother to meet and get to know him, she commented on what a nice young man he was. Bottom photo at Anchorage Museum Jamie, my mother and myself.

His grandmother in Ohio had a stroke and we all converged there. It was a horrible time for me emotionally but I was grateful Jamie and I had the opportunity to spend some time together. His father ran errands for his mistress who was also from Dayton. Jamie personally saw how his father treated me and was horrified. We talked and he was of two minds. He thought I should get out of the marriage because no one deserved to endure what he saw me going through. Yet he pled with me not to divorce his father because he was afraid it would sever the loving tie we had. Being cognizant of his father having a mistress, he knew it was the end of our marriage. Neither was his own marriage destined to last. It was some years before we reconnected again.

His father was dying and Jamie flew to Alabama. He then was tasked with cleaning up the whole mess his father had left behind and it was ugly. We talked on the phone nearly daily, I think he really could not tell anyone else all of what he found. I was glad to have the opportunity to be there for him, as he took care of a task that could have fallen to me, even though we had been divorced for many years. He was thoughtful to find one special thing for each of his brothers amid his father's things.

As I said before, I believe to his dying day Jamie's father was in love with his mother - they just could not get along well enough to stay married. Neither was happy with any other partner. I think because my ex-husband was so angry at losing his first love he chose not to be a part of Jamie's life. This was a very sad thing because he never even took the time to visit Jamie and meet his first grandchild, even though Jamie asked again and again. I personally think that God intervened, because having Jamie not be raised by his biological father made him a better man—that is the cake. Meeting his lovely wife, and best friend, Wendy, is the frosting on that cake.

Wendy's grandparents were full blooded Native Americans. Her grandfather was a Creek Indian and they were considered to be of the civilized tribes. He was quiet, only spoke when necessary and actually was raised with Creek being his first language. There is a plaque in the Oklahoma House of Representatives naming him the first Native American elected to the Oklahoma House of Representatives. Her grandmother was Kiowa Indian, which Wendy said is of the Plains Indians and considered a non-civilized warring tribe. Her mother, it was decided, would not grow up on a reservation so Wendy, like her mother, was not raised in the Native American culture and only has been exposed to it since she made the choice to find out things. Wendy told me that the Kiowa Indians had many people who were story tellers and passed down the culture through story telling. She had one professor that was an Elder Kiowa who told great stories and Wendy got to meet her and hear her story telling and purchased tapes and a book of these stories.

In 2013 Jamie and Wendy adopted a boy who had been thousands of days in the foster care program. His ancestry was Native American and he needed to be adopted into a family with Native American blood.

I am very proud of this man. After all he endured, after all that was done to him, he could easily have been like his father, neglecting his kids and mistreating his wife, but he is not. He is a kind and loving husband and father. He holds great interest in his children and is there by their side encouraging them in every pursuit. A good husband and partner, a great father, he is a person that both Don and I really like. Photo top left is their first family photo with Will; Photo top right Jamie with his wife Wendy; Photo center left is Jessica Czikra, my ex's only blood grandchild so far; Group photo below (left to right) Will Czikra, Josh Blackwell, Me, Don, Wendy, Jess and Jamie Czikra. Bottom right photo: Brothers Jamie and Chris Czikra.   Other two bottom photos are William Czikra and Jamie carving with Don.

When I worked at Data Automation in Altus, Oklahoma there was a Chief Master Sergeant in charge of the division. Under him were two civilians who were supervisors over the personnel in the two areas. One area was the operators who ran the Burroughs mainframe computer and worked in the computer room. The other area was the monitors who wrote the programs to run on the mainframe and dealt with the customers. I was unique as the Secretary because I alone worked directly for the Chief. One of the civilians, we will call him Mr. Data, had nine daughters and I think he decided I was one of his daughters.

One weekend day I turned around and he was in my kitchen. He had come in the yard from the alley behind the house and walked in our back door which opened in the kitchen. He lectured me that I was not controlling the household appropriately because my husband had spent money on a big television when we didn't even have a washer and dryer.

Another time he told me that I needed to learn to use makeup and be appropriately made up and dressed up before ever leaving the house. In my normal fashion I just let it all roll off my back and went on.

He commented, usually negatively, on my hairdos and my fingernails that were never polished. Thank goodness I wore a uniform or he would be commenting on my clothes choices as well.

One of his daughters was getting married. I had been doing Wilton cake decorating as a hobby and taken some of my cakes into work. He asked if I would do the cake, and promised that he would even buy the fancy Wilton round 4-tier cake pans. Then they asked if I would cater the reception. I didn't know anything about catering but he insisted it would be easy... they would buy all the food and would be happy with things like pigs in a blanket and other finger food that would be easy enough to make.

I learned a lot making that 4-tier wedding cake and it took me hours. Thank God for Jamie who kept the boys busy and gave me time to decorate it. If I had known what I was doing I would have known to assemble it at the reception, but no, I had not yet learned that. Then we faced the heat of Altus in June and even with the air conditioning in the car going full blast I was afraid the frosting would melt right off.

Jamie worked hard helping me set all the things up for the reception while the boys ran wild around the place. As I cooked and arranged on platters, he carefully carried the food out to the tables. Once the reception started, we each were busy replenishing, the food and assist the people.

It was a very long day and I had told Jamie at the beginning that I would pay him $20 for the day if he helped me through it all. Seeing how hard and diligently he was taking the job I was thinking I would add a bonus.

We were almost always broke due to the purchase of cars my ex wanted (at one point we had nine cars – his, mine, and Mopar's my ex was parting out), and tools for working on cars and other things he wanted. Things needed to run a household always took second place.

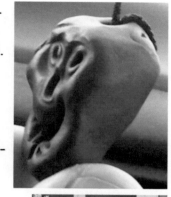

The reception lasted a long time, I think about five hours. When we were all done, we had to clean up because it was a base facility and would have to pass inspection. We got all that done and the boys loaded up in the car and Mr. Data came over to pay me. He gave me $40 and said, "Thank you, and you can keep the pans too." I learned that you should always talk money before the job is done.

1525 Lee Street, Altus, Oklahoma. Top house photo is when we lived there, bottom house photo is as it looks today from google maps. Top right photo is a clay piece Nicholas, who always was very artistic, made for his brother Jamie that hangs in Jamie's truck still today. Below that is a picture of me and Andy at the back door of the house from where Mr. Data came waltzing in to our house.

AMAZING CHILDREN STEPS CONTINUED.

When Don and I got together there was an added bonus that would prove to be one of the biggest blessings in my life—his children.

From the first moment Don and I were together, Don's son, Joshua, accepted me into his family. This really meant a lot to me because we were just laying the foundation for our new relationship, struggling with difficulties with my children and his quiet, loving acceptance, really the first, with no judgement or questions, meant the world to me.

This man has the biggest heart of almost anyone I have ever known. His deep down kindness, his acceptance of everyone, his perception of trials and issues others have, his quick wit and deep thoughtful stances in life are so refreshing. I have learned a lot from him in regards to social aspects, politics, and life in general… he is a very smart man.

Having been a younger brother to Jen all his life, he jumped feet first into being the older brother to my boys—and my boys were not easy to deal with at times. To this day Chris gauges many things on Josh's opinion because he loves and respects him so much.

Photos: Top right—Josh and Jen at her wedding; center right—Josh and Don on the deck of the Beachhouse on Yukon Island. Bottom right: Tickling Josh—Christmas Eve 1996; Bottom left: Thanksgiving Family Photo 1996.

Josh is an adventurous soul and willing to tackle any new thing we spring on him. He participated in the Abbott Family Yukon Island games, even braving the tedious rope walk (photo top left).

He joined us in a big sledding party at Arctic Valley near Anchorage, Alaska (photo bottom right). The run down the hill was a 20 minute ride so we used cars to get from the bottom of the run back up. All four boys joined us—it was so great.

He made such a positive difference in our holidays and celebrations that it really made us feel like a melded family right away.

Photo bottom left: Thanksgiving family photo from 1997. Back row Joshua and Andrew; Middle row Don and Phoebe, Front row Christopher and Nicholas.

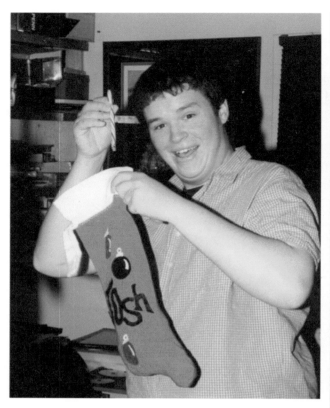

Joshua enjoying holidays with us.

Top left: 1996 first stocking with us.

Top right: 1998 Thanksgiving Family Photo.

Bottom right: Christmas 2000

Bottom left: Josh is a very generous man so we had to rethink the size of our Christmas stockings.   They are now just short of 36 inches long.

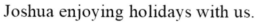

When I witness the true friendship between Josh and his dad I know several things. Don has always been a great father and he really raised Josh up to be a fine man. I also know that if we had kids together he would have raised them up to be fine people as well. But we decided God in his wisdom did not introduce us at a time when we could have kids together because we would have just been having kids and nothing else... all the dreams we are realizing today would not have come true.

Photo below: Father's Day in Anchorage Alaska.

Every project we undertook in the last 27 years Josh has been there to lend a helping hand. The photos below are of the unloading of the parts for our cabin on Yukon Island. Otto Kilcher brought the pieces over on his barge, we had to unload them on the beach, move

them with a 4-wheeler and bulldozer to our site, and place them ready for the builders. Our military friends Rusty Kendall, Steve Gordon, Hector Navarro and Elin Locke helped with the big unload. Josh not only helped but brought buddies to help too. The contractor was so amazed at the efficiency of the operation and the by size and type piling at the site that he wanted to hire our whole crew to work for him.

Josh hardly got out of his car, having driven from Alaska to North Carolina, before we put him to work building a deck on our barn to facilitate future building projects—2021.

When we expanded our school in 2022 he was digging ditches; buying, hauling, and unloading lumber; helping install the electricity and more… anything that needed done he was there.

Bottom photos 2023 renovation of his apartment (which was once a garage next to our house.

Not only lending a hand in every aspect of the Raven's Wing School of Art from planning, to building of the school, but agreeing to become a manager in the LLC that manages it.

And never forget that his assistance is not just in construction but in the every day lives we live together... jumping to unload the car if we've been shopping; gallery trips with his dad, carrying laundry down the steep stairs for me and boxes and tools for his dad; buying groceries and running errands; cleaning and setting up for classes, yard work and gutter cleaning; technical assistance and guidance in purchasing and maintaining computer equipment and other technology… the list is just too long but he is multi-talented and a really good friend.

How can you quantify the depth of the friendship that has Don asking Josh to be his best man (top right 1999) and Josh asking his dad to be his best man (top left 2008).

Bottom photos: Dollywood 2013

Josh is a talented artist. His dad always told me he thought Josh was a better artist than he himself is and Josh is working on proving it. Top left: Josh and Don collaboration Woodspirit; Top Center: Josh testing out air dry clay for adhesion to wood. Top right: Josh enrolled in his dad's beginning drawing class and this is a partially finished piece from that class. He is also clever and the life of the party. Bottom left: with his cousin Beth at his dad's surprise birthday party. Bottom right: Giving massages—Gabi with her Grampa Don and Uncle Josh.

Top right: 2023 Don's surprise birthday party planned by Phoebe, Josh and Beth. Left to right—Phoebe, Don, Grace and Paul (Don's brother and sister) Josh, Beth and Faith (Paul's daughter and granddaughter).

2021 We love to play cards when the grandkids come to visit and it is one of their favorite things. Photo below—We roped Josh in, taught him to play hearts and he beat us all his first game—how rude Josh.

Photo center left: 1999 Paul and Josh in our home in Anchorage, Alaska

Top left: Josh and his dad.

Top right: Josh and his cousin Beth.

Bottom left: Alaska 2007—Josh, Don, Phoebe (holding grandson Kaden) and Chris.

Bottom right: Josh laughing.

Bring out the camera and Joshua Paul (like his name sake his Uncle Paul—Don's brother) will be making a face. He even enlists his sister in the silliness.

Since Josh arrived in North Carolina he has been exploring. He knows the nearby towns and roads far better than I do, and I've been here 20 years. He is happy to act as tour guide and share all the great things that he has found with his sister and her family.

Top left: Josh and Gabi, Top right: Josh and Nico. Bottom photos: Joshua and his sister Jennifer.

Always an animal lover, Josh has loved every family dog from Pepper (photo upper right) to Gabe (photo center) to Deacon (photo upper left) to Kody (all the rest of the photos). Rain or shine, too hot or freezing wind, he gets up early every morning to walk Kody with his dad.

AMAZING CHILDREN STEPS CONTINUED

With Jennifer it was a bit more complicated. She was getting married. She never lived with us. She and her husband were getting their college completed before having children (always the smartest way). They were deciding on where they

would live, moving first to Seattle, then to the Phoenix area of Arizona where they bought their first house.

We were so broke back then that family trips were out of the question. Don went to Arizona to meet our first grandchild and I went to Alaska to see my oldest son get married.

In 2007 Jennifer came with her husband, Leo, and children, Gabi and Nico, to visit.

At that time she didn't really even know me. I had prepared crafts to do with the grandkids. The first opportunity to do crafts, she wasn't sure about including her son who was only 2, and assumed I would only want to do crafts with her older child. She told me that she could keep him busy while her daughter and I created. When I asked that he be allowed to participate too, and asked if she really thought he would be happier staying up with the adults than going to play with us, I think she changed her mind about me. From there we began the process of forming what is now a solid friendship between the two of us.

Nothing will ever change that Jennifer loves her daddy hard and will always be a daddy's girl.

Because of the way he raised her, and believed in her, she is a fiercely independent, highly educated, principled woman.

She has instilled these traits in her children with the help of her husband, and they are good kids, a joy to be around.

They have come to visit almost every year since 2007 allowing us to see the grandchildren grow and change. We have enjoyed wonderful times together.

Jen's oldest child looks like her but has her husband, Leo's, coloring. Her second child looks like Leo but has Jen's coloring.

Jen is also a fantastic photographer as you can see in all the photos center and bottom rows.

AMAZING CHILDREN OF MY HEART

Beth is technically a niece on Don's side of the family but she is a daughter to me. From when she came to stay with us in Alaska for the summer, to the tradition of our Wednesday evenings together, she blesses our lives.

If I had birthed a daughter just like me, it would be Beth. God has allowed us to experience similar things in our life times, ugly things. We are both stubborn and insist on doing things the hard way most often.

We have been through so much and yet, survived to be where we are now in a great place in our lives and with a cherished friendship.

Beth had a special relationship with my son Nicholas and we nearly lost them both. God brought Beth back to us after she died on the way to the hospital.

She has shared her children and now grandchildren with me and they have become the grandchildren and great-grandchildren of my heart.

She keeps us amused reading her text messages and Facebook posts and one day I hope to read her story in a book form, because she is a born writer.

Beth's daughter
Faith Anne and to
the left with her
baby Findlay Elias,
named after my brother
Findlay.

Wednesday evenings with Beth and Elias.

Beth

Sewing with Phoebe; Working out with Don; Birthday surprise; and Wasp work with Don.

November 30, 2023

Our bathroom floor is tiled with alternating white and pink 6-sided ceramic tiles. Also on the floor in our bathroom are two rugs – one designed to fit around the toilet, one a bath mat.

If you are sitting on the toilet and you gently lift the upper left corner of the toilet rug you will find below that one of the tiles is cracked across it. The crack hits just below center about where a mouth might be found if the tile were a face.

Today he is frowning… I wonder if he frowns because it is winter and the tiles are bitingly cold. Perhaps he frowns in general, all the time, because the bathroom can be an unpleasantly odiferous place. I am a cockeyed optimist and I hope for the day I lift the corner of the rug and find him smiling at me.

Tomorrow is Friday and Fridays in our life, are very important. I carry on a tradition, in a different way, that my mother started. I don't want to use the title 'Friday Night Adoption Society' because that title was hers alone. Ours is different because first of all, it happens in the daytime not at night. Ours is a meeting of artists who are friends working together. Hugs, smiles, laughter, inspiration, ideas, friendship and companionship are shared in this weekly meeting. For some it is a quiet time their lives do not have. For some it is an escape from the trials of life. For some it is like a fun club meeting. For some it is life blood. For us, it is all that and more.

We have had many dreams in our time together. First, we dreamed of a lifetime together and God has been great to give us that. Next, we dreamed of our children sharing time together and growing in the sharing as children were added. This dream as we dreamt it more than twenty years ago has not come to fruition. Though two children share our lives, we have lost a child, a child is distant, and one child is mad at the world.

I worry so for the angry boy. He has a disability and he lets that disability lead his life. He is brilliant and could soar like an eagle but, he insists hacking away. He has his machete in hand and is choosing to chop his way through a complex and thick jungle of life. He lashes out in angry because he chooses to believe that we insisted he take the jungle route, when nothing could be further from the truth.

I don't worry for the distant boy, he is smart, competent and driven. He is making a good life for him. The distance between us is his choice just as his brother is making his own choices. I am saddened that the distance exists but cannot make his life choices for him.

I am deeply saddened by the lost boy. He had such tremendous potential and zest for life. We don't know if he died by suicide or homicide. I choose to believe he was the victim of a homicide. My boy could push people's buttons like no body's business. I can easily imagine that he pushed someone to kill him, I saw it in people's eyes when he was young. I can't imagine with all his talents and wit, that he would ever choose to kill himself.

It is the last day of November. Today we have a grandson who turns 18 years old and I hardly know him. He is handsome and I am told he is a responsible, kind and dedicated young man. In the times I have seen him it was clear that he worshiped and copied his father, and those words also describe his father… a Mini He.

Sign above, in vintage retro tin metal, at 8 x 12 inches in size, with predrilled corner holes, is available at this date and time from Amazon dot com for a bargain price of $16.50

I cannot worry over those things that I cannot change. I always loved this prayer (photo left). Google send me to the Marquette University who claims it is "Attributed to Reinhold Niebuhr, Lutheran theologian (1892–1971)"

Sandstone Care.com submits that the original reads: "O God and Heavenly Father, grant to us the serenity of mind to accept that which cannot be changed, courage to change that which can be changed, and wisdom to know the one from the other through Jesus Christ, our Lord, Amen." It goes on to say: The full version goes as follows: "God grant me the serenity to accept the things I cannot change; Courage to change the things I can; and wisdom to know the difference. Living one day at a time; Enjoying one moment at a time; Accepting hardships as the pathway to peace; Taking, as He did, this sinful world as it is, not as I would have it; Trusting that He will make things right if I surrender to His Will; So that I may be reasonably happy in this life and supremely happy with Him forever and ever in the next. Amen".

Bathroom Tiles

There are four tiles in our bathroom that are broken. The ceramic tiles are 6 sided and the crack splits the tile and reminds me of an expression leading me to name then and explore their personality. Top to bottom they are:

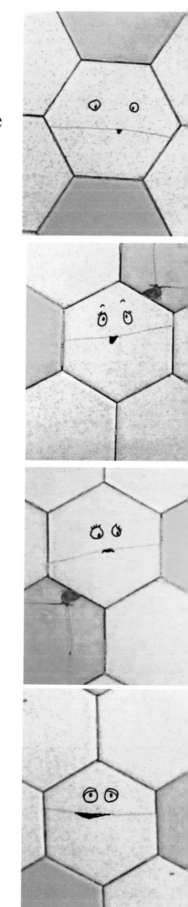

Taylor Tile who hides under the toilet rug. His expression may change when I am not looking so sometimes when sitting on the pot I will pull up the corner of the rug to see how he feels today.

Talia Tile is very curious and always looking around to see what is going on. She does close her eyes when there are naked people in the bathroom and we find that very kind of her.

Thea Tile always has an attitude and wonderful expressions. As I take the photo she is looking startled… perhaps one of the many bugs of North Carolina is heading her way (maybe it is even… EEK… a stink bug.) I most like it when I find she is wearing her big beautiful smile instead of this apprehensive look.

Tucker Tile is one totally laid back dude. He gets that silly grin on his face and his eyes seem to glaze over and I have to wonder exactly what he is thinking, or day dreaming about.

A DIFFERENT CHILDHOOD

I have really had a good life overall. My childhood was with two wonderful, amazing, loving parents. I am one of six children and we were raised very differently. The oldest three were mostly raised in California. My dad worked, my mom was a housewife, and we had a life like on the show, "Leave it to Beaver." When I was five we moved to Alaska and homesteaded, a grand adventure. Then there was a few years back East in Virginia and Maryland, and finally we moved to Washington State. Here we lived without my father. My mother worked and was a single parent to us four youngest kids. We lived in Bellevue until my just older sister graduated high school, then we moved to Bainbridge Island, Washington. This difference in our upbringings has had lasting effects on all of us.

As a teen I was tasting life and what my parents were up to was just circumstance. When I had literally just gotten my driver's license on sleepy little Bainbridge Island, my dad sent for me to come to LA to help him drive these Swiss ladies around.

First, he picked me up at the airport, gave me the keys to the car, and told me to get on the LA Freeway back to Santa Barbara. I had never seen the like of that freeway. I was unsure of myself as a new driver. Everyone was going 60 miles an hour bumper to bumper in traffic. It was horrifying and of course my dad is yelling directions and to hurry and get over three lanes, I took the very first exit I could find. I was shaking and almost crying as I told him I could not do this. This would not be the first time on this trip I would vastly disappoint my father.

He disappointed me too though. I had just come from Bainbridge Island where my mother was working her tail off for poverty wages. She still had three kids at home to feed and raise, bills from back East, and we were eating lots of tuna. I arrive in LA and not only is my dad having a grand old time working at the college and hanging out with all these hip young adults, but one is his girlfriend. She is closer in age to me than to him. He is the life of every party and living life to the fullest. What a contrast. At one party he hooks up with this other woman. He finds an old family friend, Ricky, shoves me in his arms and says, take her home for me. Ricky was about 10 years older than me and our families had been friends since the 50's. He was a handsome, tanned, California surfer boy and I was 16 years old. He was a nice guy. He took me on his motorcycle, stopped at a beach along the way for a friendly chat and a gorgeous view, and then dropped me at home safely.

We left shortly after to drive down into Mexico. My father drove and gave me annoyed glances when I knew he would have liked a break in driving. There were two Swiss ladies, a mother and daughter, who were friends of friends that he had offered to drive down into Mexico. The girlfriend took one look at the daughter and decided she was coming along too.

We got a very late start and just crossed into Arizona and it was blazing hot. A puddle in the shade of a tree was bathtub hot when I waded in. That night, we slept in a park. The Swiss ladies instantly claimed the front and back seats of the car. My dad happily pitched a tent. I was miserable. Even sleeping at the back of the tent the mosquitos swarmed right past him and his girlfriend and feasted on me. The next morning, I had the audacity (in my father's opinion) to complain out loud and got the "I raised you to be a frontier woman." speech. The next night we had already seen our first snake, and were again pitching a tent. I picked my sleeping bag up and got up on top of a picnic table, zipping myself in away from the mosquitos.

I woke up to the sound of yelling. I popped out of my sleeping bag, glanced around, and saw both Papa and his girlfriend had moved from the tent up on to picnic tables sometime in the night. This cow with the longest horns I had ever seen was mooing. Those horns were as long as the picnic table and both side benches. It was leaning over my dad on the picnic table, its neck all stretched out long, drooling on him and mooing. I could not help but laugh out loud. I wanted to yell, "Hey Frontier Man, how is it going?" but I didn't. My dad is pretty good at interpreting things unsaid. I admit at different times of the day I remembered that picture and a giggle escaped. I suppose I did legitimately earn both the dirty looks and that silent treatment.

When we lived in California it was all sunshine and oranges. We were a happy family, hiking and dressing up on Sunday for church. I am too young to remember places and miles and all that. I do know I was baptized in the Trinity Lutheran Church in Ventura, California where I was born. In the family photos of me with my little sister, Melissa, it says we lived in Ojai. Ojai is about 24 miles from Ventura. Each Sunday we would inevitably be late getting started and my father would drive like a maniac with all of us kids in the car.

My oldest sister had a coin collection that she would show to her little sisters. She would spread them out on her bed, show us all of them and tell us about each one, then wave her hands over them all and say reverently, "Money."

One Sunday the offering plate, with lots of coins, was passed down our row. Melissa was just a baby and had not yet begun to talk but when she saw that shiny gold plate with the coins all piled in it she sucked in her breath in surprise, pointed her chubby baby finger at it in pure delight, and in the loudest voice she could managed, burst out the word, "MONEY!" The entire church turned to look at us and I believe many judgements were made on the spot.

The reward for dressing up, going to church, and behaving while there, was an A&W Root Beer float. We would get our floats at the drive up, spit them happily in the heat of noon. Then we would head off for Ojai. As usual my dad drove like a mad man. These days we would say, "that is just who he is!" I can remember being jostled side to side as he hit the curves. Papa drove, my mother sat in the front with the youngest on her lap. If I was lucky, she would let me lean on her other side or curl up on the floor at her feet. This spared me being roughly jostled by the three oldest sitting in the back seat. I liked to ride in the back window but sometimes it was needed storage space and in the summer months it got too warm up there. Every Sunday my mother would try to hold herself upright, protect the child on her lap, and the one at her side or at her feet; ensure the rowdiness in the back seat did not get completely out of control which would anger my father and maintain her dignity throughout. This was not easy and finally she would have enough and chide my father in an angry whisper, "You are going too fast Bill! Slow Down!" Twenty-four miles of speed and jerks is a long ride, especially in a car with no air conditioning on a California summer day. Nearly every Sunday the curves and all would be too much for the youngest of us and she would puke. To this day I have no desire for root beer, I still associate the taste with the smell of puke.

Another Sunday my sister just older was being mean. We were to sit still and she did not do that well. I was sitting next to Papa on my right and her on the left. When we were naughty in church the accepted punishment was a quiet but deadly pinch. Abbotts have always been good pinchers. In this instance she purposely shoved me hard enough that I bumped in to my father on the other side. Then she sat demurely as if she were listening carefully. My father looked over saw me still wavering a bit, no one else doing anything but listening, and pinched me hard. At four years old I responded without thinking and burst out with, "Papa, why did you pinch me, I didn't do it!" Again, with the judgements. I can't remember going to church again in California after that.

My family often went on trips around America in the summer. We visited the grand canyon, and hiked up into the cooler mountains. One of the scariest moments for me was when we were hiking and about to cross a small creek by stepping on the rocks when we saw a huge rattlesnake. He had just eaten a frog or something and had this huge lump half way down his body. I had nightmares about that snake swallowing me!

I can't remember if these were both on the same trip but we got to drive through the big redwood tree in the Redwood National Forest. We also visited Paul Bunyan I think that was in Klamath, California. The Paul Bunyan could talk and he looked down on our family with all matching outfits and commented. My brother, in particular, was horrified. We also loved the Burma shave signs on trips and would all read them aloud together. When I had children, I found myself doing what my parents did. Throwing my arm out to stop whatever child standing in the front seat, might tumble forward.

We lived back East for a bit in Virginia and Maryland. We had a nice house. We got (for the first time) fashionable store-bought dresses for school, and new shoes before they were worn out. We got more than one toy for Christmas. We went to the Smithsonian Museum; we rode on a real Dentzel Carousel in Glen Echo Park; we climbed the 890 some steps to the top of the Washington Monument; saw fireworks over the Jefferson Memorial for Independence Day; gathered at the Lincoln Memorial; saw Michelangelo's Pieta at the National Museum of Art; collected sharks teeth at the Atlantic City Beach; touched the Liberty Bell and walked in Independence Hall in Philadelphia; attended the World's Fair in New York; saw the horses run at Chincoteague Island; went to Iwo Jima memorial, Arlington Cemetery and the US Naval Academy in Annapolis. Though this was a prime time in my family life with both parents it was a horrible time for me with schools. I learned to hate school.

Then there was the period of no money when my parents separated. My mother still had four kids to raise. All these years later her science degree was worth nothing. She got a job as a model maker for $2.50 an hour. Then my dad went bankrupt and she had to pay off the furniture in our home, the IRS as well, and feed and cloth us. The only store bought clothes I got were ones I purchased with my babysitting money. Never once did she take out her stress on us. She was a fair, kind, and wise parent.

(Photo right—book by Charlie; photos below of me taken by Charlie in photo top right.)

I was the first of my siblings to ride in hot cars, to listen to rock n roll, to bring boys home, to be a "teenager."

When I found myself floundering in an abusive marriage with a husband who spent all the money we made, who didn't help with anything, and I was working full time in the Air Force and corralling two over active boys... I would just think how my mother had to survive with four kids and $2.50 and said to myself, "If she could do it, so could I!" Later I would tell my mother this story. To my amazement she just laughed. When I asked

her why she told me that she was 13 years old when her father died and her mother had to figure out how to raise three children. When all was desperate for my mother, she would think of her mother and say to herself, "If she could do it, so could I!"

All the moving around and new schools was very hard. When I entered 9th grade at Bainbridge High School it was technically my 9th school. I had no friends, and a hatred of school. One saving grace was a man named Charlie Siegel. Charlie was a photographer on Bainbridge Island who had a shop in Lynwood Center. My cousin Jimmy was interested in photography and worked sometimes with Charlie. When Charlie needed a model for his photograph advertisements Jimmy came and collected me.

I will always be grateful to him for introducing me. I spend every free moment I had my Freshman year in his studio. He taught me about developing pictures and photography techniques and filled the role of the father that was not there. He remained a mentor to me even when I joined the Air Force.

The summer before my sophomore year, we move across the island and I met the buddies (see cartoon of some of them). At first we rented a house near Rolling Bay and there I met them that summer. A short time later we moved up the road to a cheaper house but I would still be part of that group (Scott, Mark, George, and Jim) who would remain my bosom pals through high school. Later we added Cindi, Bill, Paul, Lindalee, and Maurice. These were the first real friends my age I had ever had, though many of them were a grade behind Cindi, Maurice and I.

The day I graduated high school I found an apartment in Seattle and moved. It was a three bedroom with two roommates, one from my high school named Debbie, and one I had met at a party named Joan. We got ahold of some red wine, mixed it with orange juice and well into the homemade Sangria, pledged to move out together.

All was fine for the summer tourist season and even through the holiday hire period. Then they both lost their jobs that were actually holiday hires at local department stores. Soon I was stuck with all the bills and sinking. My grandmother died and left me $5000. I paid off all the bills and moved into my own apartment.

My apartment was on Queen Anne Hill in Seattle and had a pool. I was working as an offset pressman and actually made enough to afford my apartment and food. Pretty soon Joan got kicked out of her parents house (disagreement over her first of many abortions) and begged to live with me. She did get me to go to an Elvis Presley concert but that's another story. She was most cooperative for the first month.

The first worrisome incident was when I came home from visiting my mother on Bainbridge. My mother had been on me to be more careful as I had broken some bones in my foot falling off my 6 inch high heels, cut my foot badly on a hole by the pool, and gotten my pony tail wrapped up in the drill press at work. As a joke I had taken two popsicle sticks and taped up one finger like I broke it as well. Tho I told her it was a joke I waiting to get home to get all the tape off. I walked in the door of my apartment and found a woman I had never met, with two children, and all there stuff filling the living room. I tripped on one of the toys, landed on my hand and because of the popsicle sticks wound up breaking that finger. She was a friend of Joan's who had a fight with her husband and needed a place to stay. It took a week to get her out.

Then I came home from work one day and there was a wild party going on around the pool and into my apartments. There were people everywhere, dancing and jumping in the pool with loud music from my apartment. My landlord met me at the gate as I entered the complex and informed me I was kicked out. During the move he confiscated all my fish tanks and gear for "damage from the party." I lived with the two of them again, in Edmonds, Washington and again got stuck with all the bills. Would I never learn?

In the summer of 1972, I moved to Hawaii with my boyfriend, Kerry. It didn't work out and he returned to Seattle, while I, with a good job, stayed. Debbie came to visit and loved Hawaii. She begged me to just let her stay until she could find her own apartment. I came home and found her in bed with my boyfriend and I was flat done with having girl friends!!

EVER SO LONG AGO

Ever so long ago I was fighting my life, or fighting for my life. I had escaped a pedophile in Washington by moving to Hawaii. (Top Photo) Hawaii cradled me in it's warmth and aloha and nurtured me back to health. I had good friends and a good job and was successful in my chosen career. At 21 years old I was the general manager of a print shop with three branches on the island of Oahu, Hawaii. I had expanded my career knowledge tremendously and renewed some of my lost self confidence. Then he came to Hawaii.

I left Hawaii by joining the Air Force because of him. Also, as if that one thing were not enough to make me leap from the frying pan into the fire, things at work were bad. I was notified I would be called as the primary witness in the trial of my boss versus the IRS. I considered hiding but all those people who had offered me jobs dried up and blew away. I knew why after my boss called Chicago and the events that followed. I obviously had to leave.

I was still under the impression that I had made the biggest mistake of my life by joining the Air Force. I had survived Basic Training (no mean feat) and passed F-4 Fighter technical training (center photo). I earned a leave home (bottom photo). I had time on the island of my parent's homestead in Alaska. My mom was there and hugged me close. My brother and sisters were all there, together, for the first time since before my father had passed away. Actually we have not full family photo because when my youngest sister was born and we took a family photo, my oldest sister was in college (19.5 years difference between the two). This time we took a family photo my father had already passed away.

I was free to enjoy relaxing on the beach in the sun and not think much about the 3 more years I was committed to the Air Force. I painted flat rocks with my artist sister in the homestead house and many fond memories were shared over those rocks. I had the opportunity to begin a friendship with my mother. Before, she was the mom and I the child who felt so often unjustly accused. She did not know of my pedophile and I felt I could not burden her with that, and that too made me angry. I was defiant in my anger, defiant enough to smoke a joint of marijuana in her face. Of course that did not turn out well for me.

It seems like ever so long ago my mother was still alive. A day doesn't go by without her being in my thoughts. I might be experiencing something in life and hear my mother saying just what I need to hear. Or maybe not. When my boys were young and rowdy and wouldn't go to bed no matter what I tried, I found myself at the bottom of the stairs saying, "Don't make me come up there." Those were the exact words my mother would say when we lived in Maryland and had a two story house with stairs.

Speaking of Bowie, Maryland... The photo bottom left is the front or our house on Milburn Lane. My mother took us to the community pool as often as she could in the summer. Photo bottom right at the pool having ice cream. I am in in back and my younger sister is in the front, second from the left, in a green and white bathing suit.

I had an even younger sister who was born when we lived back East. She was 10 years younger than me, smart as the dickens and into everything. My father called her 'Denise the Menese.' When we moved to Bowie, she was in a crib in my parents room but she got out of her crib and made a huge mess, so my mom moved her in with my other younger sister. She destroyed many of that sisters things so my mom moved that sister in with me and the youngest got her own room. At first I was miffed. For the first time in my entire life I got my own room and it only lasted a few months. It wasn't long before I realized it was just so much fun to be with my new roommate that it was all worth it.

One night we got a hold of a ball of string. We strung that stuff all over the room. We had one string that attached to the door knob which was strategically left a jar so my sister could pull it and open the door. Another string I had was with a loop on the end that fit over the light switch, threaded up to the ceiling and down in my reach so I could turn the light on. We had other strings that did things like make the blinds raise up. That night we purposely made enough noise that Mom didn't stand at the bottom of the stairs and yell, she came to our room. We opened the door for her, turned on the lights, raised the shades, and other string effects. She was so delighted she laughed aloud and did not get mad at us for being up late.

My mom was a truly amazing woman, I like to say she was formidable. She was capable in any circumstance. She was intense and strong. When you did something bad she was alarming and powerful. I can't remember her ever spanking me. She didn't need to because she was a queen of psychology. She could make you feel quilt like no ones business. Because of the impact of the first time I lied to my mother, I to this day do not lie effectively it makes me so nervous.

I guess knowing the trouble my three older siblings caused, and then doubling the amount of us by adding in the cousins, she had gotten some excellent training before I came along. The tales of our clan were epic in and around Homer, Alaska.

THE ALASKA LEGISLATURE

In Memoriam

* ALICE P. ABBOTT *

The Twenty-second Alaska State Legislature is proud to honor the life and achievements of longtime Alaskan Alice P. Abbott. Alaska lost a graceful and dignified Alaskan with her passing. She was 79 years old.

Mrs. Abbott was born July 29, 1921 in Missoula, Montana, later moving to Seattle, Washington. A lifelong outdoor enthusiast, she climbed Mount Rainier and other Pacific Northwestern peaks. She attended Whitman College and the University of Washington.

After marrying William F. "Bill" Abbott in 1943, she and her husband homesteaded on Yukon Island in Kachemak Bay with their children in the 1950s and '60s.

Following her husband's death, she returned to Seattle and built architecture and engineering models for Naramore, Bain, Brady, and Johannson architects. In 1974 she returned to Alaska and founded Abbott Scale Models, a successful business lasting more than 20 years. Examples of her work are in the Anchorage Museum of History & Art and donations of her models helped the Alaska Zoo raise funds for Binky's [the legendary Anchorage Polar Bear] cage.

A wonderful mother and grandmother, Mrs. Abbott encouraged her children to be independent and to develop lives and careers they loved, yet to stay close as a family. She had great strength, wisdom, and spirit while living her life with great compassion, energy and adventure. Recognizing her support and activities within Alaska, the Alaska Air National Guard awarded her the Alaska Community Service Medal in January 1999.

It is with heartfelt appreciation for her many contributions that the Twenty-second Alaska State Legislature extends its sincere condolences to the family of Alice Abbott. Her grace, dignity, and love of life touched those who knew her.

I think also I was usually one who never caused much trouble until I was a teen. I was happy to be outdoors any time, season or reason. When a sister younger was born, I was happy to be with her inventing adventures and tales of wonder. All that went well until 4th grade for me. That was when we moved from Alaska to Virginia and I was a fish out of water. My parents got us correspondence schools when we homesteaded. Every time my mother got back to work I snuck outside. I did not do well that critical year and was behind when put I school in Virginia. In my opinion from 4th grade to 8th grade were the worse years for me both in school and at home with my father's health issues beginning with his first heart attack..

Top photo is an Alaska Legislative Memorial issued about my mom, like I said formidable.

The bottom photo is in Bellevue, Washington. My mom is in the dark V next shirt with her mother next to her. I'm not in the picture because we younger kids were relegated to another room. That's not another table, like the kids table, but another whole room… in this case the kitchen.

Mom adventures… yes she had many. She loved to sail as did her brother Fos. Top left photo is her on a sailboat. Next photo down is her in turquoise heading up for a hot air balloon ride in Anchorage, Alaska. It was our joint sisters 70th birthday present. The next photo down is when she was in England and the bottom left photo is her in Finland. The bottom left photo is Mom in Trier, Germany with my first born son in the carriage.

The photo in the bottom right is actually my sister and I on the beach in front of the homestead house in Alaska. We lived in the reddish building and the white building held our big diesel electric generator. We did have lights in the cabin. If you look closely you can see eleven 55 gallon drums of diesel fuel in front of the generator shed. Also in front of the main building are three 55 gallon drums of diesel oil that fed the heater in the back bunk house room where we kids slept. Look closer still and you see that the only insulation on the windows in our bedrooms was some Visqueen plastic sheeting. The main house had three windows facing the beach, the largest on the right was the living area window, the center one our parents bedroom and the farthest left our bunk room. There was also a window on the back side on the house in the kitchen area.

When the barge came to deliver the load of 55 gallon drums of diesel it was rough weather. The drop had been timed to hit at high tide so the drums would be closest to their final resting place. But the wind was driving the barge on shore and he could not afford to be beached. He proceeded to dump the drums as close to the beach as possible and we kids were sent into the waves to corral the drums of precious fuel.

You have to imagine living in this house on an island in the middle of nowhere in Alaska. First it was my parents, me and three siblings and two cousins so we could have a state supported school (you need 10 children). We had neighbors then, the Hortons, who had three kids. We also borrowed Otto Kilcher from Homer. I don't remember why it didn't work, but I suspect it was that the Horton's abandoned ship and went back to California. Otto and the cousins were returned to Homer and later one sibling joined the other living with our aunt and uncle in Homer.

The bathroom was an outhouse 20 feet away from the house. With that many people in that small a space 'honey pots' (or chamber pots as they were once called) were not practical and we did not have them.

All food had to be basically made from scratch. I remember how I loved the meat grinder attachment that made the meat come out like a whole herd of worms. Our drinking water was stored in a big 55 gallon plastic trash can and had to be filled in the creek, and brought on a sled to the house. Once a month or so a whole day was spent heating water and bathing each individual in the plastic trash can and then they were scrubbed carefully several times before retuning to water cache duties. In between there were sponge baths.

After dinner was family time and my mother would read to us, our favorites were the Winnie the Pooh stories. Sometimes the whole family would play games. We played battleship and Guggenheim with just pencil and paper. We did have several commercial games but Monopoly took too long and Racko only four people could play. We always several decks of playing cards and knew many versions of solitaire. We even played Blind Man's Bluff. It was a game where one child was blindfolded and tried to find the child, or children, that were not blindfolded by feeling their way. It was cold enough in the cabin to find people by their body heat. This caused one younger sister to be burned badly by hitting her arm on the pot belly stove that was at the center of our living space.

My mother tiled her own bathroom and renovated her kitchen in her home in Anchorage; She added a big front window living space to the old homestead house; and was the only architectural model maker in Alaska in the 1970's, 80's and 90's. She was amazing.

Let it be known to all that there is in the town of Anchorage, in the State of Alaska, a Society called the

Friday Night Adoption Society

The Friday Night Adoption Society, hereinafter known as FNAS (pronounced Finesse), was begun in the early 1980's by Alice Powell Abbott. Her house, being so welcoming and warm became the gravity point for a large number of individuals who benefited from her presence. First the daughters came, because their lives were so busy they found no time for social events and as their lives revolved around Alice Abbott as their mother, mentor, friend and confidant. Then the friends came as they knew there would be a gathering. The first official recognition of this society was noted by Alaskan Author Sue Henry in her famous first mystery book "Murder on the Iditarod Trail." The society continued to meet into the new millennium and became firmly established as "An Abbott Family Tradition." The FNAS celebrated diverse friendships, good company, excellent food and fine wines, the tradition of gaming, art and instruction, debate, a weekly social update, a cunningly concealed support group, impromptu think tanks, quests of skill and competition and an enormous amount of love.

Photo top left is at the sign entering the Olympic National Forest in Washington State. My mom loved to hike and it was about the only family entertainment she could afford. My father was gone, she made only $2.50 an hour at her job, and still had kids at home. This really solidified my love of nature and hiking. Good times-favorite hike! The photo was taken just before we left on our longest hike, 40+ miles through the Olympic Forest. We started at the Dosewallips Campground and ended at the Lake Quinault Lodge. We took it easy going only 6 or 7 miles a day, a whole week to do it, and enjoying our selves. We felt bad for the California Sierra Club we met exiting the forest just as we began our hike. It had rained on them for the whole week they had been hiking. We had gorgeous sunny days the whole time.

Top right is the Friday Night Adoption Society Charter that I wrote. Alaskan author, Sue Henry, named it the Friday Night Adoption Society and had a star named after it as well. She also dedicated one of her mystery books to the same. There could be a whole book on all the interesting people who attended my Mom's Friday night gatherings. I met world famous musicians, Russian aircraft designers, the man who would be the curator of the Grand Canyon Museum, the man who was the geologist for the Exxon Valdez oil spill, and many more interesting people at her house. So many people not blood relatives fondly called her Mom or Grandmother.

Ever so long ago I was a child, with two amazing parents who loved each other and were on the pinnacle of their lives together. Not long after these photos it would all fall apart and they would separate for my father's health… six precocious kids can be a lot for anyone.

When the two oldest siblings were off to college my Mom became a single mother with 4 children. In 2007, when I was in correspondence writers school, I wrote this about my mother and her mother, both truly amazing women.

NEVER SAY CAN'T

By Phoebe Blackwell

Have you ever felt overwhelmed by events in your life? Have you wondered where you would get the gumption to go on? To get through difficult times I always used this thought, "If my mother could do it, I can do it!" Imagine my great surprise, when I found that my mother, and her mother, used the same sentence when they needed that bit of extra push to help them go on.

My grandmother was from a well to do family and married a man who was from the same background. After they were married in Massachusetts, they migrated to the West. For a few years they ran a dude ranch in Montana. They then moved to Seattle, Washington, where my grandfather started his own bank. In 1934 when the stock market crashed there was no federal government backings to banks that made the funds secure. When my grandfather realized all these people who had trusted in him by putting their money in his bank, would lose most of their money, he had a heart attack and died. After more than twenty years as a housewife, my grandmother would have to find a job and support three children.

Although my grandmother was unusual (being a woman with a college degree in 1934), that did not mean there were many jobs open for women. In particular there were almost none that took intelligence, and almost none that paid anything substantial enough to support a family. Since she had no professional working background my grandmother looked to politics. She ran for and was elected to the city council. Thus, she became the first woman ever to serve on the Seattle City Council. My grandmother was not defeated by having to start over after having lost almost everything (home, bank account, etc.); find a job and go to work with no work experience; and still raise three children without a husband.

My mother was a scientist in 1942. She was one of the few women drafted in World War II. She worked for the Chemical Warfare Services (CWS) prior to the United States entering World War II. After Pearl Harbor the U.S. Government issued draft notices for everyone working in the CWS labs to ensure the necessary work would go on. They were doing research into gases that might be used during war. In particular my mother was testing the product of a company making activated charcoal for gas masks. Their job was to determine if it would work for all the different gases, before the government would contract the company. At any rate, her research was on the leading edge of technology. She got married to my father in 1943 and with the end of the contract she had been working she was allowed by the government to quit her job.

From 1943 until 1966 my mother was basically a housewife. In the 1950's my parents moved to Alaska to homestead. This made her life as a housewife much harder. We purchased grain and had to grind it down to get flour. Our homestead was on an island 6 miles by water to the nearest town. There was no running down to the corner store or borrowing a cup of flour from a neighbor. It was hard work being a homestead wife in Alaska. We grew our own vegetables in the short summer months; for meat we caught fish and hunted for moose and bear – which my mother had to clean and prep for storage without refrigeration; and put up fruit and vegetables in jams and cans for the winter. In Alaska during the winter months almost seventy-five percent of your time is spent in the pursuit of keeping warm. My father felled the trees and sawed them up. He and my mother shared the task of chopping up the wood and we kids brought it in to the house several times a day. The fire had to be kept going all day and be banked carefully each night so it would not burn down. First thing each morning the cabin was dreadfully cold and we would snuggle in our beds as my mother got up and stoked the fire. We only got out of bed when it was starting to get warm. Besides all the things to do with basic living she had to monitor our home-schooling. It was a very hard life.

In the mid 1960's my father took a contract in Washington D.C., so we left the homestead behind for rural living. Now my mother did not have canning and home-schooling to deal with. Instead she had five children from the back woods of Alaska, plopped in to rural Virginia and Southern living. Then in 1963, at 42 years old, my mother gave birth to her sixth child. When this youngest sister was only 4 years old, my father had a heart attack and my mother had to go back to work to support the family. Since her science knowledge was now twenty years out of date she could not work in that field. She finally found a job at $2.50 per hour working in the model shop of an architectural firm. My father had another heart attack and died. Here was my mother, making $2.50 per hour, with still the three youngest of her children to raise. We ate a lot of tuna casserole and tuna salad during those first few years. My mother worked during the day and in the evenings as well as dinner, housework and making sure the school homework got done. She was also taking a correspondence course in drafting to make it easier for her to trans-late the architectural plans into physical models.

When I got married I did so for all the wrong reasons; I knew in my heart that it was a mistake to marry the person I was marrying. But when you are young you do foolish things. I probably would not have stayed in that horrible, abusive marriage for thirteen years if I had not been convinced by my husband that I would never make it on my own with three children to raise. When my oldest son tried to step between my husband and I during a messy fight, I knew I had to protect my children by removing us from that situation. My husband spent every penny that came into our bank account. It had gotten so bad that I secretly started several bank accounts just to ensure I would have money to feed the children. What little I saved certainly did not leave any for a lawyer so I had to make my own divorce paperwork and defend my request for sole custody of the children in court. I have never been so scared in my life. During this particularly awful period in my life my mother was always there with her wise and loving council. One day I confided in her that she was what motivated me through the most awful times. She who had been a housewife for more than 20 years then had to start over from scratch with three children to raise was what helped me through the worst of times. That's when she told me that the same was true for her. When she found herself with three children to raise and no job, she reflected on how much easier that was for a woman in the 1960's than in the 30's when her mother had to do the same thing. She said in the very hardest points of her life she just thought of her mother, who always had everything she wanted in life, then suddenly became a poor working mother. In her mind she was saying, "If my mother could do it, I can do it." This same sentence would get me through the worst of my times thirty years later.

So, if you should ever find yourself in a difficult period of your life, just think of what other people have struggled to conquer in their own lives and you will find your burden a little lighter. Most likely you will find that as large as your problems are, there are always people with bigger challenges. Just pick one that you admire and by thinking of all they went through, it will give you that extra boost to get through your tough times just as it helped me.

EVERYTHING I COULD WANT

Good morning, God. Thank You for giving me everything I could want. On a soft Sunday I can reflect on what I want in life and how I want to live and walk each day… I want to feel that my actions reflect what You would want me to do and be. After You, I want to make my mother proud, my dad too, but my mother was so much more in my life. I hope she and you are having delightful conversations. I bet my dad is up there inventing something new and fun. I feel blessed by You, God, who has given me everything I could want.

Blessed is to go through life with a partner that is extraordinary and especially, specifically, perfect for me… for my soul, for my heart, for my mind and for my life. Blessed is being given the enormous gift of true love. You can have a good life, even a great life, with everything you need and yet it is just not the win. The grand life is a great life blanketed by a shiny, sparkling, dazzling love that heightens you both to the win. To partner with someone who, like myself, tries always to think of others first and acts on it every day is so wonderful. This wonder gives us both the peace to explore, together or comfortably alone. To partner with a man respected and admired, a genuinely nice guy, is like us being the king and queen at life's prom night.

Blessed is having sons and daughters to love. To have earned their respect, and to even have them think I am cool, is like winning the lottery for me. They bring youth and joy and love into our lives. They bring grandchildren in many flavors that are like fireworks of fun.

Blessed is having a special great friend in a sister. It is to share a communication that adds glitter to your days. It is to have someone who understands from the earliest days what your life really was like. It is to have someone who tosses out small memory nuggets and together you have the joy of sharing that memory.

Blessed is having true friends. These are friends who have been there through sick and well. These are friends who have contributed their ideas, their hearts and their hands in building the magic we have today.

Blessed is to have the talent, skills and means to express the wonder I feel at all of life with art. Art that touches another in a good way. Art that makes people feel and react.

Blessed is to have celebratory times of fellowship where we share our thoughts, our triumphs, our trails and our hearts. That's everything anyone could want.

FALLING IN LOVE

Both Don and I were married before and had children from those marriages. Since we did not have the 40 years of time together to survive the ups and downs of life that is the foundation of a strong marriage, God made it so we squished so many crisis's into a few short years that it nearly killed us. The top of the horrible list for every parent that loves is the loss of a child. I assure you that nothing comes close to that horror. You can see it as another survives it, but that is only a single lick of a 4-scoop ice cream cone. I am so fortunate to have survived this, and I know it is because of Jesus. We had grand and mighty plans. A favorite joke I heard somewhere in the past, "You know how to make God laugh don't you? Tell Him your plans for your life!"

We fell in love but we were still not listening to God. He gave us a wakeup call during which we cleared land and built a cabin in Alaska we hardly have time to visit; then we cleared land and built a house in Hawaii where we never lived before we sold it. It was paradise but it could lull you into a lost-time leisure and we had things to do on another path... a path that we could have seen if we would have listened, but we were newlyweds, we were "one-true-loves" sharing life, we were ravens finally set free to fly.

We could never have afforded what we were signing up for in Hawaii, now in wisdom we see this and we see the clear intervention by God (arson, theft, damage and loss oh my) that brought us to these mountains where we surely belong. We did not belong there in Hawaii so God plucked us up like an eagle with his talons and kicked our butts all the way back up into the mountains. As I quote from one of the ladies at church, "You can take the man out of the mountains, but you can't take the mountains out of the man!" That was their welcome, with a hug, no judgement, just open welcoming arms. Jesus gave us a homecoming on earth. We are fortunate. Blessed Indeed!

You see, we may not have the exact same goals and dreams but the ones we have mesh well. My goals focus on our love and happiness and that of those we surround ourselves with and having fun of course. I have goals to have us both find our fulfillment in life. I have a goal to making this the best darn nest ever a raven made. His goals focus on honoring the gift God gave him—his talent; on giving and sharing his immense love and joy of art; on being the knight in shining armor I always wanted and needed; on showing me each and every day how our love has evolved and grown over our journey together; and on gifting people with his pure smile, his genuine pleasure at meeting, seeing, or teaching them, and his heartwarming response. Its enough to totally make a person's day and very often does.

Don gifts me with quips and giggles, we have fun together… and we have fun together in a group too.

We don't make crutches of each other, or be a burden of dependence. We bolster each other… I know I am a better person because of him.

Do you remember the Burma Shave Signs that could be found along the road. We would all read them aloud at the same time as we came to them during my childhood family journeys..

God

Has

Blessed

Me

so,,,

TRUE

LOVE

PREVAILS !!

We have endured lots of unpleasant things and yes, having a partner through them has made half the impact on both of us. The joy is easily doubled because of how we are together, each better than otherwise, and because we both love sharing that joy with others. We have both been with someone who jealously demanded much solo time without meaning. Now we laugh, we hug when we can, even in a brief passing. We kiss often, we radiate happy and fun and our life has great meaning.

Two of you in love is a subject that everyone knows could fill volumes. I am sure there has been, is, and will be lots of love but not much of it will be as magnificent as ours. Ours is as deep as our souls, it sparkles our eyes and smile, and is too big for words to describe. It permeates our school. It has the power of healing… us and others. It is almost magical and has in fact been called that.

Well, now you know how I feel about my partner in life. Thank you, Jesus, for giving to us this great love, this amazing life, this incredible journey.

Why start here today saying again how blessed we are to be one of a great love story? Well, because I am again, this morning, as every morning, grateful for my life as it is … living in the glow of love.

That smile with your twinkling eyes...

Gives me heart rush and true love sighs

Here we are where we exactly belong

Years together make our love strong….

One thing I disliked immensely as a child was being ordered around. My mom never ordered she asked, unless you were being obstinate. I hope I always ask and never order. There were people older or larger than me who unreasonably thought they could tell me how to think and what to do with my life. I avoid that kind these days. My pay back on this lovely personality trait was to birth a child with the same trait and bright red hair to top it. For my kindergarten photo the photography man was, in my opinion, quite mean about me standing **very still exactly on the line** for the photo. He demanded I quit squirming around and that is not easy for me. I was not going to grace him with a smile.

Someone else had an early attitude as well. You can see in his photo he just returned from a fight. I bet he was standing up to a bully or showing some one he was no chicken. What fun it was to have Luke Hunter, building a house in Flat Rock, come to ask Don to carve a stump in the yard and have him say that he wanted it carved by "The Legend of East."

That brings us back around to the blessings. What seems like yesterday and yet one hundred years ago, I was blessed by marrying Don. This incredible journey will always be interesting. I never fail to be amused by how things happen in life, though at times it is only much later I excavate that humor. I guess seeing the funny side of things is just one quirk of optimism.

I enjoy the aspect of my brain that allows me to re-see situations not unlike a mini-movie. That is one of the reasons that make me think I am an alien. I often cannot completely or correctly interpret human actions when they happen, particularly when there are distractions present. For this reason, it might be necessary for me, preferably in a calm moment, to actually study for a time a past event before I come to understand whole purposes or small subtleties I missed. My husband can attest to the fact that I might come to him and directly ask him if my reaction to something someone said or did was appropriate. More often I come to him and ask him to explain someone's words or action.

There raises another reason I think I am an alien. What is common, normal and even appropriate to you, might be vastly different to me. When my husband explains that most people believe this or that, I find myself at times amazed that they would. I have to ask him why. What series of events created that social behavior? Also, I definitely have an out-of-sync understanding of when it is or is not okay to laugh. This could be because my humor gene is larger, or because my giggle gadget is more finely tuned than others, or because I am an alien.

This journey maybe interesting because God knows we get bored easily and He's doing this to keep us on our toes. Sometimes I have felt in our life that we were like ballet dancers that enthusiastically leapt up on pointe, and then were tediously stuck waiting for the opportunity to relax flat-footed. Yet that adage, "Use it or Lose it" might apply here. As we get older our muscles don't work as good as in our youth. We have to practice more than someone younger to keep them viable. I guess (with a sigh of defeat) I admit that its good for us to have a bit more time on pointe than others.

Our journey will always be interesting because you just never know what is going to happen next around us. I began a book about the three boys I birthed and named it, "Never a Dull Moment." I only thought things were crazy then, I know now how much crazier it could get… double crazy or triple even.

And lastly, this journey will be interesting because our shipmates on this journey are amazing and wonderful. We have been gifted with the very best of family, friends, and neighbors.

Dear Don,

I tell people I won the lottery and I totally did! We were young and in love. We were lost then finally found. We had met our one true love. We wrote poetry to each other and whispered endearments. You were the bravest man I had ever met with such a core of gold, smart as well as handsome—Oo-la-la…. You do so stir my blood.

You were so brave to take on my children. Any man who walks in to a three-normal-sons-and-their-mother situation, is brave. My children were never normal. Nicholas carefully calculated the size of the hole he would need to be able to breathe for a bit, loaded sand around his head, rocked it back and forth to create the space and completely buried his head to test the theory.

You encouraged me to trade them in on a spotted pony and a blue-tick hound when we had a chance. You survived.

Still today, you fill my life to the brim with love, patience, understanding, joy, laughter and so much more.

Thank you, I love you,
Phoebe

At a party my boys took up root on the open beams above my sisters living room. They conspired to help their little brother out there with them. Below is the lengthy process of me trying to talk him down. [Chris in a voice of terror saying over and over frantically, "Don't Touch Me!" "I'm going to fall!" "I can't move my limbs!".] Theoretically I could blame this on my sister. Factually, she did invite them to go out on the beam to hang her Christmas decorations for the occasion of a party. By this request, in the mind of a hormonal teenager looking ever for a loop holes, she gave direct permission to hang out there.

These days I bask in the glow of one true love. He understands when I need a day just to create, to write, to play. We just realized it was lunch time. We were both busy working and had not noticed. We had nothing planned. "What about those corn dogs?" he asked. "Sounds good to me!" I replied. Just minutes later they are cooked in the microwave, served on paper plates, happily consumed together, and I am back to writing. We are ever so rich in our lives of freedom of creation. When we finished our meal today, we looked at each other, grinned at each other, and gave a thumbs up. He had that delightful, full of joy sparkle in his eyes and on his face. I cannot say enough how we are rich in love.

We are rich in friendships. How can we ever repay Art and Larry for hours upon days, upon months, upon years of assistance in building a physical place people could come and be renewed. Rain or shine, food or not, they come. We planned and step by step it has become a beautiful reality. We did it pinching pennies and hammering thumbs by accident. Larry likes to quip, "You are building it and they will come. This will be bigger than J.C. Campbell." We know full well we won't be bigger than J.C. Campbell Folk Art School - it is hundreds of acres; there are scores of mediums, skills and crafting taught; it is located in a healing and encouraging atmosphere… well we do have that last one.. a healing and encouraging atmosphere. But we have lots of admiration for that folk school and what they are doing. From their website I quote their wonderful motto: "I sing behind the plow," the Folk School's motto since its founding in 1925, reflects the importance of lifelong learning and growth while finding joy throughout every step of the process."

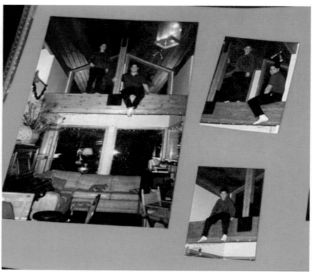

All you have to do is read our book (Raven's Wing School of Art) to know how very much work our family and friends have put into building this dream of Don and I. We have supped, and laughed, cried and talked together. We have a matching set of M&M cups for Larry, Art, Josh, Don and I. When Monique became part of the Flat Rock Woodcarving Guild there was not another M&M Mug so she brought her own mug in— Wonder Woman. Smiling big, she told Larry he couldn't use it. Do you think that is because he got the sexy lady M&M Mug?

Again, we are rich in friendships because when Don teaches, his students become his friends. He is just the nicest guy, as you well know. How I love to see the exchange between Don and Norma… "Make it darker!" "You are The Master!" Norma told me that the first time she teased him and called him 'The Master' he got this shocked look on his face, a tinge change to his skin, and began to excitedly explain how he is not nearly skilled enough, not nearly learned enough to be called a master at art.

He is humble, and because he is humble, he is like a sponge for learning. He knows he doesn't know it all and is happy to explore to learn any where, any time. Because he is humble, he gives his students the power to succeed. He believes in them and they know it. Because he is humble, he makes a great friend and people love to be around him. This is why so many students, like Norma, so enjoy his Open Studio. No matter what your week is like, there's always Friday (or Monday). Laughter, talking, sharing, all these things happen on Fridays and Mondays. Don is simply an all-around nice guy. Really, won the "Perfect Partner Lottery" is what I did.

It is obviously time for another rabbit hole. Laughing As We Go is the title. Last week when I sat down to write, I made a list of my thoughts to address. The last on the list was Laughing As We Go. When I begin writing I lose track of time and had not gotten to that last one on the list, and I had to make dinner. I never got back to it. Now I don't know what the thought was about, but I do know that Don and I share a lot of laughter. I wonder, what causes you to laugh. Wikipedia says: **Laughter is a** pleasant **physical reaction and emotion consisting usually of rhythmical, often audible contractions of the** diaphragm **and other parts of the respiratory system. It is a response to certain external or internal** stimuli. **Laughter can rise from such activities as being** tickled, **or from** humorous **stories or thoughts. Most commonly, it is considered an auditory expression of a number of positive emotional states, such as joy, mirth,** happiness, **or relief. On some occasions, however, it may be caused by contrary emotional states such as embarrassment, surprise, or confusion such as** nervous laughter or courtesy laugh.

It is that last sentence – nervous laughter - that has gotten me into so much trouble in my life. I have been known, when under duress, to spontaneously burst out in laughter. This is mostly misunderstood by others I have found, and definitely misunderstood in the ranks of the military. I am a klutz too, but that is one reason the military was a better fit than fancy tea parties. I am a nervous giggler and that is only acceptable in the best of company. Don is the best of company.

There is such joy in laughter! I think the vibrations of the joy loosens your muscles down to relax so laughter can just tumble out. From there it sinks down into your heart and like a firework, explodes with pleasure. Pleasure. I am a panther in my soul and like to stretch out on a rock on a sunny day just for pleasure. This must be why, since pleasure and pleasant are related, that I enjoy laughter so much. Did you appreciate how I circled back around?

Hawaii now has twice offered me sanctuary with a shark at the end. There's no pleasure in that. The first time I lived in Hawaii I was young, adventurous and it was warm and fun and carefree. The shark was joining the military because I had to get out of there. The second time we lived in Hawaii the shark drove us from a home we built but never lived in. Good thing too, because we have seen the uncountable ways why we are supposed to be here, not there. We know the ways our lives have been changed so ever much better by the people that we love here in North Carolina.

I realize how silly I was to ever believe I was in control – God was. And a giant, THANK YOU GOD, must be said because all my paths led me to Don. Books have been written, songs have been sung and poems composed on the subject of love and yet to those who have it not, it is a mystery beyond explaining. I can't see how anyone could get through life without being loved. There are so many people who thrive on dishing out love, just go find them. I recommend a good church.

Don is my sanctuary. I never have to run again because this man is willing to stand back-to-back with me against the world. I describe the warmth that permeates me knowing that I am right with God and am with the person He meant me to be with. It warms me on cold nights and wraps me in comfort like the perfect blanket.

We are so alike, Don and I. Wanting to do the right thing if possible; willing to work hard to achieve a goal; loving to work with others, to see delight and joy in their faces at their success; and to work together to build a place to share where people can feel the glow of love that surrounds us and find their own passion in the peace of friendship.

Yet, we are so different Don and I. Man and woman, such different views and ways of dealing with life. The differences are perfect. I think every child needs a mother and a father growing up so they learn those differences. So many things are different like the way we do art. He takes his time and works hard to create. I am throwing the paint and "gone in sixty seconds." He goes into an artistic mode, almost like a trance, the world ceases to exist around him in sight, sound or feel as he pours his passion into his work. Many people get this zoned-out thing happening with art. Dr. Betty Edwards speaks of it in her book, "Drawing on the Right Side of the Brain." (At least I think that is where she says it, but don't hold me to it…). Me, I don't 'get' the zoned-out thing, I live the zoned-out thing. I love to observe the world, nature in particular, see how it works. Don is fascinated with people, faces. I have had ample opportunity to be disappointed in people. I don't like to look deep into their eyes in case it is evil I see there. Where he can go on patiently forever, I must force myself to stick to the project until the goal is achieved because life for me can be distracting. I know I may never get back to it in the same manner, or remember where I was, and then I may be disappointed, or never finish it.

We are the same. We both have a pride inside that we served our country honorably.
We didn't just do a job, we did it up right. We both want to be able to express our
passion in art. We both want to avoid needless drama in the worst way.   We like to
have opportunities to share, be that the giving of a portrait that changes a person's life,
of the insignificant matchbox car given to a child at church, we find joy in both
extremes. We are blessed being in a place where people love to come. We both know
that only God's grace got us here.

So, are we alike, are we different, are we the same? No one is the same. Even twins,
identical twins are different. We like to celebrate our differences; we know two heads
are better than one and five can be a party. I miss parties you know, the pandemic has
stolen our parties. Now we find ourselves completing the circle (all of life is a circle
after all)…   I am completely Pandemiced out!!

IT'S LOVE

The love that naught sits dormant
Is the love I feel for him inside
True blessings from God
Who brought me to be his bride.

It is love that is healing
Every wound in heart and soul
Like we found a peaceful forest
And upon the moss we stroll.

It's love that has movement
grace like a dancer shows
It changes and adapts
And lives because it grows

It is love that rejuvenates
Like food and drink give us life
Thank you again, God.
For making me his wife

Sept 5, 2021

This isn't a tall tale or a fictional story, it all happened in real life. I have it all. I won the life lottery. I met the man of my dreams. He is handsome, debonair, kind, smart, funny, adventurous, romantic, sensitive… I am the luckiest girl ever born. Don took on the original wild Indian tribe (my three boys) and survived "initiation most thorough." He helped them, changing them in such good ways it just made my heart sing. Our life as a family was fun and full – full of laughter and fun times together. Don coming in to our lives provided me adult companionship and he insisted on helping with all the bills, even those left over from my divorce. He demanded that the boys show me respect and would not tolerate when they tried treating me as they had seen my ex-husband do. He is a   fabulous money manager and we soon had all our bills paid off and even had money to spend on the kids. We took our very first family vacation and flew to Hawaii for a week.

We lived together for four years before getting married. Our honeymoon was like a family party; all the kids – his and mine, which was five, his visiting brother, my four resident siblings, my mother, my maid of honor and her date, and it was fabulous. Later we would build a cabin there in the wilderness where we had our honeymoon. We would lay in bed together, giggling, as we picked figures out of the ceiling made from wood grain and shadows. It was similar to finding creatures in the clouds.

Don survived the terrible things the boys did to him when he first became a part of our lives, and that included twenty-nine holes in the sheet rock walls, the youngest setting his room on fire the night Don moved in, four broken windows, and much, much more. I was hesitant to get married again because I felt I had failed so utterly the first time. Also of concern was whether he could stand to stay with the boys.

When we finally got the boys settled down to a more normal family life than they had ever had, other things happened. It seemed like one crisis after another. We tried to talk to them about the abuse they had endured. We tried to get them some counseling for the abuse and the divorce issues, but the two older boys just took the counselors for a ride. They could have written the script for "Good Will Hunting" by recording what my boys did to those poor defenseless military psychologist and psychiatrists. My middle son convinced his counselor that I had just been impacted by all "such a terrible divorce", but he was fine, any smart counselor could see that. When I asked her about why then was he banging his head on the wall until he got bruises, she accused me of exaggerating. The oldest son begged to be release from counseling because his was group counseling and he was the only one in the group who had never been to jail, had never been kicked out of school and the only one who had ever gotten an A in school (much less been on the honor roll.)   The youngest was still undiagnosed and in counseling weekly but started having severe problems at school. He could not pay attention. He did not participate correctly, or at all. We switched teachers twice and finally he was just in a resource classroom, not even in a regular classroom. We began trying to get an accurate diagnosis which we would not get until he was 13 years old—Asperger's Syndrome or High Functioning Autism. What baggage this man has taken on with me.

My oldest son was free to do things on his own for the first time in his life and he wanted to live life large. He joined the wrestling team and made friends. He discovered girls and wanted to be out and about doing all these things he had never been allowed to do. He joined the swim team, he went to dances, he learned to drive (and almost totaled my Subaru.) He graduated high school, got his own apartment, got in financial trouble, moved back in and chaffed at being under rules again.

The middle son started getting into alcohol and drugs and running with a wild crowd we didn't like. He was sneaking girls in after we had gone to bed, and having underage alcohol parties. He was angry, always angry, beating up his little brother, who became terrified of his older brother. We had to separate their bedrooms to give the younger a protected space. Finally that middle son quit participating in school and flunked out in his high school freshman year. We forced him to choose to either (a) finish high school in the public school; (b) take his GED and go to work; or (c) go to the state Military Youth Corps Academy where he could get his GED and be out in 6 months. He resentfully chose the Academy. Somewhere in that time frame we began renovating the house "in our spare time." We were always so busy solving problems that it seemed time just flew by and before I knew it we were both retiring from the military. We had a plan for retirement; we just never got to finish that plan.

Now, when the two of us are down in the basement, getting cramps in our legs from bending down; watching a you tube video on how to open the front of the washing machine, I know I am fortunate. My hero, my champion, remembers the words of our most excellent GE Repairman, Mark. There's this little plastic tube and it can get mold built up in it and it will affect the flow when it drains. I deliver tools and assist as he cleans that tube out of all the mold, and even flushes it with Clorox… because he is a smart man. He is a man that likes to do the job well. It could be that he had noticed that I was missing in the basement for a time; it could be he noticed me buying flex seal (being bothered by the overflowing water in the basement, not for the first time); or that he noticed that the washer was pulled out from the wall and a stool pulled up before it like I was contemplating my attack to investigate the problem. He worries about my adventures. Whatever was noticed or thot, he jumped right on the job. That is his heart. When he expresses that, he can pour it into a piece of artwork that will speak to people. He has done this so many times. It makes me so proud to be his wife.

This photo will be in this book twice—it is a music box Don gave me.

The one time it was in the Mary Engelbreit Art piece discussion. This time it is here for a different reason—the message. The message on this precious wagon is: "Love is a journey together." Yes it is!!! What a beautiful, fun, fulfilling, adventurous journey it is with Don!

On each flour sack the girl sits atop in the wagon has a title, "Hopes" and on the other "Dreams." It is a statement about our journey together. We bundled up our hopes and dreams and loaded them up in our wagon. With this wagon full we journeyed until we found the Blue Ridge Mountains and now our Hillbilly Hearts are content. As we live our hopes and dreams, this piece becomes a prophetic statement about our lives.

FAMILY STORIES

There was always an endless flow of family stories when we all gathered. My favorites are the burnt trailer and the chlorine tank.

The Burnt Trailer Tale. Apparently, my brother had experimented with matches when we lived in Ojai, California. God knows he was still making fire displays in my mother's kitchen 50 years later. So, there was an empty lot next to our house that seemed to my parents to be a disaster waiting to happen. My parents cut all the high grass down and it was in piles of loose straw or hay.

Then they rented a trailer from the nice people at the gas station down the road. They loaded up all the straw and the trailer was heaped high. With my two oldest siblings in the back seat, he drove to the dump. The children happily wave to the gas station folks as they pass them by.

The dump was like the sides of a bowl. You backed up at maybe a 10-degree angle, there was a peak, then on the other side rolling down a gentle slope was the garbage. Imagine a man standing there on the peak and flinging his garbage bag like a shot putter.

My father is always looking out for the easiest way to do something. I think this is what makes him such a great scientist. He backed up to the peak very accurately. He opened the tailgate on the trailer and some of the straw slid out. Half or better of the straw remained in the trailer. He must have thought to himself, surely, I don't need to get up in that trailer and scoop it out. He gets back in the car and using quick changes between forward and reverse he manages to get a bit more of the straw out of the trailer.

Now in these days there were not the massive plastics yet and they still used to burn all the garbage at the dump. We were never allowed over the peak on the garbage side because it might always be smoldering in different places.

At this juncture some of the straw which had slid town the hill found one of those smoldering spots and with a whoosh became fire.

At this point my oldest sibling begins giggling nervously. That is her natural reaction to stress but a great irritant to my father who may have taken it as a comment regarding his lack of success.

It did not take long for the fire to follow that trail of straw right up into that trailer and set its self into a nice blaze. All the while my sibling is giggling and Papa is desperately jerking the trailer. Actually, I think he was trying to move it off the peak. In his efforts to dislodge his tires, they had crested the peak and were stuck on the dump side.

After all was said and done, the fire burned off most all the wood that formed the box of the trailer leaving a charred, black, smoking metal frame. There was just enough wood left to keep it smoking.

Here they come back down the road from the dump. The gas station folks are standing out front. They pull up at the front of the station, and everyone silently stares at the smoldering remains of the rented trailer.

The Chlorine tank. By family moved to Point Mugu Naval Station. In those days only the rich and famous had movers. The family acquired a trailer and all their goods were strategically packed. You had to make sure it was well balanced so as to not cause driving issues. You also had to arrange things to accommodate daily unpacking of necessities if the journey was more than a day long. A dresser might be situated so that only a portion of rope need be untied to open the drawer which then could hold daily necessities like eating utensils. My parents might have been eagles scouts so prepared for the journey they were. Among the packed items was a large steel tank filled with Chlorine Gas. I don't recall what my father had been working on with that Chlorine Gas. When they first arrived at Pt Mugu, the base housing had only been recently made. The yards were dirt so the first thing all the neighbors did was to plant grass seed. This large cylinder was quite handy for rolling the seed into the dirt and everyone in the neighbor hood used that thing. After use it was stored beside our house. One day an inspector saw it and told my parents they could not have that tank leaning against the house. They put it in the coat closet in the house. It was discovered there during an inspection and instructions were explicit that it needed to be removed far away from base housing.

My father had a friend 3 hours up the road in Bakersfield. Papa had heard that they had built one of the first recycling plants up in Baker's Field. He figured he could donate the chlorine gas, get a tour of the plant and then go see his friend.

After the hot, long and dusty drive my father arrived at the recycle plant in Bakersfield. They wanted nothing to do with the chlorine gas and would not take it. Dejected my father put it back in the trunk and drove to meet his friend.

Leaning against the car they chatted for a time of pleasant old times of their youthful selves. As always conversation wound around to science and they each shared what they were working on. As his friend was explaining about a new idea he was working on, my father listened closely and with interest. Nodding his head he agreed with the premise of the idea as it was verbally presented. As the friend reached the end of his explaining he related to my father that it was all going great until the war started and now, he was unable to get a hold of the chlorine gas he needed to continue. My dad was very charismatic and loved to tell a tale. I remember him holding his arm out like he was a presenter and saying, "Let me help you out" as he mimicked the opening of his car trunk to reveal the cylinder of chlorine gas.

My father had been in the Navy flying supplies to Wake Island and other places in the Pacific. When the US began the project to rescue all the German scientists from Peenemunde, they found out he was a physicist and discharged him to become the rocket engineer in charge at Point Mugu where they brought the scientist. The first rocket they launched from an aircraft before the bunkers to launch from the ground were built.

Middle: William Findlay Abbott and Doug Shaw. Experimental missle was strapped below the wing. Plane was armor-plated. Flew to 30,000 feet and fired missle while still aboard. Point Mugu around 1948.

FREEDOM AND LIBERTY

I don't think everyone understands freedom in all it's many facets. The obvious one to begin with is living free due to liberty. "Life, Liberty and the Pursuit of Happiness…" Thank you, America! Because I live in America, I am free to choose my own religion. I have freedom of speech, freedom of the press, and freedom of assembly. For me common sense begins with the Ten Commandments. The Ten Commandments were given to us by God and are basic rules about living right. I will tell you that I always refer to God as He. Jesus told us He is a father. Truthfully, I doubt that God is a he or a she in the sense we humans understand. I believe He is just IT! All of it, he, she, them and it.

1. "Thou shalt have no other gods before me." This one is pretty simple. Now we are smart enough to know that the sun is not some guy in a chariot. Scientists and other curious folks have shown us the incredible facets of life itself. They study what God has wrought. The intricacies of life are so vast we haven't discovered them all yet. As you look, you see the forest for the trees. I am a forest person at heart. I love nature and being close in with it. I spent well into my adulthood only seeing the trees and I still like to get up close and look at them. But now I have new perspective. I have learned how to step back and see the beautiful forest. This forest is but a grain of sand on the beach of the universe compared to all that God created. He is all-knowing, all-powerful, and supremely good. For those ed-gu-mi-ca-ted readers: Omniscient, Omnipotent and Omnibenevolent. The creator is asking you for a relationship and that is a gift to you. If you choose not to take Him up on this offer…Big Mistake. Huge. My response is a mimic of Julia Roberts in the movie *Pretty Woman.* when she goes back to the first shop that refused to wait on her. She is dressed to the nines in what is obviously the very best clothing money can buy. Her hands are full of bags from the very best and most expensive stores in town. She shakes the bags a tiny bit as she holds them up for them to see. She looks them in the eye and says, "I was in here yesterday, you wouldn't wait on me. You people work on commission, right? Big mistake. Big. Huge." Then she sings the next line, "I have to go shopping."

2. "Thou shalt not make unto thee any graven image." This one seems just as simple to me. It means simply don't worship anything but me. Refer to the above paragraph concerning all-powerful. Don't be a bug that needs squishing. Duh People!

3. "Thou shalt not take the name of the Lord thy God in vain." Okay let's refresh… The Creator is looking down on us. He has His hands on His hips and leans over and says, "Don't use my name as a cuss word and don't use it to curse someone! "Yes, Sir!" is the only smart response.

4. "Keep the Sabbath day holy." This is like a parent who while very proud of the work they see their child has done, calls for a time out. He is saying, I want you to spend one day in seven in calm reverence and prayer. Rest one day for you have worked well and chosen wisely.

5. "Honor thy father and thy mother: that thy days may be long upon the land which the Lord thy God giveth thee." I want you to focus on the last part of that sentence, "God giveth thee." I was blessed to have both a father and a mother that were easy to honor. Many people don't. I believe those titles can belong to those with whom you share no blood. When my father was gone, I had a father that was not of my blood, but who was my refuge in a terrible storm. Working the other direction, I have many people to whom I am not blood related for whom I am a "grandmother of the heart" or "their Aunt Phoebe." Find the people who serve this role in your life, love them for their time and guidance. Let them know what they mean to you – honor them. Easy Peasy.

6. "Thou shalt not kill." DUH!

7. "Thou shalt not commit adultery." I look at things this way. First there are different rituals for marriage. I define it as a partnership proclaimed and promised. You take an oath and you promise God that you will be faithful to that union. If you promise that, you need to honor that promise.

8. "Thou shalt not steal." This seems to be a big problem these days. People just don't want to wait for what they think they deserve. Many will use any method (stealing, coercing, pleading, lying and much more) to get what they want. They never think of, or disregard the importance of what this does to the person they coerced or stole from. It's just wrong people! You are not a child! Grow up and earn your own!

9. "Thou shalt not bear false witness against thy neighbor." Bearing false witness is the same as lying, and lying is a big deal. If you have lying then you cannot have trust. This Bible verse is said to be a command not to tell lies. There is a deeper meaning. I understand that in the Hebrew texts this word is used to imply purposeful deception or intentional falsification. As I heard my mom say, "You are lying and you know it!"

10. "Thou shalt not covet thy neighbor's house, thou shalt not covet thy neighbor's wife, ..." I repeat, "Grow up and earn your own." Coveting is just the first step before stealing.

When our forefathers wrote the Constitution, most believed in the Ten Commandments. According to Oxford University Press 98% or more regarded the Bible as indispensable, the other 2% were good men too. They worked together to write something that would prevent tyranny. The Constitution is considered the most sacred document in more than just our country. It safeguards our liberties. Liberties and freedom are not the same.

Liberty is defined by the Oxford dictionary as "The state of being free within society from oppressive restrictions imposed by authority on one's way of life, behavior, or political views.", while freedom is defined as "The power or right to act, speak, or think as one wants." Liberty being based on individual rights in how to live, is the opposite of tyranny. Our ancestors wanted a "Land of Liberty." Raise your hand and join our country and your liberty will be granted. Freedoms come with rules that protect other's rights as well. We will line these out in the next chapter on Bill of Rights.

But we also should consider the intention of these granted freedoms, put some reins on this horse. Consider a bit about these freedoms. These freedoms were written with the premise that everyone loved this country the most. They didn't want to go back to the oppressions that came from. They were wanting the joy of just living, not being under rule. They did love their neighbors and were wanting to share that joy of living with others. They accepted that it was none of their business or choice what that neighbor believed in unless it hurt someone else. All the neighbors agreed to live within this common sense.

"Freedom of religion." Freedom of religion was solely to allow Americans to be free to worship as they choose, even if that means not at all. "Congress shall make no law respecting an establishment of religion, or prohibiting the free exercise there of…"

"Freedom of speech." This was supposed to be the freedom to speak your opinions without fear or retaliation or censorships. It was never intended to allow others to stand and speak in hate. It does not allow speech that incites imminent lawless action or promotes or distributes obscene materials. It was based on the promotion of the public good. It was also never intended as a blanket behind which one could hide after committing treason, for some speeches given to the wrong hands is treason.

"Freedom of the press." As a person of the press, you should be obligated to consider the rights of others; you are supposedly under warrant to print the truth. Not opinions – truth. These days it seems as though too many other factors like money, ratings, and political leanings are used to distort the truth. To so many the most important part of reporting is the sensationalism. No person of the press should ever badger a person to such extent that they might cause them to die in an accident like Princess Diana did. Communications have improved thousands of times to what they are today. Somehow this has caused telling the truth and finding out what you are talking about before passing it on to go by the way side. It is way far out of whack. Someone said every-one is looking for their 15 minutes of fame. Positive or negative fame, people don't seem to care which! Frankly, today I don't believe everything I see or hear.

"Freedom of Assembly" is a freedom given to us to gather in public or private. They who wrote this wanted us "to be free to discuss and debate political actions because they understood that the rights of petition and assembly are essential for self-government.

We celebrate on this Independence Day that they achieved this liberty, that they secured this land of liberty, and that they gave us these essential freedoms.
There are other freedoms to discuss but these freedoms are choices that we make. Free from debt. We decide how much to go into debt, how much to exceed the limits of our earnings. We choose to equip our selves with golden handcuffs. If we extend into debt until we must stay at a certain level of earning to support our lifestyle, we have golden handcuffs.

Freedom of expression. The freedom of expression should not be for the purpose of hurting another, but certainly can be for the expulsion of that hurt from another. I wish everyone could find a good method of expression. I wish everyone had the time to create, but ultimately that is up to you to earn. Being free to say what is in your heart comes with an obligation to say things for the right reasons.

Free to build a place for your family. We need to figure this out, People. According to the BBC, by 26 May 2023 there were more than 200 mass shootings across the US. (A mass shooting defined as an incident in which four or more people are injured or killed). This does not mean getting rid of guns, this means figuring out mental illness and evil. Anyone who commits a mass shooting is either mentally ill or just plain evil. Things are out of hand and threatening our liberty and freedoms. This Independence Day I hope we can pledge to do better.

Now feel free to put on your favorite tune, turn it up and sway with the music. Today for me it is Tina Turner. In my opinion she rocks and I was so sad to hear of her passing. She is one of my heroine's. She sings with all her heart, her mind, and her body - "powerful vocals!" Her energy and passion, so wonderful to watch, I feel envy at her abilities and sparkle. When I just listen to the music, I imagine her up there in that sparkly sequin covered 60's short mini shirt length dress. She had a body any woman would be proud to have at any age. And she was a 'two-percenter' like me. When I broke away from my husband, and took classes at the shelter, I was told 98% will go back to the same abuse or one just like it. Now things are different, the statistics today are less than 36% of women will experience domestic abuse. Just look up this article, "20 Alarming Domestic Violence Statistics."

That was what I remember from 30 years ago. Mine was private, Tina's was bravely survived in public and she sang about it, 'What's Love Got To Do With It?'

Freedom from abuse.

LOST LOVES

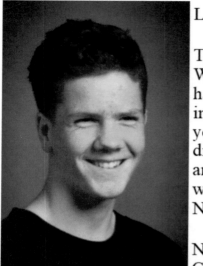

Tonight, I would like to reflect on the amazing gift of partnership. When there is two of you in love, they say it doubles the joy and halves the sadness. Part of that is true… Nothing could ever cut in half or lessen the pure tragedy of losings one's child. Shared you can make it through the horrid times of lost dreams. I know I dreamed of watching him grow to be a man; seeing him achieve and dazzle; seeing him in love; seeing him hold crowds with his wit in whatever arena he chose. It was 2010 when we lost our son Nicholas.

Nicholas could easily have become a famous standup comedian. God knows he practiced a lot on his teachers. He often tested my ability to not grin or laugh at inappropriate times. He could have smiled that devil may care grin and been the most famous extreme sport performer ever… he had no fear from birth— doctor certified ("This child has no fear factor.")! I almost see him sitting beside Shaun White when Shaun is on tv doing extreme sports… two red heads sharing their wit behind their hands and laughing together over their victories.

I know he could have been just like the guy in the movie "Good Will Hunting." He could have been in a "think tank" expounding on wild and amazing concepts and thoughts to a whole room of thinkers that only wish they could think as good or as innovatively as he could. He would discover new math theories that would rock the world. He took his SAT test in 7th grade and rated in the top 2 percentile nationally in math. John Hopkins University invited him to a summer program but he had no interest. Actually-Factually our son could have been or done anything he set his heart on but instead we lost him too soon. He was only 24 years old. We miss him every day and every hour.

So how did I survive losing my beloved son? First with God's grace and second with the best partner ever. Even though this son of mine challenged my husband, Don, mightily, and purposefully tried him, he loved him like his own. We sobbed at his loss together. He may not have contributed biologically to that son, but he love him like his own. He knew more about him than almost anyone. I do not say lightly that he *suffered* the loss with me. He also helped me to my feet when I collapsed in anguish at being told of Nicholas's death. Don has held me up and I have held him up at times as well.

At Nicholas's memorial service while everyone was on the beach talking and meeting I was on the grace side bench built by my mother's friend, June, with my brother, Findlay and my closest sister Melissa. There were no words between us just three of us sobbing at the loss of such an amazing human being.

Don wrote and read the most moving and beautiful speech about Nicholas.

(Don Blackwell, at graveside)

We come before you today with heavy hearts, Lord, to bury our child, Nicholas. We know that he is also your child, God.

In your grace and mercy we ask that you receive him into your presence with loving arms. We thank you for all that Nicholas was and is to all of us and to the memories of him we will always have.

We also ask your forgiveness, Lord, for all we have done, thought and said and for those things we have left undone, not thought, and not said.

We will remember Nicholas as a beloved son, brother, grandson, nephew, uncle, cousin and friend.

We commend his earthly remains to this ground, ashes to ashes, dust to dust. We commend his spirit to you for eternity.

We ask your blessings for all who have gathered here and for your healing grace for broken hearts. We stand secure in the knowledge of the resurrection of our Lord and Savior, Jesus Christ, and in his promise of eternal life.

Amen

Lost children. Children are a tremendous blessing. They are a gift from God. If you received a child, you should tell Him thank you every day for the blessing. Some who receive a child by friendship, adoption, or even a chance meeting, can often be blessed even more than a birth parent.

Today, I am thanking God for my son. He is gone now. It should never be that a child dies before their parent, but it happens - lost children.

A lost child makes a rift in your heart. It may heal enough that you can go on with your life, but you will often reach to caress the scar that you will ever feel.

Today another mother who has lost a son was here. I can feel the sadness that halos her. Only someone who has lost a child can feel this depth of pain that we two know intimately.

His birth date has passed. I have survived the intense ache one more year. I wanted so much to see his face when he knew the happiness of love.

I ponder laughter and sadness. Around this time of year, September 20th to be exact, I find I am more emotionally moved than other times. I laugh my head off when something is funny and openly weep at a sad movie. Some of this is bound to be a repeat.

September 20, 1984, I birthed a truly amazing human being. He was so very clever and joyful most of his life. His eyes sparkled when he was telling a joke with perfect timing or being mischievous as he was apt to do. I realized that I recognized that sparkle and, in my mind, I apologized to my mother. Upon further reflection I realized it was actually "another mother moment" when I decided she had that same sparkle and so did her mother.

Top photo is Nicholas at around 15 months old.
Center photo is Nicholas and I both at around 5 years old.
Bottom photo is Nicholas dressed for Halloween as a pirate, his all time favorite.

Lost loves—my parents

My mom once drove a car up onto a telephone pole cable. I barely remember the story because my dad was the story teller and he died before I could become a listening adult. My mom was beautiful, smart, gracious to a fault and well frankly, formidable. I so miss her wisdom, guidance and love. (Photo right around the time they got married in 1943).

My father was a real storyteller. Most were humorous and he would laugh longer and louder than anyone. It was an infectious laugh so you could not help but join in. Sometimes I would miss his words because I was so caught up in the whole visual of this charismatic, laughing, funny man. When I was in California in 1969 he was the elder among groups of college kids and he was the life of the party. (Photo right I am guessing is around 1963, but that is just a guess.) I remember well the evenings in Homer, Alaska. There was lots of drinking going on and it was loud and fun. My dad would tell stories of my mom, of his brother, of our lives, and of others close to us. With almost no   exception he made these stories into an amazing event or a tale so delightful that the crowd would break out in applause or roar with him in laughter.

Today I also ponder the subject of need. I have everything I need and most of what I want. We are very blessed. However, I feel that we are blessed because we are trying to walk what we perceive as the path God would have us walk. This creates inside us a peace and a joy. We find the peace that comes when you are not in opposition with God. Its like petting a dog the wrong way and it makes his hair all stand up and does not feel good on your hand. It is like carving against the grain instead of with the grain of a piece of wood. It is ruffled feathers and hot heads to be in opposition with God… your head is hot first in embarrassment, because of course He can see what you are doing and know what you are thinking, and second in shame. How embarrassing to snuff off your Maker! How foolish! Then, your head gets hot again because if you are in opposition to God, you are most likely acting like a spoiled child who is not getting his or her way – hot headed or hard headed. Do you stomp your foot when you demand things you want as well?

I struggle with the people who cannot tell the difference between want and need. They appear to believe that if they want it, it is a need indeed. They cannot discern the difference because they can only see themselves, their wants, their desires and getting their way. We have family that personify this. The concept of working toward something, working to earn it by virtue of effort, does not seem to click into place properly in their brains. They want it all without working at all. Do they mentally amass a list of all the reasons they deserve to have it? I used to believe they were like the grasshopper in the story where the ants work all summer, then the grasshopper wants to share the fruits of their labor. But they are not. They have mutated to being a grasshopper that believes by virtue of size they should lead the ants. They ignore the logic and efficiency of the ant's methods and insist on a change. They not only want to tell the ants how to work, but to take over the distribution of the fruits of their labor, with them receiving the largest portion because they are special. I can hear my youngest son saying, "He is such a special snowflake!" They need to talk best, loudest or longest. They will not have a discussion with you because they don't necessarily   allow the back and forth. They feel the absolute urgency to convince you of their way of thinking. They are assured their thinking is the only correct way and thus have no need of your opinion on anything, nor will they listen to arguments against their point of view. However, if along the way, they realize they were wrong they are sure to turn the story around so that they discovered the wrong someone else perpetrated and have proudly corrected the error.

Without walking on the path God has chosen, or not using the talents He has given, you only hurt yourself. You won't be happy. You will always have this big empty spot inside, this nagging need, this urgent request bugging you.

NEED
Need can make you knock-kneed
Or even make you bleed.
Indeed!
Need can be satisfied by a deed.
It is not good if it motivates greed,
Or makes it so you just don't take heed.
Indeed!
Need can possess, we are agreed
And it can halt process or impede
Progress, yet then peace exceed…
Indeed.
Need.

My grandparents were one true love's. He was red headed and she offered in the 1940s, one hundred dollars to any grandchild born with red hair. In fact, unlike all my siblings, I had auburn hair. It was not really the red of my grandfather or my son, Nicholas. My cousin had strawberry blond hair and she too birthed a true red head. I never met my grandfather because he died when my mother was only 13.

When I was restationed to Alaska in 1985, Nicholas was 7 months old. I had sent many photos to my mother, but photos never did Nicholas's hair color justice. She met me at the airport and after hugging and talking to my other son, took Nicholas from me. She fluffed his hair and they grinned at each other. Several times as we walked through the airport she stopped and spoke to someone, proudly announcing her grandmother status. Later that night she told me the story of her mother's offer. We both had tears at the thought that here was the grandfather's legacy but long after both grandparents were gone.

It's a very special thing to be given loving, kind, moral parents. I believe when you have those kinds of people to guide you when you are a child that it gives you the fiber to survive even the worst the world can throw.

My mom was an adventurer to her soul. When we hiked in the mountains and we would come around a trail that turned into a vista, we would always stop to enjoy the view. No hike was ever so rushed as to not be enjoyed. She loved the outdoors. In her last years she was not doing well. My husband and I had just retired from the military and he was running a home business. This gave him the time and opportunity to drive her to her many doctor appointments. They became great friends.

He enjoys telling the story of how they would pass the Chrysler dealer in Anchorage and there would be the newly released Prowler. She would say, "I'd like to have a ride in one of those" and he would agree. It did my heart so very good to have them be friends. She had warned me not to marry the man I married first. She was right, I was defiant. I relish the defiance for the beauty of the two sons of that marriage. She took the time to tell me that she really liked my new husband, that she knew he was a good man, good for me, and that she was very happy for me. She and my father were one true love's as well and it takes one to know one, they say.

My mother was also completely a class act. She was interested to meet each and every person with whom life presented her. She was gracious under pressure, and I was a pressure point as a teenager. She might have been as a teenager for her mother too, but my grandmother never told us that. Somehow I was tagged as the first of my siblings to be the quintessential teenager… caught up in the joy of life, running with the boys and their hot cars, and dancing carefree through life like a fairy. I have to tell you that as a general rule I am an optimist, I am quick to laugh and slow to anger. But I have never liked being told what to do.

Top photo is my mom and dad in California. Photo center right is my parents in their folk dancing outfits in California circa late 1940's or early 1950's. Photo bottom right is my mom adventuring on a boat in Alaska, a trip she took as a teenager.

My Nicholas, my lost love, was very like me in many ways… an optimist, loved nature and animals in particular. He was quick to laugh, loved jokes, slow to anger and, like me, defiant. Also like me he marched to his own drummer.

Speaking of marching to your own drummer and dancing… How can you tell which one in this picture is me? All the other little girls have their feet together and pointing   forward. I am the one in the front row, near center. My feet are not pointing forward. I am standing with one foot on top of the other. All the rest of the girls are holding their dress out so it looks like a bell or a courtesy underway. I am holding my apron pulled up so you would see the pretty dress I had on underneath that plain old white apron.

Well, there we have it… sixteen rabbit holes in a row - deviations in writing. I set out to write of how much I miss my beautiful son and I must distract myself so that I am not overwhelmed with sadness.

Photo bottom right is my mom and Nicholas.

I admit to being bad about getting off subject. I call this going into a rabbit hole. Noted Rabbit holes in this chapter: 1.Best   2.My Mom 3.My Dad 4.The Subject of Need 5..People who don't know want from need. 6.Gods path 7.'Need' poem 8.Grandparents 9.Great Parents 10..Adventurous Mom 11.Storyteller Dad 12..Different drummers.

MARY ENGELBREIT'S ART

Both Don and I enjoy the artwork of Mary Engelbreit. We buy her greeting cards to use and love her sayings and art. We had two things early in our relationship that solidified this thing we shared.

One of the first Christmas presents Don bought me was this lovely music box (photo top right). I was anxious to know what it was and although he let me hold the package I had to wait for Christmas. I concentrated on the box. Then I told him it felt like a Mary Engelbreit scene, with a girl that was what he imagined I was like as a child. I was wearing a big hat with a sunflower on it and pulling a wagon. Don was pretty freaked out by that.

The second incident was the following Christmas. By then we both knew the other liked Mary Engelbreit artwork. I bought him the book shown in the lower right corner titled, "Don't look back." Don bought me a mug for my tea with the exact same artwork! We are so tuned to each other.

Don't look back is very sound advise no matter how it comes to you. Isaiah 43:18: "Forget the former things; do not dwell on the past."

In the Lion King Rafiki tells Simba, "The past can hurt. But the way I see it, you can run from it, or learn from it." Wise words. A special interpretation because it teaches about humility and grace… "It is Don and I in a nut-shell…Yep, it hurts but we learned and we are standing our ground!

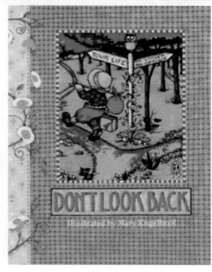

Mary's interpretation is different because she tells us flat our, "Don't look back"… Don't Do It!! This is also sound advise.

I looked for more interpretations or quotes on this but found they are just rearrangements of the Bible verse.

MILITARY HONORS

My husband and I received many military honors. I was honored to work with some of the finest Americans. This honor gave a deep richness to my life. I was honored to read what my supervisors wrote on my Airman Performance Reports. I was honored when a young airman came to me and asked career advice?" Don and I were both touched and honored when all national Pararescue Units approved making him an Honorary Pararescueman. We both were honored when 300 people came to our retirement party to show their love and appreciation and were very honored to see the front row of general officers at our wedding.

I admit, right up front, I am a social butterfly. I find nature and flowers and animals intriguing and am drawn to learn more. I find people very interesting too, and this has made me into a social butterfly who flits from place to place, feeling barred from none, and at least spreading a smile at most. I think this is what has made my life so unusual and beautiful.

Although the book will not be in chronological order, I can at least try to put the military stories somewhat in order. I will preface with saying that my husband and I had the most amazing military careers.

Here are our 'shadow boxes', a military tradition upon retirement. The yellow and green ribbon in each of our boxes was very special. It is the Alaska Legion of Merit Ribbon. We were told it had never before been given to anyone below officer or chief master sergeant, which we both were. This was because the criteria is not only that you must have 'extraordinarily distinguished or meritorious service within the Alaska National Guard' but also have had 'international impact during your career.' That both of us received this award is quite amazing. The second thing about our shadow boxes is that mine holds the American flag and his holds the Alaska flag. They flew these two flags together over the capital building in Juneau, Alaska, before putting them in our boxes. We were very honored!

Some things mean a lot more than others, particularly when you have worked hard and been recognized for the same.

In 1989 when I had just entered the Alaska Air National Guard and Don had just gone active duty in the same we both were selected as our squadron NCO of the year.

Top two are Don's award of Honorary Pararescueman. This is a very special honor because you have to have had such a positive impact to a PJ team that every team across America must agrees you are worthy of this honor.

Next down is a disc from a Burroughs Mainframe Computer, from the Altus Data Automation Division, at Altus Air Force Base, in Oklahoma. It was a traditional gift to give to data automators leaving this assignment to take a retired disc and have in engraved. Never before had this parting gift been given to a non-data automator person. Another silver lining to this assignment is that my youngest sister is still happily married to the man who was my boss at this Data Automation.

Don was honored when out of every artist in the Air Force, he was chosen to make the commemorative print for the opening of the new Air Force Professional Military Education center at McGhee-Tyson Air Force Base. A friend, promoted to Brigadier General, became the Commandant there and sent Don this picture he called, "The Don Wall" honoring Don for doing this print. The print was given to VIPs visiting the base.

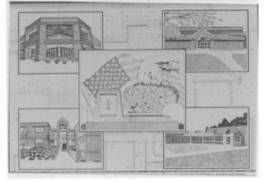

AIR FORCE BASIC TRAINING.

I found myself in my 20's living in Hawaii having a grand old time when reality slapped me in the face. I finally noticed illegal activity at my workplace, and when I asked, was told I would be the primary witness in an upcoming court case regarding that. I declined to participate by leaving Hawaii. Being young and broke the only way I knew off the islands was to join the military. I shipped out two weeks later.

Right from the get go there were issues. I had no college but was always an avid reader. When I took the Air Force entry exam, Armed Services Vocational Aptitude Battery (ASVAB) test I achieved an almost perfect score. The unfriendly test controller decided that I must have cheated, so before things could proceed I was forced to take the test again with this unhappy camper sitting in front of me. It did make me some what nervous and the second time I missed a few under the glare of impatience. Still my percentage, written permanently on the front cover of my Air Force Training Record was 95%. This caused comments throughout my career.

I should have recognized then that I would have a career marked with issues between the military and I. Recruits can come from all over the world and the Air Force forms "flights," each of some 50 recruits — male and female separated — for their time at Basic Training. Since I and two others (one female, one male) came from Hawaii, the later considered "overseas," we were brought in early to ensure we would be there for the forming of the next "flight." Now we were to be shipped from Hawaii to Texas. I was worried about this decision and I hadn't slept well for days. We flew from Honolulu to LA to San Antonio. The first leg from Honolulu to Los Angeles I cried as we took off leaving the Hawaii that had conforted me and made me laugh again. Then LA was uncomfortably hot and we were delayed for what seemed a long time in a strange airport where we knew no one. The time difference between Hawaii and Texas meant that I was now four hours off from the time my body felt it should be.

But here I'd like to canter back around to the discussion about the phrase, "EXCUSE ME!" I can tell you that military basic training was a rude, rude awakening for me. Once in San Antonio, we were escorted off the plane and led onto a bus. When we got off that bus we were under the watchful eye of some tall dude in a hat with an attitude. I am a leader by nature, and when we would up waiting while they tried to figure out what to do with us three, I leaned. The Air Force on the whole does not object to leaning, but a basic training it was obviously a crime. Exhausted, I slumped against the bus. I was still into my Hawaiian butterfly mode: flying and lighting, hanging awhile, flying and lighting. Really, I just leaned back against that bus for a moment. Who-lee the tall dude did enjoy his job. Why do folks like this not get laryngitis when they yell so loud it can blow your hair back Why didn't someone advise me that there would be some slumping rules – that's what he called it, "Slumping Rules."

After that wonderous experience we were put in a holding area. There were three of us who had come in from overseas. The military does not want hold-ups in any of their coveted processes believe you me! I got that message loud and clear. I can now assume that normally the overseas recruits did not come in a full three days early. We were shuffled and then shuffled again, finally winding up in the personnel office. By now my fun meter was well and truly pegged. I was exhausted and pretty much freaked after the anger of the bus guy. We were taken to the Personnel Center and shoved up to the counter and our escort told someone why we were there and then he hit the door running. This second angry man must have been using the facilities in the waiting area because there was no break in the counter for him to have snuck through that I could see and he definitely first appeared behind me. In my exhaustion I could have sworn that he yelled so loud that the words blasted around the room, ricocheted off the stupidly high ceilings and hit me twice. He definitely got his point across about his room also having slumping rules! I genuinely would have appreciated a modulation of the volume as he spit out, "EXCUSE ME! NOBODY **LEANS** ON MY COUNTER!" What? I thought to myself, "Are you working for the government that uses the lowest bidder and are thinking your counter might fall over?" It occurred to me that I could have responded with a little sashay and said, "Well, if you could have offered me a chair this wouldn't have happened!" Lucky for me that my instinctive self-preservation skill kicked in and the words did not come out of my mouth. I'd like to share that it is my opinion that when people like this get on a roll there is no stopping them. Just stand back and let that bull charge on through! He could not have cared less how tired we were! He did not want to hear all the places we had been shuffled from and to and when I tried to explain he talked right over me loudly advising us that he didn't even care how long we had been on this earth. It became obvious pretty quickly that he was operating under the immovable belief that airmen and recruits are not even allowed an opinion. Welcome to basic training. Dripping in syrupy sarcasm I should have said, "Well Excuse Me!" but it is a darn good thing I did not.

He then told the three of us to go sit on a bench that was to one side of the counter. The sergeant, who had returned to his desk after harassing me, looked directly at me and said, "And don't lean over there either!" The bench was about 8 feet long, like a church pew. At one end was a really pissed off looking guy and then at the other end huddled together were the three of us. Waiting on the bench reminded me of the Arlo Guthrie movie 'Alice's Restaurant.' There we were, Group W, on a bench in CBPO (Central Base Personnel Office).

By the end of the day a trickle of other recruits had come form overseas. We first dropped off our male recruit, and the powers that be placed the three of us women in a dorm with a flight of women who were in their last two weeks of basic. Several of their members had washed out leaving empty beds at the end of the rows. When we arrived the dorm was empty except for the dorm guard as the women in the flight had earned a pass to San Antonio for the day. When they returned Sunday evening, they realized they had not done their weekend chores, so they rushed around doing them.

One person was buffing the floor, several were cleaning the latrines. Everyone was bustling around and I was bored so I offered to help. The other overseas two recruits joined in and they gratefully put us in the break room with around 10 pairs of shoes each to polish. We were hard at it. At this point in time I didn't realize several things which would be apparent later. One, there was a firm lights-out curfew at 9 pm and the time was later than 9 pm. Two, the way the dorms were constructed, the windows (with light shining out) from the day room were not visible on the outside of the building as they all faced a roof area. Three, the speaker in the (Charge of Quarters (CQ) worked both ways and the training instructor on duty there must have just listened in and heard the buffer going when it should have been silent. Four, she loved her job yelling at recruits.

Polishing away, suddenly the loud speaker came to life and a very angry voice yelled, "It's after lights out, do I hear a buffer going? I am coming up there now!" One girl ran into the day room and said, "Get rid of those shoes and get in your beds!" I scooped up the shoes I had been polishing and as I ran to the end of the row to the bed I had been assigned, I was throwing shoes under the beds along the way.

The dorm is locked against intruders and anyone requesting entry must be approved by the dorm guard stationed at the entry point. The entry point is one door with a small window about 8 inches wide and 10 inches high. The dorm guard looks through the window and the person requesting entry must show their badge, be approved for entry by the list at the door, and only then is the door opened. There is an exception to this rule. In an emergency an emergency access card can be used to by pass the waiting and the list. When it is shown through the window, the dorm guard must open the door immediately.

This woman slammed the access card on the window and yelled, "Open Up! Now!" which the dorm guard did. By now we had just had time to turn all the lights out and get in our beds. She reached and pushed the whole row of lights on and yelled, "Everybody Out Of Bed!" I just followed what the others were doing and stood at attention beside the bed I was assigned. She was not done. Swiping the row of light switches again she turned them all off and yelled, "Everyone Back In Bed!" We did this aerobic exercise, out of bed, at attention, jump back in bed, for several rotations. All the while I was thinking to myself, "You have made a huge mistake joining the military!" The result of all that fun was that flight of ladies got "set back" and had to repeat a week of basic training. I learned a valuable lesson about the dorm guard who stood at the door and was the only person in the whole flight not in trouble at that particular moment.

For three days those girls in that flight were in trouble. We three rainbows* just tried to stay out of the way. It seemed a relief when they came and got us to join our flight. It was foolish

---

* When I was a basic training "rainbows" were newly arrive recruits sporting a rainbow of clothing choices. "Pickles" were new recruits who had been issues their plain olive drab uniforms. "Canned pickles" were when you finally got your name tags on your pickle suit.

relief.

As an assembled flight, originally we were assigned to a dorm in an old World War II wooden barracks. We had two male training instructors. One was younger and overly enthusiastic. His favorite thing was to get right in a girls face and yell until she cried. At this time in my life I was not crying for anyone; I had my stubborn on. We were assigned beds alphabetically and being Abbott I was first in line. We were asked to dump out all our stuff on the bed into one big pile. Everyone watched as the Training Instructor went through my stuff first. It was not fun. He accused me of trying to bribe him because there was loose change and stamps in the pile; he accused me of threatening him with my weapons which were (God Forbid) a jack knife and a pair of scissors. I witnessed the other recruits putting things from their pile into their pockets as this man ranted and raved at me. At that time I wished my name started with Z.

Not long after we arrived we were briefed on the Air Force form 341. This was an Excellence/ Discrepancy Report. These forms were folded neatly into a narrow strip and hung under the flap of our right side breast pocket. At any time, any training instructor could ask you for one of your forms. He or she would fill it out with some action you had done that was either excellent or demerit worthy. Once filled out they would turn it into your training instructor. When our younger male training instructor failed to get one of us crying, he would pull one of our forms and write some made up discrepancy on it. During my time at Lackland I never received one for excellence, but my second training instructor told me I had set a record for the number of my discrepancies. When we were reassigned to his flight, he called me into his office and asked about this. When I explained about the crying he threw them all away and I never received another one.

Photos above—P1 My Basic Training Annual. P2 Air Force Form 341. P3 the Quad you can easily see the drill space below the dorms. P4 bottom is an aerial shot of the Quad. You can see the two stories of dorms that stick out and in the center of the complex was a roof with windows looking out from our day room. Our dorm was on the second floor, level with the roof, while the dorm above was on the third floor. The ground floor held the Charge of Quarters (CQ), offices, chow hall and the classrooms in the center while the other end, shown better in the top photo was open to the weather and offered covered drill space.

I still to this day do not know exactly what happened to get us, as a flight, kicked out of the living quarters we were in, but that, too, was fairly traumatic. The silver lining was that the training instructors we got when we moved into the Quad area were far better for us.

First, this man barged into our barracks and rudely yelled at us to pack everything we owned into our duffle bags. All us women with these 36 inch high backpacks full loaded were then marched across the base to what was known as 'The Quad.' This was a relatively new building with covered drill space under the 2 story dorms (see photo left from my Basic training book. Once there we were left at attention, which gets old pretty quick. One girl had volunteered to be the dorm chief, and after the man left, she told us to go to rest position. We put our backpacks on the ground and assumed the parade rest position.

We had been parked near the chow hall entrance. There were spots on the pad under each dorm wing for flights waiting permission to enter the chow hall. Each time a flight arrived for chow, their training instructor would meander over to us and harass us with fun little things like, "Attention!" "What did you recruits do?!" "Face Left!" "Face Right!" "Face Forward!" and so on. In the other spots whole flights came, went to chow, and left. We despaired that we would get to eat that meal; I believe we were the last flight called in. It is my estimation that we were always destined to be in that quad and that first week in the WWII barracks was just while it was cleaned or readied for us, all the while implying we had done something wrong. But is was just an opportunity to indulge in their fondest pastime—yelling.

Speaking of meals, I learned quickly to be very   observant. Three times a day we went to the chow hall for meals. Before the flight could enter the chow hall one person from the flight had to enter the chow hall, stand before a row of training instructors at their table, execute perfect facing movements and with exact proper wording request permission for the flight to enter the chow hall. It went something like, "Flight Zero-One-Five requests permission to enter the dining facility, Sir!" If you did anything wrong you were sent back to the end of the line to try again. We called that 'The Snake Pit.' I learned to copy those who had been here longer, and to do these movements well. Mistakes were made, like when the lead training instructor was a female and I ended my request with "sir."

Once you achieved permission for your flight to enter you went into the chow hall line and received your food. People on 'The Fat Boy Program' were given different food from the others. I had partied hearty for the two weeks before I shipped out and was immediately put on that program. I lost enough weight in the 6 weeks at Basic to receive a whole new uniform issue at my training base. When you had your food you proceeded to a table for four. Until all four persons were there you were not allowed to sit down and had to stand, at attention

This photo of the snake pit I found online but cannot find the photo credit or I would list it

with your dinner tray in front of you. Once the last trainee arrived at the table they would say, "Ready, sit." and you could all sit down in unison to eat. The Air Force mandates 30 minutes for chow time but if you are at the end of the line, or waited a long time for your last dinner mate you might have only minutes to eat. Once everyone at the table finishes eating you all have to stand at the same time, turn your tray in to the KP folks, proceed out to the pad and back into formation.

Another observation I made was that the dorm guard monitor controlled who was on duty and when. I immediately signed up to perform that duty. When my flight was doing drill on the pad in the cold of January and February, I was scheduled for dorm guard duty. This only came back to bite me when my flight was on the pad drilling and a VIP party came to see the dorm and I had to show them all around our living quarters. They wanted to see my bed with perfect hospital corners, my locker with the hangers spaced just so, and my clothes drawers with my under pants folded perfectly into six inch by six inch squares and my nylons in a perfect jelly roll*. Although I made it through saying proper Yes Ma'ams and all, it was nerve wracking.

By week three I was feeling like Bill Murray in the great movie, "Stripes" and wanting to go AWOL (Absent Without Official Leave). Looking out our day room window and across the roof, I could see that one of the dorms was empty and there was a window open. My recruiter had told me briefly what it would be like, not that I believed him at the time. But I held on to him telling me that they were just going to push us as far as they could because they could not afford those that would fold under pressure. Only 6 weeks—they will try to break you but they won't, anyone can endure 6 weeks, right?

Above photo shows one side of the inside of the dorm. It was situated on the left side as you entered. There were windows above the lockers on the left, and a wall behind the lockers on the right. The other side of the dorm was a mirror image with another set of two rows of beds, and their outside windows on the right side.

We encountered a problem with our flight from the start. One young lady was from a military family and had father, brothers and cousins in the Air Force who had briefed her on what to do. Day one she jumped up and volunteered to be the Dorm Chief. She was allowed to choose her Squad Leaders and showed her prejudice in

---

- A jelly roll could only be made with garter type nylon stockings. If you chose to wear panty hose once we changed to wearing our dress blues, you had to store them in your dirty clothes bag. Most of us never wore those jelly rolled nylons as the jelly roll was a pain to achieve. It was made by rolling up the nylon stocking toe first slowly and carefully so all edges were perfectly flush on both ends, not an easy task.

- Photo found online or scanned from my training book.

her choices. When we were moved to the new facility our Dorm Guard took charge. There were no training instructors that first day ready to greet us. After chow we were sent back to the pad and stood in formation. Finally a female flight training instructor came and marched us up to our dorm and left. Our Dorm Guard parceled us off to the four rows of beds with one side almost completely white and the other side, where I was in the second row, was a mix of white, brown, and black.

I can tell you that every unpleasant duty from cleaning the latrines to cleaning the pad fell to our side of the dorm. There was a big blow up of the unfair distribution of chores and one young black girl was set back for what she said to the dorm chief. She was put in a training flight that was not as far along and had three weeks added to her time in training.

After that I tried to be the negotiator between the sides, and wound up mostly a listening board for complaints. We had two training instructors, a male and a female. The female was in the hospital for most of the 4 weeks left, but the male training instructor noticed what I was doing and commented on it in my training book (photo top right).

Photo above is my buddies in the break room. We had now graduated to our 'blues', the women's dress uniform. It was 1979 and we were told this uniform was designed by Jackie Kennedy's designer. I guess that was supposed to be a complement but they were, in my opinion, ugly uniforms.

1 ABBOTT W015
PHOEBE
WARNER

I only had two professional photos taken in my 23 years. One (top right) looked like a prison induction photo in black and white, and there I was first in line again. The other (bottom right) looks more like a high school senior photo. We were in dress blues, the photo was in color and we were allowed to smile.

AIR FORCE TECHNICAL SCHOOL

I was shipped off to Chanute Air Force Base, Rantoul, Illinois in March. We were to ship out the 28th of February but Chanute was snowed in so we spent three days on hold and, for a full circle, were back in the WWII barracks we started in. There was a whole plane load of us going to Chanute and we were so relieved to be leaving basic training alive, and free from all that craziness that it was like a celebration plane... then the stewardess announced that no alcohol would be served on the flight. I was afraid we weren't going to make it but finally the booing and hissing died down. I met my friend 'Boo' (short for Bouchard) on the plane to Chanute Air Force Base. He graduated basic training at the same time I did. He told me the story about the recruit at Lackland who, standing duty as a dorm guard, was bored and held a trash can out in front of him, dropped it on the floor (which made a terrific noise) and in a low calm voice said, "Bomb, bomb, bomb." One of those friendly people on duty down in the CQ heard that and the base experienced a bomb alert. We got a good chuckle imagining the person on duty, leaned back in their chair with their feet up, just about falling over when that noise came over the loud speaker. They take those things very seriously in the Air Force. I heard that guy was set back the full six weeks of Basic. Boo and a girl named Sam (her real name was Sandy) were my best friends at Chanute Air Force Base.

I was assigned to Chanute to under go training in the Automatic Flight Control field. A summation of my time at Chanute would be to mimic the quote Bill Murray makes in Stripes, "Gentlemen, It's party time, Illinois Style!" I hadn't gone to college or been in a sorority but I imagine that it is similar. You go to school all day and party all night.

Upon arrival, as we left the bus and were escorted down the sidewalk to our dorm, a guy came flying out of the second story window, in full horizontal belly-flop attitude, and landed beside us in the many feet of snow. He jumped up and ran back in the dorm. This surely tickled my funny bone and I laughed aloud. I was going to like this change of station! The temperatures dropped to dangerous and the snow froze. We were confined to the dorms and served bag lunches for our three meals a day. In the girls dorm everyone contributed a bottle of alcohol and we spent the three days experimenting with mixtures of the same. Having listed Alaska as my home state everyone thought I should be completely used to this, but I had been in Hawaii for six years.

At Chanute Air Force Base my friend Boo lived on the first floor in the same building as I did. He had a roommate named MacAfee. Boo was from California. He acted like I imagine a surfer dude would and loved a good joke. Someone had given him a hair comb that folded up and he had practiced snapping it out like it was a switch blade. Boo whipped that comb out and his roommate, who came from inner city Chicago (I think), thought it was a switch blade, and was not amused. Boo graduated before me due to me being set back to go through an algebra course. He too had orders to Germany. His orders were to Rhein Main Air Base (Gateway to Europe) while mine were to Spangdahlem Air Base in the Eifel Mountains. When I arrived in Germany at Rhein Main, I had the opportunity to see Boo before I had to catch the bus to Spangdahlem. I would see him once again later, but that's in the next chapter.

3362 SCHOOL SQDN.

I was housed in the third story of the dorm. The first floor was men from my squadron, the second floor was men from another squadron and the third floor was our floor, the few women in our squadron. Ladies would bring a pillow and sit on the floor to congregate at the top of the stairs. If a man came up we had to yell, "Man on the floor." This would be an authorized man—$300 fine to unauthorized airmen caught on the opposite gender floor. Photo right is me in my third floor window taking a nap.

I have to add something from basic training that I forgot. I was reminded when I saw my hair in the picture below (it had finally recovered some). At Basic, I quickly found that having hair long enough to sit on was a real hassle. When we were given the opportunity to get a hair cut I had them lop it all off and it looked horrible—not as horrible as it could, but pretty horrible. A few weeks later we were given a chance to go to an actual beauty parlor on base and I got my hair done. I had never been a beauty parlor but I imagined myself looking like Shirley Temple and told them to give me lots of curls. They put the curlers in and the smelly stuff on and put me under a hair dryer. Soon my forehead itched and felt like something was dripping. When I wiped it with my hand my fingers had blood on them. The hair dresser had forgotten about me and left me with the solution on too long. My hair was one huge frizz and with those ever so black complementary thick frame military glasses, I looked worse than be-

fore I went in to have my hair done. There was a photo booth beside the beauty parlor and I sent my mother the strip of four. My sisters said I looked just like the actor Woody Allen. I knew that was not a compliment.

Marching at Chanute was a whole new experience. In my 20's I was very agile. I could march with the best of them, but I could also time it just right to give a little kick on the bottom of boot sole of the person in front of me.

It was only natural that I would become a 'Road Guard.' In this photo you can see a flight marching. I quote from the 33rd Fighter Wing site: "As tech school students motion-blur through the day, some Airmen stand out amongst the rest. These Airmen are distinguished by either a green, yellow, or red knotted cord around their left arm. The stoplight-colored ropes distinguish the individual as an Airman Leader. The entry-level green rope, secondary yellow rope and final red rope level retrospectively displays the leader's level and responsibility." The Air Force loves its ropes! If you are on a drill team your uniform is dress blues with a white rope. If you are security police, like dashing Don to the right, you wore a white rope.

So we had one, ultra serious, determined to fly into space, airman who was appointed as our red rope. The red rope, although nice enough, was all business. He told the yellow ropes what to do and they echoed his command to the green rope. When marching at tech school as in this picture the ropes and road guards can be distinguished by their red vests. The yellow ropes march along side each flight about 1-2 feet out on the left. The green ropes march within the flight, in the front left position. The red rope marches 1 or two feet to the left of the yellow ropes and in the center (front to back) of the whole squadron made of flights. The group you see at the front of the flights in vests, are road guards and "The Points" (or "Point" if there is only one). In our flight we had two people who were The Points. They carried the standard (flag) for our squadron and marched at the very front of the formation. They led the flight so must be careful to execute first the red ropes shouted command. Next came the Road Guards which in our case was a 16 person formation 4 across and 4 deep. Road guards rotated. When one road guard was sent out someone from the second row rotated up to the first row, someone from the third row to the second and so on, with the returning road guard taking a place at the back of their flight. If the road guard was sent out on the right of the flight the first row moved over that direction and the rotator came from the left end. At each road that joined the road the squadron marched on, a road guard was sent out to guard the flight from any cars coming down that road. The road guard stood with legs apart like a parade rest stance with right hand raised level, palm out, in a signal to stop. The left hand held a flashlight. This was not an ordinary flashlight, this was an air force issue flashlight with a lime green, translucent, plastic cone protruding from the front. At an airport, you might see ground crew use something similar when guiding in a commercial aircraft. We fondly called these 'Lackland Lasers.'

I had a friend named Jeff that loved to substitute the Lackland Laser with a banana. I might have joined him a time or two. This angered the red rope but he couldn't stop our flight while marching to chew someone out. Our red rope was ultra determined to be the best red rope ever, no kidding around. Bananas were kidding around. When this was brought before the proper authority (we were blessed with a commander with a sense of humor) we were fortunate not to get in that much trouble. But I realize my fellow point began plotting his revenge for being reported, at that moment. Did I mention that the road guards were the bad girls and boys. If you tripped during marching you became a road guard. If you had no rhythm, you became a road guard. If you were on report, you became a road guard. If you pissed off one of the ropes, you became a road guard.

We rented two hotel rooms off base and all the road guards were invited. We practiced all weekend so we could march with dazzle. Instead of just rotating we practiced snappy facing movements slapping our boots together to add sound. We were looking so good and there was no regulation against it. Our commander was a great fan—we could do no wrong.

My fellow point at the time was my friend Jeff and we were pals that liked to have fun. Jeff and I both had received orders for Spangdahlem Air Base, Germany and this would be our last time of marching as the points. We were doing everything right and our red rope was chest out in pride as we passed people on base. To get to the school building we marched across base, down the front of the hangers where the airplanes were on static display, to our school beyond the hangers. The points led the way, the road guards followed the points, the flights followed the road guards. When we got to the front of the hangers my fellow point said, "We're marching into the C-130!" I was game. We made a slight facing movement, executed flawlessly, and headed straight for the aircraft. The Road guards followed us, executing as a flight perfectly and willing to follow their fellow road guards anywhere. The flights followed. Our red rope was so frustrated he could not think of what to say so he yelled, "Hey!" and we marched on. There were a couple other inappropriate commands that no one followed gleefully marching on together. By the time he yelled, "Squadron HALT!" we were just about nose to nose with that airplane. It was delightful.

When you move from one base to another the military calls it a Permanent Change of Station. Military troops call it a PCS. My orders were to Spangdahlem Air Base in Germany and fellow Point Guard Jeff was going there too. It is always easier on a move to know someone when you get there. Sadly, my friend Jeff died on Spangdahlem. The Air Force paid for his brother to come collect his remains. The brother was a staff sergeant so they asked me to escort him while he was there. He looked just like Jeff except a few years older and we were both very sad.

Serious Study was done at Chanute. There were blocks and sets (or sets and blocks I can't remember…) in the classes. The first blocks were classes teaching all the fundamentals like introduction to tools and their usage, safety, and technical data. Once you passed those you moved on to the sets which were classes on electricity (diodes and capacitors), flight control surfaces and movement, reading schematics, understanding common avionics problems, gyros and other flight instruments, and so much more. We would get even more specific training when assigned to a base that would be for their specific airframes. These were called FTDs or Field Training Detachments —mine was for F-4 Phantom Fighter Jets.

One block was for algebra to understand vectors. While I can do geometry all day long, algebra was never my forte... leave those x's and y's for some one else. I flunked this course. First I was put into a remedial algebra class and passed that. Next I was put into a holding pattern until the next group for that course came along and I could be fitted in. I was lucky that the next group was only 4-weeks behind me. For those 4-weeks I worked in the squadron office answering phones, taking messags, painting the Tips Stand and the stairwells of our building. The Tips Stand was a small building maybe 6 feet long by 5 feet deep with a large open window in which the commander would stand each morning and give us the 'tips' for the day. These were usually short briefings on events coming up, directions for the day, an occasional callout to someone recognized, and whatever else they thought of. A blessing then was that my commander was also a Pink Panther fan and I got to paint a pink panther on the Tips Stand.

Did I mention that it was a $300 fine for being caught on a floor housing the opposite sex? So we were assigned to paint all the stairwells. The other person I was working with was named Costello so there were Abbott and Costello jokes. In fact, when we finished at the bottom of the stairs in small letters I wrote, "Painted by Abbott and Costello." My commander loved it and it stayed. We had a break and I ran up to my room and got one cup full of Pink Panther pink paint from my hidden gallon. I figured there was no one on the male floor since they were all at school (except Costello who was off to collect something.) I snuck into the male dorm and painted, "You've Been Struck." on one certain male's door. Just as I finished I heard the outer door slam, I panicked and ran and hid in the bathroom. While waiting there I painted little pink footprints in the shower as well. I heard the outer door slam again and figured I was alone. I rushed out of the bathroom to the door where my commander stood with his arms crossed waiting for me. Again, so glad he had a good sense of humor.

During my time working in the office I noticed a big board with a floor plan for each of our squadrons dormitory floors. There was the female dorm rooms just as they were laid out on the floor. In each 'room' there was the last name of the occupant, their ethnic code and their rank. When there were two people assigned to the room, two lines in the 'room' made it obvious which rooms had space for another occupant. The standard in the corner of the board read: 1-White 2-Black 3-Hispanic 4-Other. I saw that almost every room now had two occupants and there were only four left solo, me being one. When no one was looking below my name "ABBOTT 1 AB" I added "PINK 5 AB" Everyone knew the pink panther was getting painted everywhere by then so I figured anyone who looked more than a single glance would know there was no Airman Basic Pink. Besides which there was no such ethnic code as 5 at that time. I had my defense in mind. I never got a roommate.

In each Chanute classroom there was a slot that held a sign with the instructors name. The sign or name plate slipped in and out. The instructor would arrive with briefcase and books and their sign. The first thing they did was slide their name sign into the slot before getting behind the teachers desk. There were lab room like class rooms, where we learned about transistors for example. It was interesting to watch some airman put his instrument leads on both ends of a transistor and get kicked across the room in one of the labs.

As I mentioned, the name plate came with the instructor. These name plates were approximately 5 inches by 36 inches made of what I imagine was high grade aluminum. Some instructors had signs that looked brand new. Some had signs with dented corners indicating they had been dropped. A few of the name signs looked like they had survived a fierce battlefield. I had one young staff sergeant (Rank E-5) instructor whose sign was so bent in such odd shapes and places that I felt it was a miracle it could still fit in the slot. I should have thought through the reasons why it looked all beat up. He was small in stature and red headed. He was in his 30's and very enthusiastic at his job, especially waking sleeping airmen.

This red-haired instructor's had a teaching style that had him striding about the room while he instructed. I thought this was just his restless style. His rhythmic pacing back and forth could almost be hypnotic. To face him as he spoke you would have to turn your head one way and then another, back and forth, until your eyelids just dropped. No! There was a method to his madness. Based on the gleeful looks on his face, his favorite thing in the whole world was finding a sleeping student. He had many methods of torture. One was to silently slip his sign out of the slot, tip toe across the room, and slam it down on the desk of the sleeping airman. You would be amazed the decibels he achieved with this method. Another of his favorites was to use any handy book and forcibly slam it on the desk of a sleeping student. While this did not reach the decibels of the sign slamming, it was very effective at startling awake the person in the desk. Still another method was to take any one that seemed overly inclined to sleeping, having been sign slammed more than once, and make them stand in the corner holding the classroom trashcan directly out in front of their body. Between the weariness that soon invaded your arms holding that steel can, and your already dozy state, it was a good bet you would drop that can. Military issue trashcans are charcoal colored steel round wastebaskets weighted in the bottom just enough to promote staying upright. When dropped directly on to the floor they made a surprisingly loud and startling percussive sound. Clever airmen woke up mid drop and caught it. Resuming correct position so quickly that the instructor couldn't turn fast enough to actually see it, could earn you a smile and a nod. I just know he slept through all his sessions of school. Warm and humid sleep inducing days were those that really pleased him. If he could get a can dropper and then the joy of other students being startled out of their seats he was positively gleeful.

In the last weeks of class we received our reassignment orders and this instructor knew Spangdahlem was assigned F-4s. He surmised that being small I would be a prime candidate for crawling back down the fuselage of the aircraft to change the Aileron Rudder Interconnect (ARI) . He picked me out and said, "Learn this—Aileron Rudder Interconnect. To me at that time it might as well have been Greek but I rolled it off my tongue until it seemed a common phrase. I know he was still laughing long after I was gone.

The control surfaces on an F–4 are hydraulically actuated and for stability the ailerons are mechanically connected to the rudder. The ailerons are the hinged surface on the trailing edge of an airplane wing that control lateral balance. The rudder is the shark fin looking thing sticking up on the back of the fighter that controls the yaw of the aircraft. This interconnection is done to reduce the side slipping that happens when turning a jet, and improves the turn rate response.

In my days at Chanute, I had two distinct set of friends I hung out with. In the first part of my time at Chanute my best two friends were a guy named Boo and a girl named Sam (photo right). Sun on the door painting was Sams door. I took the photo after she left and there was already a new name on the door. Boo graduated earlier than me and was assigned to Rhein-Main Air Base in Frankfurt, Germany (I might have mentioned that already). Sam was a cute and naïve young lady from Minnesota. She was raised by her grandparents. When we approached our final tests at Chanute she got notified that her grandmother had died. The Air Force would not grant her leave until she took her final tests. Upset and crying she did her best but failed them. After school they called her in, and advised Sam that she was being discharged. They presented her with money for a phone call and a bus ticket home. She was to go from Rantoul, Illinois, transfer in Chicago, and the second leg was Chicago to Saint Paul, Minnesota. They decided Saint Paul was close enough that her grandfather could collect her and that's what the money for

the phone call took care of. We were all pretty ticked about that. Sam was scared. I went to my commander but he had tried already and there was nothing he could do to change the decision from higher up. She could no longer stay in the dorm and had the weekend to evacuate. Sunday morning she had someone drive her to the bus station. I could not imagine Sam alone in Chicago even for a 5-hour layover.

Meanwhile I had gotten busy asking around the squadron… Who had a car? Who would be willing to drive to Minnesota. We wound up with a whole crew of 6 and picked Sam up from the bus station before her bus arrived. Photo right is me in the orange dress at the Rantoul Bus Station. Sam had been crying and didn't want to be in the photo.

We took off and drove more than 500 miles to Minnesota and dropped Sam right at her front door. I will never forget the relief in her grandfather's eyes. He shook hands all around and thanked each of us personally. All along the highways the truck drivers watched out for us both ways. I had a long conversation with one trucker when it was my turn in the front seat and I adopted the handle 'Panther.' He passed the word up the road and truckers beeped at us, waved and wished us luck. It was a close thing. We arrived back at Chanute at 5:30 am on Monday with just enough time to run and change and appear before the tip stand. After school the commander called me into his office and demanded to know what went on. The vehicle owner was restricted from leaving the base and had anyway. I was nervous and blurted out details of the whole trip in great detail explaining how we could never have done it without him and the heartfelt thank you from the grandfather. When I finally wound down he thanked me. He too was uncomfortable with sending Sam home that way but unlike us was under orders not to interfere. He understood and we got off 'Scott Free'.

Commander on the floor! One of my most embarrassing life moments happened at Chanute. I had been sick with the flu and was sent home to my quarters for two days. I was told to just go ahead and sleep and take the medicine they gave me. I was good with that and stripped down to my underpants and fell into bed. I slept the rest of that day, all night and half way through the next day. The girls on my floor knew I was sick, so when the pounding on my door woke me up, I was not a happy camper. I ripped open the door and yelled, "What?" My commander was standing there and his eyes got wide... I slammed the door, grabbed my full length rain coat and put it on. When I opened the door again I calmly announced, "I did not hear 'Man on the Floor!'

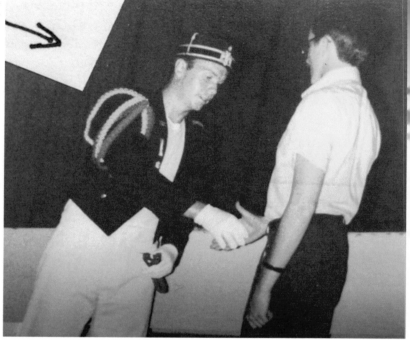

Once a month we had a 'Commanders Call. This was when the whole squadron met in the base theater. The commander would discuss important thing for us to know—changes and updates—as well as any recognitions that were due. This commander was really the bomb. To amuse the troops at one commanders call he arrived dressed with his formal officers dress mess jacket, a shoulder full of ropes, a funny box hat that might have been a mason hat, white navy bell bottoms and his combat boots all unlaced. When we had a squadron picnic he knew that we had spiked all those watermelons with vodka but he let us have a good time and steam was released.

He and his lovely wife were both in Sports Medicine before he joined the Air Force. He was not only the youngest, but also the lowest ranking squadron commander on Chanute

Air Force Base. The other reason that I really liked this commander was he was a Pink Panther fan. He bought an Aston Martin car in Europe and some jerk had taken it for a spin on the dock after it came off the boat and wrecked it, bending the frame. Although they fixed the dents, the frame damage had pretty much destroyed its monetary value. After seeing my painting of the Pink Panther on the Tips Stand, he decided that I should paint his car. I enthusiastically bought a gallon of the Pink Panther shade of pink.

We painted his car and his gracious wife, Sandy, made dinner and I stayed for that. It was a long day and I guess I didn't have the lid tight on the gallon of paint. As I reached the landing on the second floor of the dorm I noticed that I had left big drips of paint every six inches or so. I followed the splatters back down the stairs and saw that it must have leaked all the way from the parking lot. I figured no one would even notice the pink dots on the sidewalk but something needed to be done about the ones that crossed the lobby and went up the stairs. I had no cleaning supplies so I treated each dot like the sole of the foot and added three little toes at the top (see painting on Page 5). The second floor and technically part of the lobby belonged to another squadron and that commander was really mad "at the defacing of government property". I guess he left in a huff when my commander burst out laughing.

When it approached time for me to leave for Germany I received this letter of appreciation (below) and was presented with my very own, specially hand knotted, never before made, pink panther pink shoulder rope.

After I was reassigned to Germany I received a letter from him and his wife. Enclosed was a t-shirt with the Pink Panther on it and 3362 (our squadron number) above it. He finally got permission and in a squadron wide effort painted the Pink Panther on the end of the three story dorm building as we had discussed doing before I left.

DEPARTMENT OF THE AIR FORCE
HEADQUARTERS CHANUTE TECHNICAL TRAINING CENTER (ATC)
CHANUTE AIR FORCE BASE, ILLINOIS   61868

REPLY TO
ATTN OF: 3362 SCHS/CC   23 Aug 79

SUBJECT: Letter of Appreciation

TO: PHOEBE ABBOTT, Airman, USAF

    1. It is with pleasure and pride that I submit to you on behalf of the 3362 School Squadron, Chanute Air Force Base, Illinois, a letter of appreciation to you, Amn, Phoebe Abbott.

    2. This letter is submitted in appreciation for all of the hours that you have spent listening to other people's problems; for offering your efforts and time to improve the morale and welfare of the 3362 School Squadron; and for helping to establish the Pink Panther as an Honorary Staff Member.

    3. On behalf of the 3362 School Squadron, "Yo, we're into it!"

Neale L Caffin
NEALE L. CAFFIN, 2d Lt, USAF
Commander, 3362 School Squadron

Photo right is my dorm room door. It was really more of doddle painting on the inside of my dorm room door. It couldn't be seen from the outside and remained open, hiding the painting, during inspections.

Photo bottom left: Abbott and Costello in front of newly painted stairwell of our dorm building. It was right after this photo that I added in the white area, in small letters, "Painted by Abbott and Costello."

Photo bottom right: Training certificate reads as follows— AB Phoebe W. Abbott has successfully completed the C3ABR32530-1 Automatic Flight Control Systems Specialist Course, PDS NCW (602 hours)

FIRST ASSIGNMENT—SPANGDAHLEM AIR BASE, GERMANY

First Choice on my dream sheet, Germany, here I come! A dream sheet is a tool used in the Air Force for a person to choose their next assignment. I had chosen Germany in the very first block, and could not have been happier. After you have been in the military you come to know that its called a dream sheet because you are dreaming if you think the military will send you anywhere but where they need you! I know this intimately because when I turned down a special assignment to D.C. I got tornado alley Oklahoma.

My time at this first assignment has sort of two phases… Before Andy and After Andy. Andy is my first born son. He was born while I was stationed in Germany on Bitberg Air Base, but that is another story. 1979 and 1980 were carefree times Volksmarching with my boy friend in Germany and Luxemburg, Paris for New Years, and Experiencing Fasching with the Germans, and deciding to get pregnant. 1881 and 1982 were the role of motherhood, Wine Fests on the Mosel, House parties and finally marriage.

Here is a rabbit hole—Speaking of Phases: My life is a series of two phases grouped. Now I can tell that much of my life can be divided into two phases, but only at 69 am I noticing that. Parents: Phase I with Papa; Phase II with only Mom. Home: Phase I Yukon Island; Phase II—Everywhere else. Work Experience: Phase I civilian offset pressman. Phase II—military airman. Chanute Training: Before and after set back.

I loved working on F-4 fighter jets. I learned the economical leap that got my foot in the bottom rung of the step ladder up the jet and climbed like a monkey. I got to legitimately sit in the cockpit. I could walk under the wing without stooping and yet learned the jump that allowed me to place my tool box on the wing above me. I was running with the big dogs. In my mind there will never be a more patriotic sound than to hear close up an American fighter jet launching. It shakes you like an earthquake and you just want to yell, "YEAH!" then the afterburners kick in… amazing! I was hooked. I was going to be Rosie the Riveter Air Force style. I won Airman of the Quarter and then Airman of the Year for my base.

Those old GI's were not used to women on the flightline and they played on me every trick in the book… asking to get me to go find a yard of flightline, hooking up the hydraulics backwards so the fluid rolls down your arms. I can take a joke like the best of them but the one I felt was unfair was not telling me my first time on the flightline that when you start the flightline generator it simultaneously sounds like a bomb going off and shoots flames out the smoke stack. I got my aerobics in that day cause I was still a pretty fast runner and made it to another pad before looking back to see my trainer waving his arms and laughing.

I was 90 pounds and five foot two inches tall. I did not appreciate that being small meant I was the obvious choice to change any faulty ARI. The ARI, or Aileron-Rudder Interconnect, is a flight control system that falls for repair under the Automatic Flight Control system. I remember well one of my teachers at Chanute telling me I needed to remember the phrase 'aileron rudder interconnect'. It did roll off the tongue nicely and I had even made up a few notes to sing it. Now I understood!

One of the things to be endured at Spangdahlem was 'Black Flags.' Black flags were an exercise where we practiced for a gas attack. They were usually during exercises, sometimes were very short and you just sat and waited, and some times could last as long as your whole 12 hour shift. In these cases you wound up working in full war gear which is difficult with test equipment and fat gloves.

Phoebe in war gear

Spangdahlem Air Base is located in a place where it was only a 7 hour bus ride to Paris and the Rec Center offered a 3-day trip, over New Years, with transportation from base to city and back, hotel, tour of Paris, and continental breakfast for $72. Andy's father, Ken, and I jumped on board. I leaned a lot that weekend. I learned that many French folks were not fond of Americans, but think Alaska is part of Canada, so with an Alaska divers license I was accepted. I quit showing my military ID card because they just would not believe it was real. I saw my first strip show and nearly had my camera taken. Photos: (right) At the Eifel tower; (bottom right) Watching the artists in the Artist Square in Paris; (bottom left) Another favorite trip with Ken was to Luxembourg City. The center of the city has a valley that looks like a giant crack, 10 stories deep. The walls are straight and a river runs through the valley there with a lovely park beside the river. We watched a whole circle of children dancing and laughing. That is me sitting in the doorway of a stone

church that was built right in to the canyon walls. We were told this was called The Valley of Death. It earned that name because when the Nazi's took the city, the rounded up all the members of the resistance they could find, lined them up along the walls and shot every one of them.

I loved the tasks of autopilot tech. Changing out the black boxes, taking them back to the shop for testing, looking at schematics and technical orders (T.O.s) (that showed everything down to the last resister or diode), and even chasing wires trying to discover what the problem was. The first months passed quickly. I seriously did enjoy looking at T.O.s until of course they stuck me in the tool crib for some weeks and I had the mindless job of changing and updating the T.O.s all day long for days on end.

I will inject here two stories about older maintenance guys. First, I initially arrived on base it was just about at quitting time. My sponsor met me at the bus and gave me a choice of going to the dorm or going up to the base bar where much of the shop would be having an after work drink. When introduced this one guy swung down from his bar stool and grabbed my butt. "Welcome…" he began to say. I take exception to people doing things like that and I decked him. I would say that surprise that I would do that was as much responsible for laying him out as my actual right hook. I was excused from being disciplined because I was in civilian clothes, because I was perhaps unable to see his rank in the poor lighting of the bar, and because it was much easier to just sweep that whole mess under the rug. Second, the first time I worked the flightline with this same guy I was eager to show I could do the job. I jumped up and got on the ladder of the fighter jet and he, still on the ground, drawled, "I don't want women out here on the line but I can get used to this view." I was mortified.

I noticed that some of the older men didn't really want women on the flightline and didn't really care that the Air Force was determined to integrate women. More than any of the young male airmen, we females were assigned many off the flightline jobs. This was not entirely the Air Force's fault. In Technical School we were tested on lifting weights. You were supposed to also hold that weight over your heads—'sustained hold'. This determined whether or not we were capable of carrying the tool box necessary to make repairs for that career field. I saw girls run up, swing that weight up above their heads then drop it. They could not sustain the 70 pounds over their heads. But the Air Force were set to make a quota of women working on the flightline and many were as they say, 'pencil whipped'. One girl on Spangdahlem clocked in a 82 pounds, 4 foot 11 inches tall, and worked in the hydraulics section. She was more than a foot shorter than the front strut on an F-4 which it was hydraulics job to change if it developed problems. There was no way she could have changed it. This meant that when she was assigned to a task, a stronger and taller male would have to accompany her to help her do the job they could do alone.

For winning Airman of the Quarter I got to drive the FODmobile. FOD stands for Foreign Object Damage and it is a very serious issue for jet engines. Photo right is me with 'Smitty' the Instruments Shop Chief on a Mosel River Cruise. I was around 6 months pregnant.

I finally realized that I was not getting back out on the flightline. For weeks I had been doing every boring off-the-flightline support job (posting technical orders, working the tool crib, driving the launch truck, etc.) that existed in my career field. I asked to be cross trained. Overseas there are no technical schools so I was told my two choices to cross train into were cook and administration. I chose administration. I took a bypass test, passed and was reassigned out of automatic flight control. Since I had to stay in the same squadron to which I was assigned until the end of my tour, I first was allowed to paint murals in the flightline buildings. When a spot in Aircraft Debriefing opened up they put me in there to work for a few months. I loved being in Debrief.

On my base there were three fighter squadrons: The 23rd or Blue Section, the 480th or Red Section and the 81st or Yellow Section. When I arrived on base, maintenance was set up in a complex of buildings off the flightline. Each specialty, like Autopilot and Navigation, had their own shop in the maintenance complex. Then the Air Force implemented the very unpopular POMO system. If memory serves, POMO stood for Production Oriented Maintenance Organization. Some guy in an office somewhere without even a view of a flightline decided that if the specialist was out there on the flightline they would save time and money by not having to be transported to the flightline. To implement this change, they built a maintenance building within the restricted flightline area at each section. Specialist like autopilot and navigation were split up into these three squadrons. Here the maintenance leadership had offices, and there was an area for all the specialists to hang out until they got a call. That area was like a big break room with couches and coffee. The first step in converting to POMO was to take similar career fields, in my case Automatic Flight Control and Instrumentation, and merge the two fields. We all were obligated to devote time to learning the ins and outs of the field new to us. I spent many evenings in civilian clothes hanging out with the test equipment and learning. My favorite instrument component was the CADC or Central Air Data Computer. It was like the brains of the F-4 and controlled most of the front panel instruments. It was a big learn. Finding out that one of the jobs of an instrument troop was to go to a crash sight and remove the cockpit panel and instruments. Upon crashing the instrument would imprint on the front glass the last reading. The instruments were in heavy steel tubes and the hope was the glass survived the crash. Most of the crashes happened with the crew not being able to punch out.

Revetments were these round top buildings where each F-4 parked. They were shaped just like the Quonset huts we lived in in Homer, Alaska, but were more than twice as big and made of concrete and steel. They had huge electric doors that ran on a track and closed tightly. In front of the revetment was a pad of concrete large enough for the fighter to turn around. The entered the pad pointing at the revetment, executed a precise 180 degree turn facing away from the revetment, shut the engines down and disembarked the aircraft. Next a cool low Air Force vehicle was driven up, hooked to the front of the fighter, and used to back the fighter into the revetment.

To enter the flightline area you had to go through a security check point. These security police were guarding valuable assets and they took their job very seriously. Unless you wanted to experience being abruptly forced face down on the pavement of the tarmac, you did not joke with, harass or even converse with them when they were on duty.

When I worked in the 23rd squadron it was as an autopilot troop. While there I painted a mural on the wall of the waiting area. I had come to know the cartoons of Jeff MacNelly and his obvious insight into military life. Particularly the Shoe character Loon resonated at the time. There was one strip where Loon is sitting on a big tree branch and lined up beside him were all these musical instruments. Loon was holding a book titled something like Flight Manual and reading, "Before takeoff ensure all instruments are in working order.." The 23rd mural was a strip with Loon. In the first panels Loon is sitting in the cockpit and is going through the pre-flight checklist aloud. In the last panel you see him sitting still in what looks like one of the little coin-operated airplane rides for kids outside the grocery store. You can see the base of the ride and that it is not moving. Loon is saying something about making sure you have enough nickels.

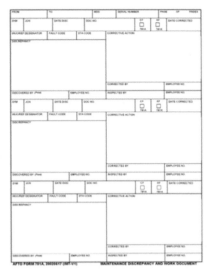

I worked for a time in the Debriefing Section of the 81st squadron. It was very busy for a time and then longer waits between crews. This staggering of crews was done on purpose I surmised. I had seen the mischief light crews made to wait could get into when bored. This was great because it afforded me time for painting murals in between debriefing. Again using the Jeff MacNelly cartoons I copied one he had the summed up the high rivalry between the 480th Warhawks and the 81st Wild Weasels. The first panel showed a bird flying along, the second that bird flying into a flock of smaller birds and getting one in his mouth. The last panel showed him spitting it out and saying, "Redhawk in the intake!" For non aircraft people a bird in the intake of a jet engine is called a bird strike and often requires immediate landing as the jet engine is no longer functioning well.

Back to Debrief… the job entailed talking to the aircrew after each flight. The aircrew (pilot in the front seat, weapons officer in the back seat) recorded any problems experienced during their flight in the aircraft forms. These forms were AFTO 781a, 781f, 781h, 781k etc. I only dealt with the 781A. We would accept the aircraft forms which were kept in a binder about 1 inch thick, ask for any clarification needed, and if necessary write above illegible entries for interpretation. The forms would then go to the aircraft crew chief to ensure each problem was corrected. The crew chief then worked with the individual specialist (like automatic flight control, navigation, instruments, sensors, etc.)

As I did the debrief I got to know the aircrew in the Yellow Section and I decided what cartoon character they each reminded me of. Then I drew a cartoon of each. The senior debriefers thought they were so cool they put them up on the wall. We made a sign to go with, "Aircrew Recognition Program." It got me a spot in the base newspaper.

Just a little recognition

TSgt Douglas Cardwell, 81st AMB debriefing NCOIC, left; SSgt. George C. Gatewood, debriefer; A1C Phoebe Abbot, debriefer; and Lt. Col. Larry Peters, 81st TFS commander stand in front of 81st AMB recognition board. Airman Abbott drew the cartoons representing 81st TFS aircrews. She received themes from the section debriefers and other aircrew mem-

After some months in Debrief an actual administration slot in the squadron opened up. When it did open up I was assigned to Maintenance Technical Administration or Tech Admin. Having enjoyed painting murals out in the revetments on the flightline, I got permission to continue it in the office area. The top mural (right) was like our squadron patch with the three aircraft sections (blue, red and yellow) flying in formation. It was approximately 40 inches by 60 inches. We had recently changed to the POMO way of doing things, there was much grumbling among the troops about this change, and this was to be a joke about that. It read, "THINK POMO! And that's an order." It was about 36 inches wide and 30 inches high. Again with the Jeff MacNelly cartoons the third mural was Roz holding a newspaper with the following three headlines: "TODA found alive under stack of T.O.s. 52bd AGS tops in Phantom Phixing. $25,000 available—submit a suggestion today." This had three significant digs: 1) The TODA was the person assigned to update the Technical orders. A Technical order set might be ten 4 inch black binders. Updating them was tedious I did not enjoy. 2) The F-4 fighter jets nickname was Phantom. Using the Ph like in my name I changed fixing to phixing. 3) The suggestion program gets a whole paragraph later on. I can't find the photo of the weapons that the F-4s carried but that was the 4th mural.

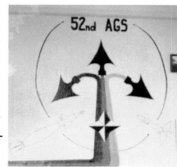

I had been in Tech Admin long enough to paint the murals when we got a new commander whose last name was Flint. Someone quipped, "Our Man Flint!" and they all laughed. Now I know that there was a tv show in the 1960's called 'Our Man Flint.' The story of my life is often getting jokes after the fact, days and even years later, or never at all. My husband has been particularly kind in explaining every day things to me without ridiculing me for not knowing. B-D-B! Been there. Done that. Blessed not to be doing it still.

So our man Flint was a hard charging, high intelligent officer. He had great ideas and so many that I often thought he might explode. The day I met him he strode into our Tech Admin Office, stopped in front of my desk and said, "You paint these?" I nodded. "Can you draw?" I responded, "What kind of drawings?" "Technical and slides." I quipped, "Yes, my mother and grandmother were draftsmen." In the Mel Brooks movie, History of the World, the guys says, "Its good to be the king." In the same pitch I thought to myself, "It's good to know the commander."

He would rush in to the office, tell me the slides he wanted me to draw and rush out again. When I did his slides concerning FOD he submitted the slides for the FOD Award and I won.

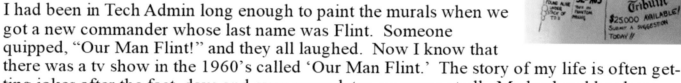

Dishonored check list is wrong

Due to computer error, some people stationed in West Germany, Italy, Belgium and the Netherlands were mistakenly added to the current dishonored check list. Even though the Army and Air Force Exchange Service has notified all major facilities to provide full check-cashing privileges to those incorrectly suspended, many people may still be erroneously listed.

Anyone finding their name incorrectly listed should immediately call AAFES-Europe at one of the following numbers: Munich civilian (089) 6220296/6220298 or 6220301; or Munich military Ext. 6131, 7163 or 8332.

H.S. Music boosters meet

The high school music boosters will meet Tuesday at 7:30 p.m. in the high school music room.

WOW briefing set

The Welcome Orientation for Wives/Husbands will be held Feb. 18 at 9 a.m. in the NCO open mess. This two-hour briefing is to acquaint newly arrived spouses with base organizations and facilities.

There will be free babysitting at the NCO open mess and refreshments will be provided by volunteers from the 52nd Combat Support Group.

AGS member honored

SrA. Phoebe Abbott, 52nd Aircraft Generation Squadron, has been selected by the 52nd Tactical Fighter Wing

Foreign Object Damage Committee as the winner of the quarterly FOD award.

She designed fix FOD posters for a campaign to reduce foreign object damage in the 52nd AGS. She also prepared a FOD briefing that was given to the FOD committee.

Airman Abbott will receive a ride in the flight simulator and a $10 gift certificate for dinner at the NCO open mess or officers' open mess.

FOD winner announced

A1C David A. Ledbetter, 52nd Transportation Squadron, has been selected as the Foreign Object Damage award winner for December.

As a driver for the 81st Tactical Fighter Squadron, he detected a potential FOD hazard in the use of tire chains of flightline vehicles.

Airman Ledbetter will receive a letter of recognition, two theater passes and a hour flight in an Aero Club airplane.

For sale

Whirlpool dryer, excellent condition, $75 (avail Feb. 12); Small kitchen cabinet, $15; one 1,500 watt transformer, $35 (avail Feb. 12); two clothes shrunks, $75; Bird cage, $5; Maternity outfits, size 12/14, $50, Mil women's mess dress blouse, size 12, $8, 1302 VW engine and misc parts, $20. Call SrA. Beaton at Ext. 6294 after 5 p.m.

Top left: After arriving at Spangdahlem I was sent to Hahn Air Base to a FTD (Field Training Detachment) school for the specific systems of the F-4 Phantom. This is my graduation certificate. Top right: In 1980 I was selected as the Airman of the Quarter.

(Left) For Fire Prevention Week I painted a sheet of plywood with the pink panther getting shocked. I won and this is the letter stating the same.

(Below) The painting was displayed on the main road leading to the exit gate of the base.

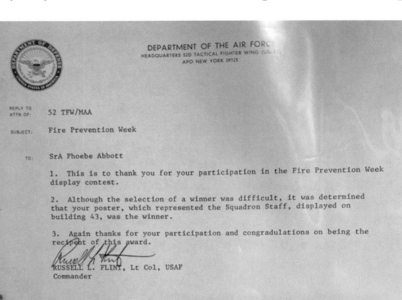

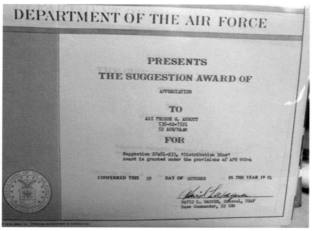

I have always had a tendency to be a smart aleck. The Chief Master Sergeant assigned to Tech Admin came out one day and said he had a directive from USAFE Headquarters, that the base needed to submit more suggestions to the Air Force Suggestion Program. He told all of us that he wanted us each to submit one within the next two weeks. I told him that I would give him ten he shook his head and walked away. The next day I handed ten in. Each was acknowledged and rewarded. Some rewards were just like, "Okay, thanks." But one got me a monetary award of like $10 (I think that was a suggestion concerning the components of the E-I Pickup in the control stick), one won me a t-shirt, one won me a squadron coffee mug and one got me in pretty deep do-do.

One of my jobs in Tech Admin was to compile the Accelerometer Report submitted monthly to Hill Air Force Base. This data let the folks at Hill Air Force Base know when the airframe had been 'Over G'd.' Gravitational forces (G-forces) are mighty. They are what has you whipping around on a roller coaster. A fighter jet G-forces are much stronger and the aircrew are required to wear a suit that mitigates the pressure experienced so they don't pass out. High G-forces can damage the airframe so there are two G-Force recorders called accelerometers in each F-4. The two accelerometers measured the acceleration which gave them the G-forces the plane had undergone. One was under the pilots seat and by pressing a button can be zeroed out while exiting the aircraft after a flight. They are not supposed to do this, but if you over G and aircraft you can be given a letter of reprimand or worse, so many zeroed it out to avoid this. The second, and then only accurate accelerometer, is a black box in the wheel well. This one the aircrew cannot peg off. At first it was interesting to learn all about this system. Then I notice that a good number of accelerometers were not functioning and had even been broken for months. Investigation found that everything that could need to be repaired, and even taking the F-4 to the wash rack to be washed, had a higher priority than this system. In other words, once it broke it was never fixed. At this point we had lost several fighters with full crew. We had one F-4 fly from Germany to Spain and upon landing was found to have a 12-inch crack at the leading edge of the wing where it joined the fuselage (or body of the aircraft). It had obviously been over-G'd and the accelerometer system hadn't worked in 8 months. Over G-s could damage the structure of the aircraft and make it unstable. F-4's were said to be "proof of an amazing aeronautical principle: that a brick can fly if you stick a big enough engine on it." They were naturally unstable and adding structural damage could be deadly.

One of the submitted suggestions was about raising the priority for fixing the wheel well accelerometer system. Unwisely I stated on it that the aircrews life could be in danger. That was like kicking a hornets nest. They sent the highest ranking maintenance Chief Master Sergeant from USAFE Headquarters at Ramstein Air Base to talk with me about this suggestion. I stubbornly held my ground but clearly learned that senior airmen three stripers are not allowed opinions on all things. I was told to work on correcting my attitude and the suggestion was torn up. (USAFE—US Air Forces in Europe.)

We had a deployment to Zaragoza Spain. It was to be my first temporary duty and I was very excited. I was also 6 months pregnant. There was snow on the ground in Germany when we left. Flying in a C-130 can be chilly so I had on Air Force issue long underwear under my uniform. When we arrived in Spain there had just been an incident with a pilot and a very rich and beautiful young Spanish woman, witnessed by her chaperoning and protective father, that nearly caused an international incident. When we got off the plane, they lined us all up on the pad and explained about the incident, what to do and not do while off base in Zaragoza, a particularly interesting part about the police in Zaragoza and the advise to do exactly what we were told to do and no joking or talking back, after all they carried machine guns. This all went on for more than an hour and standing in the sun I was getting hotter and hotter. For the first time in my life I passed out. I fell backwards on to the cement pad and my elbows hit so hard they convulsed. Zaragoza had no more medical facilities than basically a Band-Aid station and did not want to deal with a pregnant woman with convulsions. An Air Force hospital aircraft, the C-9 Nightingale, was diverted to Zaragoza and I was loaded on it and sent back to Germany. When I was on the plane they called my shop chief and told him I would be arriving at Rhein Main Air Base and would need transportation back to Spangdahlem.

When I arrived on Rhein Main they said it would be some hours before my ride from Spangdahlem would be there. I asked if I could go see a friend in the barracks rather than waiting in the airport and I was given permission to do so. I called Boo and he picked me up and took me to his barracks room. We had barely gotten there when my boss and husband-to-be, Jim, arrived to pick me up. I said, "I just got here, I thought it was going to be hours before I got picked up." My boss glared at Jim who drove a Plymouth Mopar (and took literally that there were no speed limits on the autobahn), and said, "Yeah, well I didn't know we were gonna to fly here!" Mopar was used to describe the vintage cars by Dodge, Plymouth, and Chrysler that sported high powered, big block, V8 engines that allowed sustaining speeds over 100 miles per hour.

Meanwhile, in my personal life, I had given birth to a son. He was simply amazing and I felt so blessed to have the gift of his birth. One of my friends, Debbie from Nav, was now married to an F-4 fighter pilot named Don and became my babysitter. I was at the base exchange when I heard we had lost a jet. I had been talking to Don just a while before and knew he had gone off to fly. I raced to Tech Admin but they would not disclose who the crew was. I found out later it was, in fact, Don piloting the fighter. Of the 9 crashes while I was stationed there, this was the only one where the aircrew got out alive. They speculated that only the pilots fast reactions, and his extensive flight time training others, had him punch them out safely with 4 seconds to spare before the jet buried itself in a German field. When the control stick became immobile Don said "Were punching out." The back seater began to say, "Are you sure?" but Don already ejected them. They said later if the back seater had finished his sentence they would not have made it. The back seater's parachute got hung up on a barn too far up to drop to the ground. Though unhurt, he was hung up until help came. The front seated pilot, Don, parachuted down to land on the small patio behind the home. The occupant, an elderly woman, screeched, ran in the house, and bolted all the doors. He stood there and carefully removed his helmet, mask, and G-suit until he finally looked human again before she would come out of her house.

I love native cultures and enjoyed learning all about German traditions. In February Fasching was celebrated and our German cleaning lady (Putz frau) told my friend Allison and I all about what would transpire. She invited us to join her after work. She also explained that it was Women's Day. Days during Fasching were assigned to different groups like children, grandparents, men and women. On women's day one of the rituals was to cut off men's ties. German men learned not to wear ties on this day for this reason. Our commander did not get the word and very brave Allison marched right up to the full bird colonel and cut off his Air Force tie. The Putz frau was delighted, the colonel clearly was not, but after his initial shock took it in stride. That evening Allison and I met her in her village. The ritual was for all the women to form a group and stand in the middle of the road. Any car wishing to drive on had to pay a monetary toll. Once enough was collected we adjourned to the nearest pub and bought drinks until the money ran out. After that we returned to the road to collect more and so on.

Interestingly enough I was told that it was illegal to divorce in Germany based on things that happened during Fasching. Any woman was allowed to make any man do within reason what ever she wanted. Any man that wanted some hanky-panky outside his marriage could once a year to safely, and by Germany law, legally, use this day as a free pass. The pubs were filled with jeering, leering men willing to be used.

One of my sisters had married a Swedish man and they were staying in his hometown. When Andy was 7 months old I took a train from Germany to Sweden to stay with them for a week. It was a trip fraught with problems but as always God was watching out for me. Two men had come up and sat down close to me. They were way to interested in Andy for me to be comfortable. When we arrive in the station I grabbed my bag and ran leaving my brand-new expensive goose down coat hanging where I had been sitting. Before I realized I had forgotten it, the train was gone. Once I changed trains for the overnight leg into Denmark it turned out my ticket was the wrong kind. It was simply a train ticket with no assigned seat much less a bunk. Cold and exhausted I must have looked forlorn. This wonderful Danish group took me under their wing. They had booked a whole car full of berths and had two of their boys share one and gave me and Andy a berth. In the morning they woke me up and escorted me to the next train.

In my experience the Scandinavian people were the best and I thoroughly enjoyed my time there. Most Swedes could speak at least some English and were happy to use what they could, even seemed delighted to try out their language skills. In Sweden I saw someone play a saw like an instrument. I saw how the war had effected elderly people so they saved even a tablespoon of food from a dish to serve it the next day and more. (Top photo is Andy and I in Bollnas, Sweden. Bottom photo is Andy's passport photo shot when he was 10 days old.)

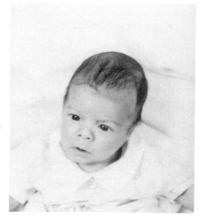

A few more photos:

Top three photos are Valley of Death in Luxembourg City. You can see how far down from the city level it was and the children dancing I referred to earlier.

Photo right is my Volksmarching book.

Internationales Volkssport-Abzeichen

D   Kilometerwertung

500 km   Teilnehmer - Ausweiskarte

ABBOTT
PHOEBE
BOX   4811
5561 SPANGDAHLEM FLUGPLATZ
2nd Book
Find Book #1 1979

Bottom two photos were highly amusing to me. Spangdahlem used sheep, rather than lawn mowers, to mow the flightline grass.

A couple last stories. To gain entrance to the secured flightline a person must either have a current restricted area access badge (we called them line badges), or be escorted by someone with such a badge. The line badge had your photo, name, rank and all fitted on small Air Force Form which was then laminated.

My mother came to visit when Andy was just a few days old. I got permission to have my mother escorted out to the 23rd maintenance building so she could see where I worked. Just as we arrived at the building a convoy of weapons came down the flight-line. My young maintenance lieutenant tried to stuff my mother back in the launch truck so she wouldn't see them. My mother shook his hand off and told him in no uncertain terms that she had known about American aircraft weapons longer than he had been alive, she was after all, drafted in WWII.

There was a young Black girl named Bonita that worked in our orderly room and she and I were friends. Another orderly room worker I was friends with was our White Squadron First Sergeant whose wife happened to be my babysitter. In pursuit of her duties, Bonita had been out to the flightline to pickup daily distribution and she had set her badge down while she emptied all the bins and couldn't find it. We got her an escort back to her office and some time later I found her badge under the table. Our First Sergeant happened to be out there doing career advisory duties and since they worked in the same office I gave him Bonita's badge and asked him to give it to her. As was his habit he tucked the badge into his right shirt pocket where he kept his own badge.

Our First Sergeant pulled his vehicle up to the check point, greeted the security police-man and without thinking grabbed Bonita's badge from his pocket to show for clearance to pass the checkpoint. The Security Guard on duty was a new airman in his first solo duty of a restricted area check point. He was anxious to do everything correctly by the book. He never hesitated in his duty. He whipped open the door of the truck, jerked our First Sergeant out and forced him to the ground, face first, spread eagle and pointed his gun at the First Sergeant's back. Our First Sergeant realized what he had done but had to wait until another Security Guard arrived who would listen to him and allow him to reach in his pocket to retrieve his real line badfe and explain how that all happened. When our First Sergeant was getting reassigned I made a line badge as a joke. The re-stricted area badge was an Air Force form 1199 was around business card size with your photo on the front. The one I made looked the same except was the size of a 3x5 index card and while it had his name and information it had Bonita's photo.

Last but not least Todd. Todd was my friend that worked in Sensors. The laser sensors on an F-4 in the repair shop could burn a hole through a paper target on the wall from across the room. Todd would offer to keep Andy so we could have a night off. When Andy's dad had been reassigned he gave me his car. It was a Subaru made from two Subarus. His brother was in the Army and also stationed in Germany. He had been in-volved in an accident and the car which had the roof ripped off when it went under a semi and was totaled.

His brother's car was nearly new so he took the engine out of it before they junked it and found a Subaru in a Germany junk yard to put the engine into. They were not the same model and there were lots of issues trying to put it together so the whole autopilot shop helped him. At first the radio only played in time with the windshield wipers, which had to be on for it to play; the turn indicator lever activated the windshield wipers; and many other crossed wires. The wiring harnesses were so different from the two models they couldn't tell where it all went. As the time grew near for him to leave we were running out of time to get the car done. I guess being aligned did not happen. I drove him to Rhein Main for his flight. My solo drive back to Spangdahlem, first time on the autobahn, left me with blisters on my hands from holding the shimmering steering wheel so tight. Not only did the car have a terrible shimmer when driving but also the frame on the car he put the engine in to obviously had a bent frame because in a curve the car would cat walk across the road. I had experienced it driving but when I loaned Todd the car I forgot to tell him that and it cat walked right across the road into the guard rail.

Todd was smart and really worked Air Force programs. He initially enlisted in the sensors field but took night and weekend college classes his whole tour. When his first four years were up he reenlisted and since sensors was a critical career field at the time he received a large monetary signing bonus. Once he finished his Associates Degree he applied for AECP (Airman Enlisted Commissioning Program) and when they accepted him since it was their choice he got to keep his signing bonus. He was promoted and sent to Purdue University where he completed his degree in Engineering. Enlisting as an officer in engineering had something like a $40,000 signing bonus and he only had to give 6 years in commitment. He banked all the money, married his graphics professor from Purdue and I don't think he was even 30 years old when he got out of the Air Force, college paid for, free and clear.

Photos below: (left) Todd and Allison (right) Debbie and Don with Andy. They are all friends I am still in contact with today. Ken and my first husband Jim are both deceased.

ASSIGNMENT ALTUS AFB OKLAHOMA.

In my life there are always silver linings. Oklahoma has a silver lining that is my stepson. I will always be blessed with that gift. Here is the cloud—let me tell you what you never want to do in the military... turn down what is perceived to be a reward. My commander must have really sent the raves up in what he wrote in my performance reports because I received "Special Assignment" orders to Washington D.C. to work at Bolling Air Force Base.

Bolling Air Force Base was once the General Headquarters Air Force. It is where the Army Air Corp was born. Hap Arnold led a bomber flight from Bolling Field to Alaska in 1934. This was a choice assignment. This was Chief-in-Ten-Territory*. Oh how I wanted to do that.

I was barraged with helpful voices telling me I could never afford a place in the D.C. area with out adding in 2-3 hours of drive time daily. Add in baby sitter pickup and drop off and it would be 14 hour days and no time for baby. I researched, a tiny studio apartment only 1 hours drive away was $400 and I was still on airman pay. Babysitting would be most of the rest of my paycheck.

My husband-to-be reminded me daily that I "could never afford to be a single mother in D.C." and "look at the crime rate" and "the baby needs two parents." I so desperately wanted to be the very best parent.

We were married by the Air Force Chaplain at Wright-Patterson AFB in Ohio, 20 minutes from his mothers house. My mother told me in Germany not to marry him because he was not right for me; his mother told me in Dayton not to marry him because I'd regret the h* out of it. I clung to Andy and married him. The Chaplain stopped the ceremony in the middle because I was shaking so hard I shook the veil right off my head. He had his wife hold Andy and took me in a separate room. He said, "I have to know if you are being coerced because you are obviously terrified to do this."

I turned down the special assignment and the Air Force sent me to Altus Air Force Base Oklahoma, home of the roaming tornados. The sent my husband to Dyess Air Force Base in Texas 187 miles away.

He started living in the bars at Dyess, got a DUI on base, pleaded his way out of it and even finagled a transfer to Altus. But he was already mad about the whole thing and the drinking had taken hold. Every drink made him believe he was greater, better, and even best. It was now essential. My only defense was to offer to mix the drinks adding more water with every drink. He had his first affair when we were married a scant two months. He was sorry, he couldn't resist the English accent.

Chief-in-Ten-Territory. The enlisted ranks are E-1 through E-10. E-10 is Chief Master Sergeant. Established Chief Master Sergeants are like Generals of the enlisted ranks holding great respect. I have seen them back down Colonels. According to military.com, Chief Master Sergeant slots are limited to only 1% of the entire enlisted force. Special assignments. and working with General Officers, was the way to make rank quickly and be in on the stuff of the nation.

He took to reminding me that it was all my fault. If I had been the paragon of wifehood that his first wife was, this would never have happened. It is like you are this little Vienna sausage. Then this tiny abuse is done and like a small piece of dough sticks to you. Then maybe there is a big one and it wraps you like a fur coat in that dough. You look down at that dough all stuck to you, baked into you because of the time endured, and you wonder how that even happened.

Working in Data Automation on Altus Air Force Base was a delight. I had a great Chief for a boss. He looked just like the comic strip Dagwood's boss. Initially we sat down and lined out all he expected me to do as the one administrator for all the data automators. I saw how it could be done in half of my day and wondered what the person before me in the job did all day. I proposed to the Chief that if I could do it all in half a day could I use the other half for training. He thought that was a splendid idea.

At this time 1984 the administration career field, with an identifying number 70200 and was split into three distinct fields: A, B and C. Those in the 70200A field were assigned to a central base administration that handled regulations for and inspections of administration and administrators on base, and training and assistance to those "in the field." 70200C personnel (in the field) were assigned to the orderly rooms in different squadrons. Orderly room clerks were responsible for making traveling orders, handling the weight program, working with the squadron command staff, and handling small personnel matters for the unit members. 70200B was every other administrator. Where those in the A and C career fields worked in an office with a team, those in the B career field were almost exclusively flying solo. This chief went right to the base commander and got me welcomed training in all those offices on base. Training levels are 00 is nothing; 30 is entry into the field; 50 is competent in the field; 70 is supervisor in the field and 90 is Chief in the field. I tested in Germany to get my 3-level; I completed my 5 level and 7 level, passing with flying colors in the first year I was there. There I was done with my train-ing and still with a job that only took up half the day. The Chief got me promoted to buck sergeant and then staff sergeant (Rank E-5) Chief introduced me to the key punch machine and I was soon running all the key punch cards for the "Monitors." Then I went through a tape handling course and was granted pass-card only access to the mainframe computer room. I assisted with recording, storing, and

handling of the tapes that recorded the days processing, and hung out with the operators. I helped the Monitors with running off their product, ripping the jobs apart and passing them out to the customers. Lunches were spent in hot hearts games in the operations breakroom.

If I get some of the military stuff wrong I apologize. Blame my fading memory and don't make big bets on it. As I remember the data folks were split into three parts: The command part - the Chief and three other people including me; The Monitors—who wrote all the programs an dealt with the customers requesting those programs; and The Operators—who ran the Burroughs Main Frame computer.

It became impossible for us to keep up with only one car and working different shifts so we bought the last car on the whole lot I would have chosen. It was an olive green challenger that had such a small trunk it could not fit family groceries and two boys in car seats. I would discover later that it was a car impossible for Alaska. In Oklahoma it meant that strangers were apt to pull up next to you at a light, rev their engine, wag their eyebrows and suggest that you race.

In 1986 the Air Force purchased something like 90,000 personal desktop computers from Zenith Corporation. They were a Zenith model Z-100 with a whopping 128 KB of RAM. You can look at the chart below but in todays computer world 128 KB is the size of a very small digital photo and, the average computer today has an 8 gigabyte RAM. The Chief chose me to be on the team that trained new Z-100 operators on base. This cemented my love for computers. Along with training people to use it I got to learn basic programming using Z-DOS (Zenith Data Operating System) computer language.

I worked with wonderful fun people. The Burroughs Corporation provided an onsite Burroughs Field Engineer. Our engineer was named Ed. Ed could have been a stand-in for Santa with his white hair, white beard, and rosy checks. He was passionate about the card game hearts. He was not a gracious loser. He considered us mostly whipper snappers in need of fatherly guidance. I think he felt since he dispensed such valuable life information he should be afforded the chance to win. We disagreed which made him a common target. I will never forget the sight of him jumping up out of his chair, yelling and slamming his hand of cards down on the table because he just got given the Queen of Spades and 26 points. Hearts is won by the person with the least amount of points. Then again, perhaps he just did it because we all thought it was funny.

Sometimes the Air Force would send down paperwork each person in the unit had to fill out and sign. Ed delighted in unique and sometime rude answers since he was under no obligation to fill the paperwork out. With his tiny pencil he would write whole sentences in the little blocks (GRADE: A—Prime Beef RANK: Only when I don't take a shower.

There was one non commissioned officer below the chief that supervised all the Operators and Monitors, his name was Mike. Mike and Ed were buddies and usually went to lunch or the guy together. One day in the gym sauna Mike saw something under one of the benches and decided that someone had pooped in the sauna. He was hot. He demanded that they get it taken care of right away. They collected it with a dust pan and it turned out to be the broken corner of a brick with mold growing on it. Ed looked on with glee and forever loved the tale of Mike seeing poop places. "Hey Mike, Is that poop over there?" He painted a brick with gold paint and presented it to Mike to hold his papers down on his desk.

BYTE CHART: KB or kilobyte is 1,024 bytes. MB or megabyte is 1,024   kilobytes. GB or gigabyte is 1,024 megabytes. TB ir terabyte is 1,024 gigabytes.

Mike's wife brought him a helium balloon for his birthday. It kept floating away so he wrapped the balloon string around the brick to keep it in place. He went to lunch and when he returned he found the balloon taped to the wall with long strings of scotch tape. The string hung down forlornly and the gold brick was gone. Mike ranted and raved for the whole rest of the day. A few days later he received a ransom note. His name was pasted on a cassette tape with letters cut from a magazine . The tape had on it a man speaking in a heavily accented voice that might have been imitating a Russian speaking broken English. The man stated that they had kidnapped his brick and a ransom would be required to get it back. After the intimidating man spoke a young girls voice came on the tape pleading, "Help me Mikey, please help me!" The sinister man returned to describe what they would do to the poor brick if the ransom was not prayed, while the girl cried in the back ground. It was good for a laugh and Mike took it all in stride.

The next day he received a corner piece broken off a gold brick and a tape stating that they had cut off the ear of the brick.

When I arrived at Data Automation they told me this whole story and Mike showed me the gold brick with the missing corner still holding up his books on his bookshelf. He had the tapes with his name in letters and the box with cotton and the brick corner. I loved it.

Christmas that year we had a gift exchange and found that most tried to be very silly or funny with their gifts. I drew Mike's name. His present was a stack of boxes all tied together with an entire roll of curling tape. They were numbered and had to be opened in a specific order. Box 1—a doll sized baby bottle. Box 2—doll sized baby rattle. Box 3—a small ornamental brick that was 2 inches wide, 4 inches long and 1.5 inches in thickness painted gold and wearing a white cloth diaper with little gold diaper pins. Box 4—held a scroll that rolled out to tell the entire brick story, history, background and the conclusion that while his brick had been in captivity it had impregnated their brick but they were no longer able to care for the baby so Mike was responsible. It was signed "The Conspirators."

Another time I came in early and taped 20-30 little small gold footprints I had cut out of gold cardstock. The footprints game up from the drawer where he kept the baby brick, across his desk, up the wall an to the door. A week after that he was returned the baby brick by four very conscientious regular sized gold bricks sporting bright red chapeau tribe fez hats with gold tassels. They held a fancy scroll that was a ticket for negligence written to Mike for allowing the baby to attend a Mason convention.

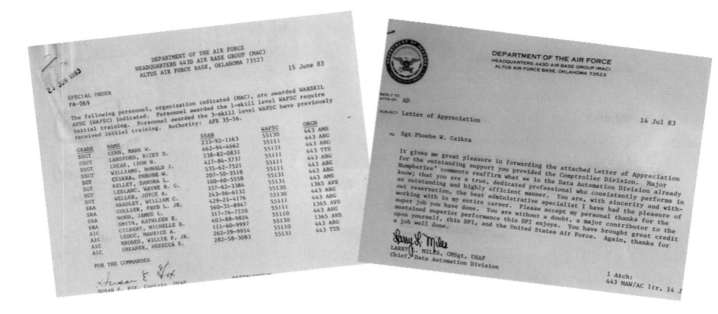

While stationed in Altus I was required to have a war skill and had to earn at least a 5-level (competent) in that job. It even had its own special code—WAFSC 55111. To train in my WARSKIL I was sent to the Civil Engineering (CE) Squadron to learn to be a heavy equipment operator. I was certified on dump trucks, snow plow, bull dozer, and front end loader. I did not like running the crane because it seemed like it would swing back into the cab and I just could not get the hang of speed shifting the 18-wheeler so I only had a 3-level in those. I got along great with the guys in heavy equipment. They teased me because they had to get a pillow so I could see over the dash when driving. I wanted to say thank you for the time with them so I baked them a cake and brought it in the last day.

I was learning cake decorating and of course the base exchanged had the whole Wilton line of cake decorating supplies. The US Air Force Civil Engineering had their own patch with a big blue bull on it. I worked hard to duplicate the exact blue in the patch on the top of that cake and it was a good job if I say so myself. I felt a twinge of guilt when I left and everyone had blue lips but I knew it would go away. A week later I ran into one of the guys from CE at the base exchange. He told me their poop was blue for days afterwards.

Every job in the Air Force was assigned a number code called an AFSC or Air Force Specialty Code. In the previous chapters I mentioned earning a 5-level in Automatic Flight Control 32550 and a 7-level in Administration 70270.

14 Jul 83

REPLY TO
ATTN OF: AD

SUBJECT: Letter of Appreciation

TO: Sgt Phoebe W. Czikra

It gives me great pleasure in forwarding the attached Letter of Appreciation for the outstanding support you provided the Comptroller Division. Major Humpheries' comments reaffirm what we in the Data Automation Division already know; that you are a true, dedicated professional who consistently performs in an outstanding and highly efficient manner. You are, with sincerity and without reservation, the best administrative specialist I have had the pleasure of working with in my entire career. Please accept my personal thanks for the super job you have done. You are without a doubt, a major contributor to the sustained superior performance this DPI enjoys. You have brought great credit upon yourself, this DPI, and the United States Air Force. Again, thanks for a job well done.

Larry L. Miles

LARRY L. MILES, CMSgt, USAF
Chief, Data Automation Division

1 Atch:
443 MAW/AC ltr, 1

While I was at Altus the Space Shuttle landed on our runway and we got to see it land and be taken away aboard a larger jet. It was so patriotic and awesome.

When I left Altus I was honored at the awards they gave me but most of all this engraved Burroughs Mainframe computer disc. I was told it was only given to data automators but I had done so much data work that I had earned it.

I did love my job at Altus but my homelife was a real mess and I was getting desperate. My second son was born and had lots of medical problems starting with jaundice at birth. He seemed to have constant ear infections one after another and had the worst penicillin reaction documented at that hospital.

I didn't know he was allergic. They gave me amoxicillin and second dosage Nicholas turned blue. He then developed something called Henoch-Schoenlein Purpura (HSP) which caused tiny explosions under his skin. These resulted in a 1/2 inch to one inch bruise and before they could get the epinephrine to work his whole body was coved with bruises and it looked like someone had beat him with a stick. I thought he was dying and had been crying as they tried to stop the reaction and save his life. When it finally stopped they needed him x-rayed to ensure there was no bone damage. It was Halloween and all the families were there to have their candy x-rayed and I carry in this beaten baby crying… it was bad.

As I said, my home life was a mess and I really needed to talk to my mom. We could not save up enough money for me to fly to Alaska or even afford lengthy phone calls with her. I discovered a loop hole. The Air Force Dream Sheet Program gives preference to those for whom the assignment is home state. It is a whole program in itself that is promoted to positively effect morale. I went to CBPO (Central Base Personnel Office) and changed my dream sheet to Alaska Home State Preference and tore up my Join Spouse Paperwork. Join Spouse is an assignment request that allows military couples to be stationed at the same base.

In 1982 six tornados touched down in the Altus area. Damaged two C-5 aircraft and their hangars, destroyed the base service station and tore the roofs from four barracks. The veterinary clinic was destroyed, and the dining hall and rec center roofs were damaged. In 1983 a tornado hit the base but only traveled 50 yards on the base. It was common in Altus to have 12 mph winds year round. This is not big wind but it does bring dust in every crack. This means if you begin dusting at one end of your house, but the time you reach the other end there is new dust at the first. There was one bad wind storm that tore roofs off, imploded a Sears shed and destroyed fences all over town. There were thunderstorms with golf ball and softball sized hail that beat down the bumpers on cars and left dimples in the roofs and hoods. There was flooding. I once asked why driving through Altus the road would dip down 10 feet every now and then. When it rains so hard and the Altus ground is so dry and hard it cannot absorb the rain, those dips become their water culverts. One flood I got up, drove to the base to go to work and the water was level with the door knob on the guard shack. Three Christmas's there we called my mom and because of wind chill it was colder in Altus than in Anchorage, Alaska. There were 7 natural disasters to hit Altus AFB while I was there three years. I wondered who would ever voluntarily move here.

Once I pulled my join spouse paperwork I got home preference assignment orders to Alaska. Boy, was my husband mad. He did not want to move to Alaska but CBPO said they could not cancel my orders. His only choice was to insist I put the join spouse paperwork back in, so I did. My orders had me in Alaska in the fall of 1985, my husband's follow-on orders had him arrive in March of 1986. Seven months alone in Altus had made him a very unhappy camper.

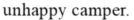

HOME PREFERENCE ASSIGNMENT ELMENDORF AFB ALASKA

I can't adequately describe the relief of moving to where my mom was, of having a safe place to go. We first sublet an apartment just 4 doors down from my mother's house on M (for Mom) Street in downtown Anchorage. My husband helped me move in, then was back to the Lower 48 as he would not be reassigned to Alaska until four months later. Even with the extra work of a single parent with two boys it was a good time for me. The assignment portion was a roller coaster. I worked for the Command Section, Headquarters Military Airlift Command in Alaska, again a special assignment. I had no problems with the Commander and Assistant Commander (also the Director of Operations or DO) (both colonels) but my immediate supervisor, the Executive Officer, was a Captain who was never satisfied with my work. On the positive side I met and became lifelong friends with two people assigned there. I will begin this chapter with 'The Beverly Stories.'

When I was first assigned to 616 Military Airlift Group Headquarters in Alaska, Beverly McGlotha already worked there. She was the administrator (admin) for the Resource Management Section (RMS). The third admin in our hall was assigned to the Operations Section (OPS). As you entered the MAC Headquarters there was a long hallway. On the right the first door was the huge Command office. In the command office was the colonel who was the Group Commander for MAC in Alaska, his assistant commander (also the Director of Operations), his Senior Enlisted Advisor (the highest ranking enlisted person in the group), and the commander's civilian secretary, Connie. The second door on the right was the RMS Office where Beverly had a desk in the front with two offices behind her for her colonel and the captain that was his assistant. On the left hand side of the hall were two doors for the long adjoining room that was all the operations people. As you entered this long room were two enlisted guys on the left, and then 5 or 6 officers on the right. At the end of the long hall was our office with two desks. One mine, one the operations admin. Office our office was a very small office where a Captain in charge or aerial operations and her assistant worked.

Many of our tasks required the three admin to work together (like the morning command briefing) because we were all one-deep in our positions. When I arrived there was a girl named Diane in the Ops Admin position. She was mean, nasty and difficult to work with. Beverly filled me in on the what, why, and wherefores of working with Diane. I was immensely grateful and we became friends then and there. About 8 months into my assignment there Diane was replaced with Wayne. We then became the terrific trio as we all worked together well.

Beverly could be mischievous. One morning when I hadn't been there very long she told me how Diane was obsessive about everything in the office and considered the whole office hers. Beverly walked over to Diane's desk and moved something about 3 inches out of place. When Diane came in the first thing she did was move it back and then start yelling about who messed with her desk. She also was obsessive about opening the blinds on the three windows in the office first thing every morning. I almost always arrived before her and if I opened the blinds she would be angry all day. I soon learned it wasn't worth the disturbance and left the blinds alone for her to open whenever she came in. Sometimes Beverly would come in our office and open the blinds just to get Diane's goat.

616 Military Airlift Group at Elmendorf had several components: Headquarters, 17th Tactical Airlift Squadron, 616 Aerial Port Squadron and 616 Consolidated Aircraft Maintenance Squadron. The morning briefing was held by the 616 MAG Commander and each of the squadron commanders of the above units would bring their slides for the briefing. These were basically an 8.5 x 11 transparency in a cardboard frame. The briefing room had a large screen behind which was a little room with a projector. We admin would stand in the little room with the 5-6 inch stack of slides and put them on the projector one at a time with the commander or person whose slide it was saying "Next." Beverly would whisper jokes and sometimes I would laugh out loud which of course got me a lecture afterwards by my boss. One time the slides got bumped off the little table where you flipped them and though we tried to pick them up in order some were out of order. I just remember one operations Major saying things like "Well, this is the slide that should have come before the last one…"

One task we all hated was typing messages. The messages were scanned and transmitted electronically and could have no errors, no white out, no corrections, and were often a whole page of typing. You would get all the way to the bottom and make a typo and have to start over—hateful. The commander had asked Beverly to sweep the hall, had given his secretary a message to type, and had left to run and errand. Connie didn't want to type that message so she told Bev to sit and type the message and she would sweep. I was just coming down the hall when the colonel returned and saw the two had switched places. He looked at his secretary and then bellowed, "Beverly!" Bev was a senior airman, not even a sergeant yet. She jumped up from the desk where she was typing, stalked over to the colonel and said, "She ripped the broom right out of my hands!" I almost gasped at this low ranking airman having that attitude and being pretty disrespectful to the high ranking commander. I froze in place. The colonel threw back his head and laughed. Then he said, "As you were." and proceeded to his office. I was very impressed. Bev and I discussed the fact that she probably was never meant to be in the military and did have trouble with giving respect to officers that did not deserve it. I was still amazed at her audacity.

There were many exercises we participated in during that assignment. This one particular exercise we were all on 12-hour shifts. There was a whole contingent of people from Scott Air Force Base sharing all the operations offices and taking notes of how everyone did. I was often asked to draw cartoons of what happened. String was put up in the hall and these cartoons were taped to the string. By the end of the exercise there would be three or four rows of cartoons hanging.

Wayne and I offered to go for pizza's and soon had so many orders we had to write them down. If memory serves, we were getting four large, three mediums and six or seven individual pan pizzas. We were on the second floor of the big white command building on Elmendorf. I was carrying half the pizza's and Wayne was carrying the other half until we approached our hall. Then Wayne took all the stack of pizza's while I got the doors open. As I shut the double doors and we stepped into the hall Beverly was right there on door guard duty. She was vacuuming the hall and held up the vacuum wand like it was a sword and yelled, "Halt!" It quite startled Wayne and I, so we stopped, Beverly walked over to Wayne holding all those pizza's. She started at the top and sniffed down each pizza in the stack. Then she stepped back and said, "Okay you can pass."

During another exercise, and of course 12 hour shifts, Bev and I had gone to the convenience store across base and bought hot dogs and buns. Then things got busy and we did not have the opportunity to eat them. When shift change came we discussed the hot dogs. We could put the buns in one of our desk drawers but the hot dogs had to be refrigerated. We also knew if they were left in there overnight the night shift would eat them. Bev suggested that we wrap them up in brown paper and mark them DO NOT OPEN. We did that.

There was a tech sergeant on night shift that was skinny, always hungry and never cared whose food it was. I know he figured there was food in the package but since we had marked it 'do not open' and someone saw him handling it, he had to put it back. Thwarted, he called the base command post and reported that there was an unidentified package in the refrigerator. First they evacuated the whole building. Then the bomb squad reported to our hall, carefully removed the package and the little white tray it was in, took it out to a field on base, x-rayed the package and determined "it *potentially* held eight sticks of dynamite", so they wired it up and blew it up. Beverly's RMS colonel was hot and said we owed him a new plastic tray for the refrigerator. Someone took a picture of the mangled Wrangler package and the pieces of hot dogs strewn in the grass. I was assigned as the typist for the inspectors and was working on the final report. Bev, like everyone else, had to go to the out briefing. She said she wanted to crawl under her chair when the photo appeared on the briefing screen and the Scott AFB Commander thanked the two of us by name for the bomb alert.

My mom lived right downtown in Anchorage, not too far from the back gate of Elmendorf AFB. Every Friday all the sisters, and one brother if in town, would go to our mom's house after work. We shared making the dinners. Friends dropped by and mom made it lots of fun with grand discussions and wild games. I invited Bev to come with me to my mom's house one Friday after work. We worked well together but she didn't know me very well on the personal side. I was white and she was Black and I think a tad apprehensive about meeting my family. As I drove to my mom's house she questioned me. "What would you think if I married your brother?" My brother was a notorious bachelor. Being the only male in our generation he was the one that was, according to my father's mother, supposed to carry on the Abbott name. I laughed aloud and replied, "I will give you $1000 if you marry my brother." She looked surprised at the answer but didn't ask anything more. When we arrived at my mom's my two older sisters and a family friend named Sue were already there. Once in the door I announced to all. "Bev asked me what I would do if she married my brother and I told her I would give her $1000." At that point my mother, both sisters, and Sue all loudly announced that they too would kick in $1000 for a grand total of $5000 dollars. There were little cat call comments at the end like, "Can I write you a check right now?" Ever after Bev just called my mom, "Mom" like the rest of us. Some months later my brother, Findlay, was in town. He lived in Homer, Alaska some 240 miles South of Anchorage. He met Beverly at my mom's on a Friday night and he was enamored, Bev not so much… he still hung on to his hippie ways in dress and appearance, and was more than 20 years her senior in age. She did flirt a bit though and could easily have reeled him in if she wanted.

November 24, 1987, I gave birth to my last child, Christopher. I might have mentioned that I had my first child at 9 months. I had my second at a documented ten months, and my third child at eight months. When you are pregnant, over 35, smoke cigarettes, are under an undue amount of stress, and are one in a million, you can have what is called placental abruption. This is where the placenta separates from the wall of the uterus before birth. If a complete separation the baby is denied oxygen at that second and the woman begins bleeding. If not stopped it is often fatal. My mother carefully cut out of the paper the article stating that in Anchorage in that five year period there were 5 placental abruptions. In all the other 4 mother and baby died. Chris was born at 5 pounds but immediately lost one pound. The muscle that stops food from regurgitating was not all the way formed and when fed he projectile vomited his milk. They gave him something called Reglan. I had to give him the medicine, precisely 30 minutes later begin feeding, and feed no more than 30 minutes, three times a day. Using this method he was able to keep his food down and begin to grow. Photo right is Chris at one month old.

Besides being extra small, Chris was different from my other two boys from the get-go. He never made eye contract, even when I was holding and feeding him and I was so afraid he was blind. I took him to the doctors and they did some tests and told me, "He is not blind, he has an enormous capacity to ignore." I thought to myself, "Seriously?"

Did I mentioned in the Altus AFB chapter that my second son, Nicholas crawled at 2 weeks old and was running through the house like a destructive tornado at six months old? At this point with Chris I am now the mother of three smart, active and often naughty boys with a husband who "did not do children!" I also worked full time in the military—challenging.

When Chris was two months old and still had not made eye contact with another human. Bev came to see the new baby. She came after church and was dressed up very nice. She had on this bright red pill box type hat similar to the one in the picture but felt. She had bright red lipstick to match.

Bev could sing like an angel and often spoke like she was singing. She leaned over his crib and said, "BAAAA-BEEEE!" like it was a song and Chris looked up in amazement and made eye contact for the very first time. I loved her for that. Chris has always been interested in music and in fact today plays keyboard, violin, harmonic, mandolin, acoustic and electric guitar and sings and writes his own music.

Photo from https://www.wye.com

Just for the sake of understanding my life with three boys and no help I have to add. Nicholas was kicked out of the Elmendorf Day Care Center when he was 19 months old. He had escaped more than 18 times and they insisted I needed a one on one babysitter. I had two on base sitters that did not last more than six months all together and finally found a woman named Judy who lasted longer. She was even willing to take on my third child when Chris was born. There are rules when you live in base housing, and the second time Nicholas made water come out of Judy's kitchen light fixture they took her babysitting license away.

Beverly decided to transfer to the Alaska Air National Guard. In that process it was discovered that she had breast cancer. Bev was very well endowed, like 40 double E. They found cancer in only one of her breasts and it would need to be removed. They discussed with her the problem that would be created if she kept her other breast because it would make her out of balance. She decided to have both of them removed.

I took her a kt in the hospital containing puzzle books, reading books, toys, snacks and a squirt gun. I told her the squirt gun was to keep the nurses in line. I was joking. I really didn't think that she would use it on them but she sure did. On my second visit the nurses asked if I would take it away from her. Bev was always such a card. The day after surgery, the doctor came to her room during his normal rounds. He had with him a very young doctor doing his residency. Bev was a beautiful woman and fully revealed as the doctor did his exam she caught the young residents eye, gave him a big beautiful smile, winked and said, "How is it looking?" The guy turned bright red, stuttered something no one understood, and literally ran out of the room.

As I said, Beverly was always singing. Some people hum, some whistle, Bev sang. Most of the time it would be gospel songs but she seriously had a voice that could have won awards had she ever done anything with it. She did sing in her church choir and it brought tears to my eyes. When Ray Charles came to Anchorage, she was the one chosen to sing with him… a great honor.

In 2008 Bev called me out of the blue and over the phone we renewed our friendship like we had seen each other every day between. We laughed a lot together and remembered things we had done together. We laughed about our First Sergeant Evelyn who ran over her black military purse and it had track marks ever after. We both admired her so much. One day she was so mad she stepped up on my captains desk to point down at him and tell him what she thought. She was 5 feet, 11 inches, of Black fury.

When Bev was in Alaska she had a license plate that read Bev-Mac. Sometimes I can be really oblivious about things. I told her that I had always thought that the Mac stood for Military Airlift Command where we worked and was amazed she loved it so much she had it on her license plate. Bev laughed long to hear that since there was no love lost with her for the Air Force. I told her it had just dawned on me thinking of her that the Mac on her license plate was for her last name, McGlotha. I really loved Beverly and am sad she is gone sooner than she should have at 57 years old.

On with the Elmendorf stories. Wayne, the operations admin, and I became great and lifelong friends. He moved in next door to me off base and we were close. His daughter was the first girl that my oldest son ever kissed. Since we were both in one deep positions we thought it would be smart to act as a back up to each other. This made trips out of the office, leave and other things much easier to handle. It did not affect my command section job much but Wayne had lots of running around base involved in his job so it affected his position a lot more. The Operations guys had never had a back up for their admin before and were very grateful. One major noticed my abilities with the computer and taught me basic programing and had me write some programs for the Group.

I need to back up one step before I talk about Wayne. The last month that Diane was stationed with us was worse than the six before because she frankly just stopped helping with anything. We had a rotation for flipping the slides in the command briefing and Beverly came to me concerned. She said that Diane was on the schedule and had not come to get the RMS slides for the slide show. There was a door between our office and the operations area that was a split door and usually only the top was open. I popped my head in and asked if anyone had seen Diane. No one had, but one person said he thought she was out in Aerial Port helping with a files inspection. I called Aerial Port but they said she wasn't there. Bev and I flipped a coin, I lost and gathering up the slides was headed out to take her place. As I reached the exit it suddenly was blocked by a red-faced, highly angry major, Diane's boss. He was hot! He began yelling at me about not checking up on his admin, and what she was doing being none of my business, and who did I think I was anyway... He was tall and thin and more than a foot taller than me. He had backed me into the corner of the office and with his finger shaking in my face was ranting and raving for the whole hall to hear and we acquired an audience. That is what is known in the military as "conduct unbecoming an officer." I only found out details later but apparently he was an alcoholic and spent the 90 days in the Betty Ford Addiction Treatment Center in Florida.

During my time at MAC Headquarters I received an award and there was a ceremony for presenting it to me and four others who has also won awards. Families were invited and my mother was there for me. She knew that the captain had been giving me a hard time since I arrived but always gracious she sat and talked to him before the presentations. He was from Oxnard, California and my mom shared that my sister was born there and her husband had been stationed at Pt Mugu Naval Station. He grinned and said his father worked there too. "Oh?" my mother asked, "What did your father do?" The captain replied that his father was a janitor there. My mother was never one to brag and I know she responded as she did only because he had been giving me such a hard time. "Phoebe's father was the rocket engineer in charge."

The first year of my assignment we had a commander was a great leader. He was inspiring with a wonderful sense of humor, fairness and was good to work for. He left and the Full Bird Colonel that replaced him was the complete opposite. He had no sense of humor, was difficult to work for, and rank not fairness was always the issue. It was a good thing Beverly didn't speak to him the way she had to the last commander. I think he was part of the reason she chose at that point to move to the Alaska Air National Guard.

Only one time did I get in trouble with my first commander (in photo). He was very personable. Once a month he held a welcome briefing with all the troops newly assigned to the group. The colonel liked to pick someone out of the crowd that he had already met to speak to in this briefing. I think this showed that he commu-nicated at all levels. Since I was his admin he had met my husband who picked me up after work. During the briefing he was talking about how some people did not want to be stationed in Alaska because it was so far away from their families in the Lower 48. He wished them luck in acclimating and making the best of the assignment.

He went on to say that there were also those who loved coming to Alaska, volunteered for the assignment knowing of the great hunting, fishing and recreation. He pointed at my husband and said, "Why Sergeant Czikra is an example of someone who wanted to come here." My husband was outspoken to say the least. "No Sir!" he announced and to the colonels embarrassment went on and on about the joint spouse trick I had played on him.

Since Wayne and I were doing our back-up-each-other deal, I had come to know all the operations officers that worked on our floor. They were nearly all pilots and liked to have a good time. One morning one of the OPS majors came to me with a request for a cartoon. It was not unusual to be asked to do a cartoon, so I really thought nothing of it.

He explained that their brand new operations section captain had his first C-130 ride that morning and was so embarrassingly air sick that he puked on the aircraft. They asked me to do a cartoon with the captain inside the C-130 with a green face and dizzy circles around his head. I could hear them joshing him so quickly did the cartoon and gave it to the major. They all loved it, thanked me and I could hear them laughing and sharing it with the rest.

Just after lunch my captain came scurrying into my office in a fluster. He said the commander wants to see you *right now.* He advised me it was a very serious matter and I was to do a formal reporting in at attention, with salute and all.

I was pretty apprehensive as you can imagine. I barely knew this commander who never spoke directly to me. Unlike the previous commander, he never wandered the offices and spoke informally to the workers. I entered the office, went to attention and saluted. He made me stand there for a good two minutes holding that salute before he looked up at me with distain and saluted so I could drop my hand. He took a folder from his desk, opened it up, and threw down on the desk with a slap a copy of the cartoon I had done that morning. "Did you do this cartoon Sergeant Czikra?" he demanded. "Yes Sir, I did." "Really...." "What do you think was the point of this cartoon?" While he glared at me in anger I tried to explain how the ops guys had asked me to do it, how the previous commander always loved cartoons about what was going on and how it was just a harmless joshing of the new captain...." He cut me off. "NO! That is not at all what this cartoon is about! This cartoon is a statement about my flying ability since I was the pilot during that flight!" After my dressing down I returned to my office and found several ops officers grinning though the half door. They had done it on purpose. When I left the group the entire operations crew took me and Wayne to lunch. They thanked me profusely for helping take care of them when Wayne was gone and presented me with a hand held stereo.

When we had Exercise Brim Frost they sent a team in to work with and evaluate us. Of course there were more cartoons lining the hall of the slip ups, the triumphs and the events of the exercise. The exercise went on 24 hours a day and we were all on 12 hour shifts. The head inspector was a colonel and he shared the office with our assistant commander (the DO) with each taking one 12 hour shift. Our DO was named McGough and the inspector from D.C. was named McKay. I noticed that right away and that evening created a big sign which we thumb tacked over their door. It read, "McOffice."

This captain that was my boss seemed to never be satisfied with my work. I know several times he wanted to ding me for something but my first sergeant was always there to remind him that my work was excellent and he couldn't just ding folks for no reason. He did find a way to make life difficult for me despite her protection. When I had Chris I was only 8 months pregnant and not schedule for maternal leave. When I was discharged from the hospital I had to go to my work to have him sign my maternity leave slip. He refused to sign it until I stepped on the scale and weighed in, knowing I might be over weight having not yet lost the baby fat. He was right, I weighed in at one pound over resulting in the harassment of two years on the weight program.

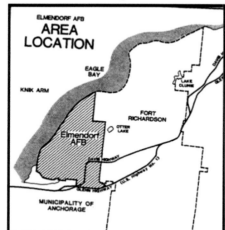

One of my tasks was preparation for the officer boards. Every quarter or so the commander would hold a board that would determine which officers in the group would be promoted. The board had to be set up just so in the conference room with extra coffee, pad and pens for notes and the complete personnel record for every officer meeting the board. In this one instance the board was set up with almost no notice. The captain gave me the list of the dozen or so officers that would meet the board and told me to go to the Base Personnel Office and get all their records. I pointed out that they required 24 hours to pull a stack of records for a board. He was mad and told me to just go over there, demand that they pull the records immediately, and have them call him if they wouldn't. I always found honey works better so armed with 2 dozen do-nuts I went and requested the records.

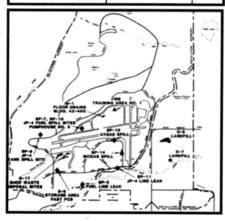

Another task that we three admin on the floor shared was man-agement of the MAC Chalet. Elmendorf AFB is over 13,000 square acres with wilderness and lakes. The runway on Elmendorf is basically a T shape with the bulk of the facilities situated at the front of the base between the runway and An-chorage. There were 8 or more chalet's on the back side of the runway in the more than half of the base that was like wilderness. Elmendorf.
On Six Mile Lake the Military Airlift Command had a chalet that was open for rental for parties and gatherings. The MAC Chalet, as it was called, was a two story facility complete with a kitchen, a 2 acre lot that boarded the lake, Building 63-621. We had to get signed contracts for rental, collect a damage deposit and rental fee, and issue out the keys. After the event was over with we had to inspect the chalet to make sure they had cleaned up or we kept their damage deposit. There were some wild parties out there. One memorable one was a group of pilots. We are not sure how they did it but the marks on the ceiling were obviously made by someone's buttocks.

The two maps on the right show Elmendorf in relation to the city of Anchorage (top) and (bottom) how the run was is situated on the base. The roads at the top of that map are the roads leading to the base chalets. Maps from 1983 Installation Restoration Program for Elmendorf AFB, Alaska.

One more side story. When I left Altus AFB I said that if anyone came to Alaska to look me up. One day, the lieutenant who commanded the data automation, walked into my office in MAC Headquarters. He had been assigned as the Deputy Commander for Shemya Air Force Base and had 4 days in Anchorage to in-process and asked me if I would show him around Anchorage. The first day the boys and I took him to Fur Rendezvous, an annual winter celebration in Anchorage with dog sled races, snow sculpting, and more. The second day I took him to my mom's house for Friday night. There he met my younger sister. They are almost the same age and I guess it was love at first sight because they are married still. Shemya AFB is now called Eareckson Air Station. It is located on the western tip of Alaska's Aleutian Islands and is as remote as it gets. On one end of the island they had a sign that read, "Just Ahead McDonalds 1500 miles."

Aside from my friendship with Wayne it was just not the same anymore. Beverly had moved to the Alaska Air National Guard (AKANG), our commander seemed to be permanently angry at me over that captain being sick cartoon, my boss was on my back, my home life was a mess, and I was not happy.

I had now 11 years in the military, a decision point of going on or getting out. I still had two years on my contract with the Air Force. I went to see the Base Career Advisor and he suggested that I could take advantage of a program they were shutting down called Palace Chase. They were shutting it down because the Air Force was actually having retention problems. This program allowed a person to trade two years active duty for four years in the Guard. If I went to the Guard as a traditional guardsman I could then apply for an Active Guard Reserve (AGR) slot. The Alaska Air National Guard had three types of workers: Traditional Guardsmen who served one weekend a month during a Unit Training Assembly and one two week period sometime during the year; Technicians served the same active time as traditional guardsmen but during the week worked for the State of Alaska at the guard base; AGR were just like full time active duty personnel and like Air Force but assigned to the National Guard. As an AGR, I could do another 9 years active duty with the Guard and achieve an Air Force retirement at 20 years. Beverly was in the AKANG and said she loved it. This sounded like a good deal to me and I put in for it. They told me I was the last Palace Chase off Elmendorf before the temporary cutoff of the program due to manning issues. In February of 1989 I left the Air Force.

THE ALASKA AIR NATIONAL GUARD

From the first the Alaska Air National Guard (AKANG) was sweet! I had a boss who was happily married, encouraged his troops, worked to provide advancement opportunities, had good sense of humor and was an all around nice guy. How many colonels do you know that for a squadron fun raiser would dress up as Madonna, complete with a metal bra and mine a song in front of the entire base. Here was how the military was supposed to work... no matter your rank your opinion mattered. I wondered if this was because of the unique mix of people with civilian lives and those holding down the military post. Perhaps I had just been blessed with a really good group of people to work with. I don't know which or what but it worked for me.

The Palace Chase Guard representative hooked me up with my boss before all the paperwork was done. I was hired as a Technician Secretary to the Chief of Supply. This was a great job! My boss was such a character. We must have some Mike stories: Mike had a long time friend who was blind, not from birth, but onset as an adult. His name was Sandy. I don't believe either of them ever got used to the change. Mike was very social and would call out or wave in passing even when he was in a hurry. He told me that one time he was escorting Sandy into this Mexican Restaurant we all loved. Sandy had Mike's arm to avoid bumping things. Mike saw a table of friends and happily waved, as he walked his friend right into a post. Another time his Sandy was in downtown Anchorage getting used to walking alone with a cane in a city. Anchorage in 1990 was not a busy city as a general rule. Here comes Mike and his wife driving down the street Sandy is attempting to navigate. Mike was thrilled to see his friend not sitting home but working to transition his life. He was excited even. He rolled down his window, waved and honked and yelled, "Sandy!". His friend had a heart check as all the commotion he thought he had stepped off the curb into traffic.

Then there was Stan and Kenny. Stan and Kenny might have been a comedy show. Kenny was our Chief and Stan one of the main supervisors. Kenny loved a laugh, almost always had a smile and especially loved a good story. Stan gave me paperwork to go on leave and I was waiting for Mike to sign off on it. Kenny's office was right next to Mike's and although technically secretary to the Mike I could handle any admin work the five in our office needed. The five were: the Chief of Supply (Technician), which was Mike; the Chief of Supply (Guardsman) who technically outranked Mike but only worked weekends (and she was one in the top five of the highest ranking officer women on base); Kenny, the Chief, the highest ranking enlisted person in our squadron; and the Captain, Assistant to the Chief of Supply, also a weekend warrior.

Kenny saw Stan's leave paperwork on my desk and he shook his head and laughed. I asked him what that was all about and he said, "You'll see!" Stan returned from leave, all in a fuss and was complaining to Kenny about things that had transpired. Kenny dragged him over to my desk and with a huge grin said, "You gotta tell her, Stan!" Stan talked slow and with great description. Apparently had purchased an RV. He was so proud and excited to use it to the best advantage. He and his wife drove up to Fairbanks, Alaska to stay in their campground. First there was an issue with water. Apparently Stan was under the belief that he had the equipment to get water flowing to his RV by hooking up to the water fountain. It didn't work and caused a flood before they could get it turned off. The feller in the tent down the way had everything he owned soaked and water logged.

Stan managed to get through the first two days of the long weekend with he and his wife eating all the snacks they brought along but the last night there he decided he needed to hook up his propane and make them a real meal. I don't know what he did wrong but he started a forest fire right there in that campground. The rangers escorted them out of the campground and on their way home. They also asked that they please never come back. Kenny was roaring through all this and I did think it was funny but not that funny. When Stan finally wound down and finished his weekend tale, Kenny gave him a nudge and said tell them about last year, well you better do the year before first. He grinned at me again.

Stan had gone to Seward, Alaska a couple vacations before and wound up purchasing a boat from a man down there. Stan knew nothing about tides in Alaska and tying up a boat but he did know his knots. At low tide Stan secured his boat to a piling in the boat harbor and as the tide came in and faced the buoyancy of his new boat and the accuracy of his knot, it pulled that piling right out of the harbor. Everyone was relieved that no one was hit by the piling coming down and no boat was damaged either. The Harbor Master was not pleased but was gracious about Stan's mistake. Kenny nudges Stan again, "Tell her about running over the lady with your boat, Stan!" I gasped in wonder and asked, "You ran over a lady with your boat, Stan?

Last years vacation they had returned to Seward, launched their boat and spent a wonderful day fishing and boating around Resurrection Bay. Stan had studied all year and now knew every boating rule. Motoring at appropriate speed for the harbor he was proudly at the wheel, captain of his ship. Suddenly from the dock he was passing was a yell. There were the couple smiling and waving at Stan to stop and talk, that he had bought the boat from. There was a slip open with a small dock connected to the walk way so Stan put the boat in reverse to backup and then go into the slip. The couple walked out beside the slip to greet them. Stan thought he threw the boat into neutral but in fact he threw the throttle all the way back and that boat leapt right out of the water and pinned the man's wife to the dock. Took four large me to pick that boat off her. The man sued Stan for lost marital privileges cause his wife wouldn't have sex with him anymore. She was probably mad at him for getting them involved with this guy. Stan gave him the boat back in payment. Kenny grinned at me and said, "Happens every year, can't wait to see what is next!"

I loved to do little pranks on April Fools Day. I had programmed Mike's computer so that when you turned it on it would wait about 10 seconds and then the letters of the menu that came up on the screen first would begin to melt off the page. I usually arrived an hour before Mike, as did Kenny. I had stayed the night before and fixed Mike's computer but hadn't told anyone. Kenny went into Mike's office, turned on the computer and my program went to work. Kenny jumped up and yelled, "Oh NO!" loud enough to startle all of us in the room out side the office. Kenny had jumped up out of Mikes chair so quickly he rammed it into the wall with a big bang. He was sure he had ruined Mike's computer.

Mike got a trip to Hawaii and Kenny and I told him he needed to take one of us along with him. We didn't care who got to go, just so someone went. Neither of us got to go. I had to do something to welcome him back so I went over to one of the maintenance shops and introduced myself to a sergeant named Sue Hilton.

I bought the super large bag of 12 inch balloons from the party supply store on Arctic Avenue. Sue helped me blow them all up, cart them over to supply and put them in Mike's office. The windows in Mikes office were so high up I had to stand on tip toe to see out them. We filled it to the window level. For the first time since I had worked for him Mike came in earlier than I did. He rounded up the troops, taped off my cubical and filled it to the top with all those balloon. I paid him back by hiring a belly dancer for his birthday. I honestly did not know a man could blush so red.

As usual there was not enough of my job to keep me busy all day so with Mike's permission, actually encouragement, I started helping in the other branches. First I was decollating listings and then I was running off supply reports that came from Elmendorf and distributing them. Kulis Air Guard Base was treated as a satellite supply office to connect to the mainframe computer at Elmendorf. We had computers that were really stations to sign-on to Elmendorf's computer and order things. Seeing this Mike encouraged me to go ahead and do the Base Supply correspondence courses and said when something opened up, he would transfer me. This worked and I transferred into the section that took all the parts orders. I worked for a man named AJ. AJ was famous for his barbeque sauce and people requested it for every event on base. No matter how much was needed AJ had containers to bring it to the base. He always cooked it at home jealously guarding his recipe. When we made a squadron cook book I asked AJ if he would put his recipe in the book. He grinned and said he sure would. I had a deadline for collecting all the parts and pieces for the cook book. Every page was dedicated to a promised recipe. AJ waited until the last minute to turn his recipe in so there was no time to find a substitute. His recipe went like this: Drive to Dimond Boulevard. Turn into the Costco parking lot and park. Go to Aisle 12 and find Sweet Baby Ray's barbeque sauce. Empty carefully into one of your own containers.

AJ was helping Stan with some wood splitting and some how or other AJ's finger was removed by that wood splitter. When AJ got ready to retire, six or seven of us 'supply girls', including one of our civilian workers, dressed up in neon colored shirts and performed for his retirement. We had signs made announcing the one time performance of "The Neons." We had a whole rap song that we danced too and at the apex of the show Carla flicked a rubber finger off at AJ. I still have that video recording. Fun times. AJ was replaced by Ralph with whom I am still friends.

From there I went to work in forward supply. It was a small three person office in the maintenance squadron where maintainers could come in and order necessary airplane parts. This was a fun place to work with two great guys. From there Mike transferred me to computer operations and made me in charge. I was the NCOIC or Non-commissioned Officer In Charge. I loved the part of the job that was going to Elmendorf and working with the mainframe people when we had problems. The other part of my job, not so much. The other part of my job was teaching people how to use the supply computers, training new people, implementing new programs, and maintenance on and replacement of the twenty plus computers in the building. Mike was promoted to Recourse Management Squadron Commander. We got a new Chief of Supply. He wanted me to not have to run help so much so had me make computer checklists for everyone and every station. He told me to start every one with. "Turn the computer on."

When Mike got promoted to squadron commander we wanted a fun gift for him. We purchased a small gorilla stuffed animal. His wife stole one of his old flannel shirts and got it to me secretly. Since I could not sew my sewing sister sewed a little flannel shirt and blue jeans with flannel in the cuffs. I had a special order for the alterations shop on Elmendorf who sewed me a perfect little uniform for the little gorilla including a doll sized name tag for it.

That reminds me of one more Mike story. Mike was a member of the Lions Club. At one point he was selected as the Alaska Lion of the Year, quite an honor. There was a fancy banquet held during which he would be given this award. He was at a table with a couple who smoked cigarettes like crazy. The table had a small ashtray that was not up to the task and unknown to Mike the couple had taken one of their napkins and was dumping the contents of the ashtray in the cloth napkin and folding it over so no one could see the ashes. Poor form!! Mike thought he knew the program but was surprised when they called his name. He jumped to his feet and in doing so bumped the table. The wine belonging to the woman across the table promptly spilled on her evening gown. Mike was horrified and grabbed the napkin on the table to help her, thereby spilling the contents of 4 ashtrays on to her wet gown. That'll be a stain.

We had a lot of fun in Base Supply. We had a winning baseball team, and we enjoyed squirt gun fights in the down times. Mike bought himself a big squirt gun and really got me good. I could not let that stand. I called his wife, found out that he was bowling that night at the Jewel Lake Bowling Alley. I marched into the bowling alley and emptied my squirt gun down his back. Not being a bowler I had no idea people would freak so much about water down in the lanes.

I implemented a birthday cake of the month program and we celebrated monthly birthdays. This one pictured left was three little Indians (one for each birthday person that month) and their teepee.

Mike let us have a lunch get together for Halloween each year . One year he was Frankenstein, one year the Zoo Keeper in a gorilla suit, and another year I made a huge paper mâché head he could wear to be the 'Head of Supply'. When he was the Head of Supply I dressed as his X-Secretary. For one Halloween my sister, her son and his girl friend all came to our holiday lunch. My sister was Uncle Fester, my nephew Gomez Adams, his girl friend Morticia Adams, and I was Cousin It.

The last photo below is Kenny, our Chief Master Sergeant, who passed in 2009.

During the time I worked in Supply the Alaska Air National Guard picked up the rescue mission. Part of the rescue squadron consist of rescue aircraft and crew, rescue maintenance workers and Pararescuemen (called PJs). Our PJs were special. The washout rate in the career field is (according to Air Force Research Laboratories) 86-90%. "Those who complete training are considered to be among an elite group of special warfare operators"— dark angels. The Pararescuemen are highly trained to rescue in just about any condition on earth. Their training, called the Pipeline, was then almost two years long. It was fondly called 'Superman School. "It is among the longest special operations training courses in the world." They must first pass the 4-week Pararescue Indoctrination Course. They then train 8 weeks at the Navy Diving and Salvage Training Center in Florida. Three weeks are spent learning basic parachuting skills at the Army Airborne School in Georgia followed with the Army Military Free Fall Parachutist School in North Carolina at Fort Bragg. Then it is off to the grueling SERE-C (Survival, Evasion Resistance and Escape) school in Washington State and one more unique Pararescue course. They are "qualified in advanced weaponry, small unit tactics, airborne and military free fall, both high altitude low opening (HALO) and High Altitude High Opening (HAHO) parachute operations, Combat Divers, High Angle/Confined Space Rescue operations, Small Boat/Vehicle Craft utilization, Rescue Swimmers, and Battlefield Trauma/Paramedics*. All can fast rope/rappel/hoist from any vertical lift aircraft to both land and open ocean rescue objectives. All PJs can perform both static line and HALO jump operations utilizing boats, vehicles, or other equipment from any fixed wing aircraft. In addition, 1 in 12 personnel are tandem jump qualified and can HALO/ HAHO both equipment and non-jump personnel into the objective area. As required, all PJs can jump in with and utilize extrication devices to remove war fighters or civilians trapped in wreckage or collapse structures. PJs also utilize the latest subsurface technology to locate and recover submerged equipment or personnel."

The PJs came to being during the Vietnam War and during that war operated mainly out of Sikorsky MH-53 "Super Jolly Green Giant" helicopters. Each PJ had two green foot prints tattooed on their butt cheek. Two notables about PJs: 1) they are a tight team. At any given training base if one is asked to drop and do pushups the whole group does them with the individual. If someone asks to see their footprint tattoo they are obligated to show it. 2) Even our base commander wound up with the footprint tattoo, wanted or not. Only Don escaped this initiation and only because they never succeeded in drinking him under the table.

Always with the art, I would often stop off to do business in the base graphics shop. Here I met Don. He was in a traditional guardsman slot in Graphics because the only full time graphics position was filled. I encouraged him to take a full time administrator slot. I told him he could do it with ease and still have time to do his artwork. I agreed to train him should he be selected. He first worked in the orderly room for the 210th Rescue Squadron and when the rescue squadron came on board Don applied for and was hired as the Pararescue Section Administrator. Here he would spend this last 11 years in the military. He loved being on the team.

---

* In he early 1990s when the PJs joined the Alaska Air National Guard they were trained only to the EMT 1 level. Statement on Pararescue from the Air Force Mil site.

You now know that the PJs that made it through all the training were pretty special but ours were even more so. First they hired the Chief. He was one of the last PJs still on active duty who had served in Vietnam. He either knew personally or knew of, every one of the PJs around America. He hand picked 30 of the best of the best. One guy was previous Coast Guard and certified on all things boating; one was one of the best parachutist in the miliary and often asked to do demonstrations; one was an expert mountain climber; one an ice rescue expert and so on, best of the best.

The first thing the PJs did when coming to our base was paint big six foot long Jolly Green footprints on our Supply Transportation Building. As you drove on to our base the road came down a hill where at the top you could see the buildings all laid out. Our transportation building was almost dead center making these footprints very obvious.

I was incensed, "Wait a minute! These guys left the jolly green helicopters in Vietnam. They are on Blackhawk now. They need to get with the times" and the Alaskanization of the PJs began. Senator Stevens and the Armed Forces committee had procured us brand new Pave Hawk helicopters for the new rescue squadron. These are Blackhawk helicopters modified for rescue and aerial refueling. I went home, researched hawk footprints, and cut out a stencil from a 14 inch piece of cardboard that gave me 4 footprints. I went on base really early before anyone was hardly stirring. In the maintenance hanger I found a pair of military issue olive green coveralls laying around and borrowed them. I pulled my military issue cap down as low as I could and still see. Armed with black spray paint and my stencil I painted black hawk foot prints all the way up the door of their temporary quarters—a prefab building in the parking lot. I was witnessed but not recognized.

Boy were they mad about that. The PJs thought someone was calling them chickens… guess that Blackhawk theme went right over their heads. My friend Don advised me that the PJs held a war party meeting, were determined to find out who had done this, and intended to paint them green. Part of my job as an administrator was distribution. This required that I go across the base and up the hill to the Headquarters Building and pick up distribution each day. This was where the Wing Commander resided so if Mike had a meeting that day he would sometimes offer to bring distribution. On occasion I would be asked to drop off distribution at operations or maintenance since they were on my way. As I proceeded with my duties the next week I was prone to gossip. In the operations section I told people that the Maintenance troops had painted the PJs door and they were mad, after all someone in a maintenance cover-all was witnessed leaving the scene. In Maintenance I said that the supply troops had done it. In Supply I whispered that the cops had done it…

Friday at Mom's I filled in the family on my Alaskanization Program. One of my sisters wanted to be involved, so Phase II began. Until moving to North Carolina I could not sew well enough to even get by, in fact my military issue pants were taped up with duct tape instead of sewn. My sister however, could sew. We got bright yellow waterproof nylon material to make a flag. I cut out a black nylon silhouette of a Blackhawk helicopter with a hawk foot print cut out in the center. My sister sewed it in the middle of the flag. We used iron on letters to put their motto at the bottom, "That Others May Live." and she added real grommets to the corners so it could actually be run up a flag pole.

Paper distribution in the military was done in what we called Holey Joes (photo left). These were brown recyclable folders with blocks on the back where you wrote who it was going to. Then these were put through distribution. I took one Holey Joe and filled in seven blocks with other places that had nothing to do with me, put the flag in the folder and into distribution. The PJs loved it and mounted it behind Don's desk, right at the entrance of their building. The PJ Chief stopped me on base and accused me of making it. Without lying I said, "Chief, I cannot sew a lick." I showed him my taped hem and skedaddled. This flag was there above Don's desk until a visiting New York PJ unit stole it. Since we had not specified the 210th rescue on the flag, it applied to them as well.

At the time Don was just beginning his career as a selling artist. One of his first series was of the Native People of Alaska and they sold well on base. He was working on his first piece using colored inks and wanted to put a totem pole behind the Aleut boy that was the subject. By this time our Chief, Kenny, had taken a job at the Headquarters for the Alaska Air National Guard and his position or desk had not yet been filled. Beside his desk was a small 6 foot tall wooden totem pole. Don came to my office and asked if he could borrow the totem pole to draw from. I really thought it was Kenny's and he wouldn't know if it were gone for a week or so. He and I carried it across the parking lot to his office. When Mike returned from lunch he immediately noticed and demanded to know where he totem pole had gone. In a panic I went to Don's office to retrieve it, but by then the PJs knew about it and were not giving it up.

One interruption here. A friend of ours from the Guard died and his prints were sold to a gallery. In 2017 Don traveled to Alaska with a group including his brother and two friends. The day before the flew out of Anchorage for North Carolina they spent in downtown Anchorage. They were wandering in galleries and noticed some of Don's Native Prints (shown below).

Don went to the gallery owner and asked about them and found the man had died. The owner then asked if he knew Don Blackwell. Of course Don shook hands, introduced himself, and spent a time speaking with the delighted gallery owner.

Back to Mike's totem pole...That is when I learned about PJs and totem poles. PJs have a thing for totem poles. On Elmendorf the Canadians had special hardware added to their office wall so they could bolt their totem pole to the wall since the PJs had stolen it so many times. These guys were clapping Don on the back and cheering for him... their admin had stolen a totem pole. I had no idea what to do and kept stalling Mike about his missing totem pole.

Once again, Friday Night at Mom's, I filled in the family on the goings on. That weekend was a Guard training assembly and I had to work at the base. My sister called me at work and said I needed to come to Mom's house.

My mom was an architectural model maker and had a shop with table saws, sanders, a big band saw and all kinds of other equipment. When I arrived my sister had fabricated a 6 foot tall totem pole of sorts. It was a wooden base and core structure and covered in the poly urethane foam that my mom made her models from, all ready for carving and painting. We planned it out and by adding a foot and a half long beak made the top two feet into a black hawk. The second two feet we made a jolly green man using Hawaiian Tikis. The bottom two feet we had a place in the middle that said their motto, "That others May Live" with a red salmon in Native motif on each side of that.

We then called in our 'inside man' and Don came to see what we had done. He thought it was really cool and then told us the story of Charlie. Charlie is a small totem pole that looked very similar to the green man we had carved except it was equipped with PJ dive equipment like mask, snorkel and dive knife. There was only this one totem in the whole PJ arena, some 35 units. PJs were allowed to do anything short of death to steal this totem from another unit. It was currently in the possession of the Alaska unit who had scaled a building in New York to steal it and they had proudly showed it to Don. No problem, we could add those things and my sister had them fabricated in no time.

Now we had something to trade for Mike's totem, but we did not want any proof that we had done it. I called up the General that was the head of the Alaska Air National Guard and Assistant Adjutant General Air for the State of Alaska. I asked him if we could use his front yard. He laughed and replied, "Only if you tell me the story." Swearing him to secrecy, especially since his son was one of the newest PJs in training, I told him of the Alaskanization of the PJs. He was raised in Alaska graduating from Anchorage High School in 1961 and loved the whole story. My nephew delivered the finished totem to the Generals front yard. We hired a company called Pony Express to pick it up there and deliver it to the PJ Section. The PJ's jacked up the driver demanding to know where it came from and found the General's address to be a solid dead end. That night we stealthily extracted Mike's totem and returned it to him the next morning.

Meanwhile my sister, a medevac nurse, was working for the State of Alaska in the office that licensed medical certification. She began talking to the PJs and learned that they had some EMT training, and some EMT II training but no certifications to use this in the civilian sector. She proposed a project to her boss and got approval.

She then put the PJs through an extensive week long course and got them state EMT I/EMT II certification. Immediately it was recognized the importance of this to the State of Alaska so an EMT III course was added. At one meeting there were three sisters" me for the Air Guard, my sister just older than me that had done the medial training, and our oldest sister who got them college credit (she worked at University of Alaska Anchorage) for the training.

After all 30 of the Alaska PJs reached EMT III certification they were then each entered into a Paramedic Course. Once the Air Force recognized what was happening they changed the criteria for Pararescue training adding the Paramedic school on to the pipeline—Alaska leads the way.

The last Phase of this program had to do with driving to Homer. My sister and I would drive with my three boys to Homer, and across to Yukon Island, as often as we could. It is a 4+ hour drive from Anchorage and I would tell her my military adventures. I told her all about the cadences we would call out at basic training when we were marching. Surely you have heard of them beginning with, "Mama, mama, can't you see, what the Air Force's done to me…"

As we drove we made up a special cadence for Don and each of the 30 PJs. When we returned from the island I printed each cadence up on an 8 1/2 x 11 page. My sister bought a bundle of slats from Lowes. We put each page in a zip lock bag and then nailed it to the top of the slat. My sister wanted to dress the part. I loaned her military pants and t-shirt in olive green and a black military issue watch cap. We used black Halloween makeup to cover our faces.

By now the PJs had acquired permanent facility which was actually not located on the base. They were located in the Spenard area of Anchorage in the old Army Guard Armory on Airport Road. That evening we proceeded to the armory and spacing them 4-5 foot apart proceeded to cover their front lawn with all these cadence signs. While my sister was hammering one in and I was holding it steady the Anchorage police cruised into the armory parking lot. I whispered of their presence to my sister who said, "Just keep doing what were doing like we belong here." Sure enough the police watched us for a few minutes and then moved on.

While we were there my sister noticed that there was a tank on static display in front of the armory. She arrived one night with a flag she had sewn. It was basically red, with a big white explosion in the middle with large black letters spelling out, "Bang!" She had found a long pole like a banister rail and we safety wired the flag to the pole and the pole inside the main tank gun. The next morning it was a big hit with the PJs and many people driving by the armory to work. The Army Guard on the other hand, was not amused and made arrangements to remove their tank from the armory.

I had the opportunity to go on a temporary duty assignment with part of the PJ team. Don had been appointed as the 'Boatmaster' and his training was to begin in Homer. The head PJ was previously a Coast Guard member and could certify his boating safety class. Another PJ went along to do some diving. They had asked about the possibility of staying on our homestead on Yukon Island across from Homer. I asked if I could come along as cook and chief bottler washer and even assured him I could cook with vegetation found on the island - I was in. Don would later complete his training in Canada at the Rigid Hull Inflatable Course given by the Canadian Coast Guard and be a certified Boatmaster.

One of the things that Don was required to do was to plot a course in 'legs' on the chart he was given. He then had to estimate the speed and his time of arrival. How close he came was important. He got all his course plotted on the chart and we headed out. Each leg was in a specific direction marked as a straight line on the chart. For example, one might go precisely in a southern direction for 15 minutes, then make a 20 degree turn to the west for 15 minutes before making another turn, etc.

Don's plotted course had over a dozen legs. The first few turns were within the shelter of Yukon Island, then Elephant Rock and finally Hesketh Island. All these turns were completed precisely, on time, and without problems. As we rounded the southern end of Hesketh Island and headed for Seldovia, we encountered open ocean with enough breeze to make white caps on the waves. Don was driving the boat and trying to keep it up to speed so he could make each leg in the time allotted. I grew up on boats and knew to be observant and helpful. The boat, the Arctic Angel, has a canvas cover, supported by a metal frame, that was used to keep the sun off the boat driver when needed. For this trip it was folded down in the front of the boat. As we bounced over the waves at considerable speed, I noticed that the canvas and frame was coming up off the deck. I knew it could catch the wind like a sail and come flying back on us. I moved to the front of the boat to lash it down. I had to get on my knees to maintain my balance while I attempted this operation. It was rougher than I had anticipated bouncing over the waves I was lifting off the deck of the boat. The instructor told Don that he could fudge the time a little and still pass, but he needed to do something about his deck hand that was coming a foot off the deck. He brought the boat to a stop, we lashed down the canvas and frame and he was still within 2 minutes of his estimated arrival.

For dinner I cooked nettle balls with lambs quarter. Nettle balls taste like spinach and are the leaves of the nettle plant wrapped around your meat and cooked. They are tricky to pick without getting stung, there is a trick, but once cooked they no longer sting. The other PJ had gone diving and caught one single scallop so I cooked that for him as well. We had a commotion the next morning when I was making breakfast and a stellar jay decided to come in the cabin and demand his share. Don had to catch it before it beat itself silly on the big window.

The last part of this trip we stopped over and got a tour of a Coast Guard boat docked in Homer. Homer had always had a big seagoing buoy tender which is a big ship over 200 foot long. They had recently been assigned the US Coast Guard Cutter (USCGC) Roanoke Island. It was 110 feet of sleek and dangerous looking ship that was commissioned in Homer in 1992, practically brand new. We were assigned a very young one striper to give us a tour of the boat.

The Roanoke docked in Homer harbor. Photo by Isaac Wedin from Wikipedia..

The PJ named Mike that had been diving was quite a kidder. We began in the wheelhouse and Mike picked up the tube that we all knew was for the captain to speak to the engine room and asked if this was a tube for peeing in, cause he had to go real bad. The young seaman grabbed it from Mike saying, "No, no, no.... Sir!" and hung it back up where it belonged. As we traveled to the engine room we passed the armory alcove. Mike was in there in a flash touching all the guns locked to the walls, the young seaman almost wet himself trying to stop Mike.

In 1995 my marriage ended. I had taken all I could take, including taking refuge at my mother's, my sisters, the women's shelter, and on the Guard base. I felt like I was losing my soul. When I went to the base with my children because he was in a rage, I admit to enjoying seeing him planted face down in the dirt when he thought he could follow me on base despite the security police at the front gate. I had all the kids in therapy on Elmendorf and there were restraining orders not allowing him in the clinic there. I filed for divorce and he left Alaska. In 1996 the General asked me to come work for him at the Alaska Air National Guard Headquarters. My divorce had finally come through. I had to do the divorce all on my own because I could not even afford a lawyer and it took much longer this way but only cost $100.

I was greatly relieved to have it finally come through. The next day at work I saw the General in the personnel office and marched up and said, "Sergeant Czikra will never come to work for you in Headquarters." For a moment he just looked at me and then noticed my name tag and laughed. I had taken my maiden name, Abbott, back during the divorce. Moving to Headquarters was a change because there were 5 enlisted and 5 officers that worked together in the office. Most places there would be one officer, or maybe two, with a whole crew of enlisted worker bees. Also a big change because of the General that we worked with. He was completely a visionary man and smart, nothing went past him. He built his first personal computer in his garage when people didn't have them at home. He had wonderful quips and quotes. Here are a few of my favorites.

In the staff meeting the general pointed out that the conference room table needed replacing. He wanted a new one purchased and he wanted it to be solid wood so it would not fall apart like the one we had. He told the Chief, "Don't get any of that laminated chicken fat." I have used this for years since I heard him say that. Another favorite was when he was briefing us on a major change in the Alaska Guard. The Kulis Base Commander had done something really stupid and the general had no choice but to fire him. At the briefing with his staff when he explained that this would happen he did it this way. First, he explained that we really all were pigeons that lived on the tree that was out unit. Second he explained that as far as examples go for the lower level troops there was nothing quite like shooting a pigeon at the top and letting everyone see it fall on by. I loved this analogy.

I need to jump back to Kulis and the time before moving to Headquarters. I was assigned to the Battle Staff during exercises. This was a secure, locked down, area of operations. This included the flight operations command post and a conference room for all the commanders. Exercises were done in two 12-hour shifts and this made for long days where levity was always appreciated. We had recently gotten LAN (Local Aera Network) systems on the base.

This allowed instant messaging between people. No one was used to the system yet and the biggest hazard was leaving your password on the system because someone could come along and see your open terminal and send rude and inappropriate messages in your name.

At least half the commanders in the Battle staff were also aircrew and it is my contention that they are merciless with each other. The commander of one squadron had really gotten another commander who left his terminal open. Revenge was being looked for. Then that first commander misplaced his flightline access badge. It was turned into the Battle Staff and that was perfect for revenge. Everything in an exercise is reported in the logs. His flightline access badge was given to a young sergeant with the following instructions.

Go on the flightline, break into the cockpit of an aircraft and pretend that you are a terrorist. This whole scenario was written up in extensive detail. As the morning debrief began the speaker announced that there had been a terrorist attack and people needed to be more careful with their access badges. I watched everyone in the room check for theirs and this colonel turn white when he realized he did not have his. They played him hard and part way through he realized what was going on and moved from looking concerned to smirking at the other colonel and nodding in his direction like saying, "Okay, you got me this time...."

I mentioned that PJ Chief that was the last PJ active in Vietnam previously. In 1995, we held a special ceremony for the retirement of one of his bosom buddies. Staged at the drop zone on Fort Richardson Army Base. PJs and Combat Controllers, many from other US states participated. I was off duty but camera in hand, documented the occasion. Sixteen PJs and Combat Controllers, parachuted out of the Herc (HC-130) and eight PJs jumped low-level from the Pave Hawk helicopter. 27 jumpers in all—very impressive. There beside the runway, the ceremony was held as the Chief had arranged it.

Remember those colonel who gave each other such a hard time in Battle Staff? Don and I each had an opportunity to get him once. During that ceremony, after the jumpers had all landed, that colonel, the squadron commander, buzzed the air strip and then went up to altitude. As he did this maneuver I took a photo that looked like I was looking directly up at the rotor and the helicopter was inverted. I took this to the Sikorsky contractors on base, handed them the photo, and told them this particular colonel had inverted the helicopter. All kinds of dust was stirred before it was discovered to be a hoax.

Chief was reassigned to Headquarters as the Senior Enlisted Advisor. All these last years Don had been 'taking care of the Chief' and no copiers or computers were damaged as a result. When Chief came to headquarters he already knew me as I had helped him with administration duties before Don was hired in the position. He told me he didn't do email so each morning I printed out his emails for him to read. Don told me later he was dyslexic and just could not spend the time to read them all on the computer so he read the printed out emails during breaks, lunch and even after hours. Each morning he would come to me with his responses—between Don and I we took care of that PJ Chief for his whole time in the Alaska Air National Guard.

That helicopter colonel took an assignment to work at the Pentagon and there was a big party for his departure. The Chief and Don had lots of things cooked up no one else was party to. One of the things was awarding this colonel the honor of being an honorary Pararescueman. Its not often done because all the units in the Air Force and Air Guard must agree on this award. When that happens the awardee is given the special maroon beret. Chief asked Don up to help him do the presentation and I knew Don was up to something. They had the colonel at attention and then put the beret on him. After that particular award was over with, in this room packed with people, the colonel took this beret off to use it for a fan. He did not know that inside the hat was green dye and his forehead and hair were now Jolly Green.

Don and I were married at that armory in 1999. We had set out 300 chairs, half on one side for the military and half on the other side for civilians. My brother made us an arbor to get married under. With a special once in a life time license my sister married us. Don's son was his Best Man; his daughter and my middle son performed a candle ceremony joining the two families. My oldest son gave me away and youngest son was the ring bearer. We had initially hoped for a small family wedding but everyone kept asking if they would be invited. On the military side we had three generals and so many officers that no one below lieutenant colonel got a seat. The civilian side was filled with family, including Don's brother who few in from North Carolina, and friends from Anchorage to Homer.

Don had painted murals and signs all over Kulis Air Guard Base. Our general who headed the Alaska Air National Guard had retired, and we had a new general who is still a good friend of ours. He and his wife learned to decorate Ukrainian Eggs attending my mother's Friday night get-togethers. He loved Don's work and had Don design his 'general's coin.' Also, for the last three months Don was in the military, the general just had him paint murals at the Air Guard Headquarters in the National Guard Armory on Fort Richardson. (Photos of the Headquarters mural are at the end of this chapter.) Photos below, left to right, are: The 210th mural inside operations; The operations sign in front of the Operations Building; The Pararescue sign on the Armory.

Don was busy painting away and that colonel who got a green forehead was featured as the helicopter pilot. He had only joined the Alaska Air Guard when we picked up the rescue mission. One of the colonels that worked in Headquarters, a C-130 pilot, had been with the Alaska Guard for more than double the years. As he saw Don painting he complained and asked Don why he, of so many more years, was not featured in that mural. He wrote his name on a yellow post it note and left it on the wall for us to find the next morning. That night Don and I stayed late and he painted on the wall a funny stick figure with the colonels name below it. The next morning when he came in Don pointed to it and said, "See, Sir, you are in the mural too. It was up for a few days before Don painted over it.

Before I end this chapter I have to tell a few more stories. You might remember the big hoopla in 1988 over three gray whales trapped in the pack ice near Point Barrow, Alaska. 'Operation Breakthrough' was a rescue operation to get these juvenile whales free. Inupiat hunters had found the whales and their people stayed involved throughout. The oil companies from the North Slope, the Alaska National Guard, NOAA, Greenpeace and even Russia were also involved and it hit national news. The pentagon sent a captain up to participate and get them first hand news. She loved Alaska, and fell in love with our Adjutant General too, so she transferred to the Alaska Air National Guard and was assigned as our Transportation Officer.

As I mentioned before the Guard was much more informal than the Air Force and the Air Force was much more informal than anything at the Pentagon. Don was in Base Supply picking up an order and the Captain greeted him. She then looked at Don carefully and noticed his mustache did not meet the grooming standards of Air Force Regulation 35-10 because it extended beyond the corner of his mouth on both sides. In a serious officer tone she said, "Don, I believe your mustache is out of regulation." Quick thinking as always, Don stretched his mouth and lips out really wide so they were longer than his mustache and said, "No Ma'am." and quickly left the area. I told him later how the captain had stood speechless looking after him as he left. He told me he immediately advised his boss, the Chief, of what he had done. The Chief laughed long and hard.

The Rescue Angels was a project Don and I did together. The mascot of the rescue squadron is the Guardian Angel. We had several disasters including a crash of a tanker at Elmendorf and three of our Guardsmen had spouses killed in the crash. Our Adjutant General and several others died in an airplane crash. We had one family lose their home to a fire, one family had a son develop a brain tumor and needed home renovations. There were also other crisis's. The Family Support function was only allowed by law to give $500 to each of these crisis's. For the family who lost everything $500 is only a drop in the bucket. We had hoped to offset this so we formed a non-profit organization called The Rescue Angels. We intended for Don to do portraits of 12 female Guardsmen as angels and make a calendar from it for sale. Don had done the first angel, Kelly (top left) and her portrait was on the front of the Rescue Coordination Center booklet. She was a recruiter who had helped recruit some of the new PJs coming into the unit. Julie was the second angel (top right) who worked in another rescue unit, I think in Oregon. Her husband was a Guard rescue helicopter pilot. The third angel was me, all three of us had something to do with the forming of the 210th Rescue in Alaska, if only administrative help. Don was over come with work and never able to finish the rest of the angels.

When we retired we were friends with the woman who ran the Family Support function for our unit. Her husband was the colonel commander of the Civil Engineering Squadron. She took on our non-profit and not only the prints of the three angels that we produced but all the extra dinner dance posters were donated to this entity with a market value of around $30,000.

Speaking of dinner dance posters. Don's artwork commemorate and sponsored three dinner dances for the Alaska Air National Guard. Dinner Dance posters: (top) "The Aleutian Tigers" 1990; (bottom) "R & R In Hawaii" (the Vietnam War) 1991; (center) Victory "World War II V-Dance 1995".

The PJ that had been Don's first boat instructor was visiting the Aleutian Islands and noticed they had a copy of the limited edition print "The Aleutian Tigers" on display in their museum. He talked to the curator who told him he had flown to Seattle and won the print in an auction. That's when the PJ told him that Don lived in Anchorage and worked on his PJ Team.

The second story is much more recent. Not long ago Don was contacted on Facebook by a woman named Violet. Her husband, Sean, was the model for the Eskimo Scout in the 'Victory' print. Her husband had passed and she had only the one print and wanted to give a print to each of her children. We explained about them being with the Family Support unit. The Alaska Air National Guard had been joined with the Air Force on Elmendorf Air Force Base and they had moved from Kulis. She contacted them and no one could find those prints since they moved. Violet wrote again and explained it to Don. When we had the prints done in Alaska we needed a negative to print from. Once the negative was done we had a letter size stat made of the print for our files. Although the children would not have a limited edition numbered print, Don mailed one copy for each child of the unsigned stat to Violet who was overcome with his kindness.

The SAREX Prints. Don produced three Search and Rescue Exercise (SAREX) prints. We were in the first unit to do an exercise on Russian soil. The SAREX exercises were joint Alaska—Canada—Russia exercises, cooperation that had never been done before. For the first SAREX in 1993 Don chose to feature James Delong. He was a boat captain whose ship was caught in the icepack off Russia. He split his crew into three groups sent off in different directions to try to find help. Two of the groups did find help but the third, containing the captain, did not. When the rescuers found them the captain was frozen in the ice with his arm in the air and his Bible in his hand. The Russian city doing the exercise was Tiksi located at the top of Russia near where James Delong and his crew died. The Tiksi Museum had a whole section on James Delong . When the Americans and Canadians arrived things were tense and stand offish. People crossed their arms. The Americans had heard about 'these Russians.' The Russians had heard about 'those wild American cowboys.' Then the general in charge brought out the original to the James Delong print and donated it to their museum and it changed the whole face of the exercise. Vodka followed and friendships were cemented. In the out-briefing the Air Force Lieutenant General who was in charge of the mission told Don that he

had international impact and his artwork had broken the ice and made it all happen. We had small letter size prints made of the Delong print and with the sales proceeds bought crayons, paints, markers, and paper for the children of Tiksi.

The second SAREX print featured Ben Eielson, an American aviator, explorer and Alaskan bush pilot. Eielson Air Force Base in Fairbanks, Alaska is named in his honor. In 1929 while attempting to evacuate furs and personnel from a cargo vessel trapped in the Siberian ice, Eielson and his mechanic crashed and died in Siberia.

The third SAREX was actually held on Yukon Island in Alaska. My grandmother bought a piece of land that was once a Russian fox farm and my parents homesteaded next to it. On that land the exercise was staged. For that reason Don chose me as the model and three horses working in cooperation (standing for Alaska, Canada and Russia), pulling a Russian Troika.

Three things concerning this exercise on Yukon Island. First, they chose the flattest place on the island to land the helicopter carrying the three generals. When we were kids it was a pond we skated on. In the 1964 earthquake the island sank some 6 feet and the ocean at high tide took over the pond. I had corralled my three children up on to an old barge of my brothers that was up on blocks near by. The pilot of the helicopter was Don's commander.

the helicopter landed, the visitors disembarked and as he got ready to take off again the commander was startled to find a boy standing, under the rotor, next to his window grinning at him.

Eldred Passage is the waterway that runs on the East end of Yukon Island and at the point of the island is about a half a mile wide. All boats heading around Yukon Island must use Eldred Passage. One local boat maker was traveling home from town (Homer). When he came around the corner of Yukon Island in his normal manner, he found himself facing a helicopter hovering 10 feet off the water with a ladder with PJs on it hanging down. From the shore it was funny to see him suddenly veer off to avoid the helicopter.

The last story has to do with our friends in aerial port. The head packer was a good friend and even helped us build a cabin on Yukon Island. After the important people had left the island and the exercise was winding down he broke down the hospitality tent and cooking facilities and rigged it for the helicopter to pick it up and fly it to Homer. There it would be transferred to a C-130 and flown home. Our friend had just motioned for the load to be taken up when he looked down and found two little 10 year old children standing beside him watching the load be taken up. He said he nearly had a heart attack imagining the danger. Yes, one of them was a son of mine.

Below are photos of the mural in the Air Guard Headquarters. All Alaska Guardsmen at work, with the logo Don helped design in the middle it depicted a rescue helicopters with two PJs hoisting up; two maintenance troops hooking up a personnel carrier to a helicopter; two maintenance troops working on an aircraft engine; two firemen, the then newly acquired space mission with the shuttle taking off; the Headquarters Alaska Air Guard logo and an American bald eagle. The AKANG is always leading the way, in diversity and other ways so African American, Native American, Asian Pacific, Hispanic, Slavic, and plain old American Guardsmen were chosen for the mural.

Addendum One—Naughty boys and girls. As I write I remember some pranks and acts that went on…

F-4 Fighter pilots had a favorite entertainment at Spangdahlem and other bases. In the officers club they would line up 3 or 4 of the dining hall 8 foot tables, oil it down, and have carrier landings. A carrier landing was done by having the individual run across to the tables, launch themselves on to them and slide. The best landing was one that left the individual hanging off the table but not falling off completely.

TDY stands for Temporary Duty and was the name of trips that we made in the military. One TDY to Incirlik Air Base in Turkey nearly started an international incident when some airman stole the 4-foot in diameter brass gong from the NCO club. When the plane landed at Spangdahlem everyone was held at attention on the flightline beside the aircraft until the gong was recovered and could be returned to Incirlik. The base is shared by the US Air Force and the Turkish Air Force. It was their gong and they were royally pissed.

A TDY to Denmark came close to an international incident. Personnel from Spangdahlem traveled to Air Base Karup, the main air base of the Royal Danish Air Force for a joint NATO exercise. Everything went well for the first part of the exercise but then some airman got drunk and stole the Danish Base Commanders personal Mercedes Benz to go joy riding.

Last but not least is this story. When an officer makes the rank of colonel he should be pretty astute in his social graces. This one particular colonel was in the rescue business and knew me from the base. He also knew my just-older-than-me sister that offered the medial training to the PJs who were in his squadron. I have one brother and four sisters with ages stretching just under 20 years apart. He was at a social event in downtown Anchorage and saw my oldest sister. He went over to introduce himself and told he that she looked so much like the two of us that she must be the mother. With icy distain my oldest sister related that she was actually an older sister. Then she asked, "And who might you be?" At this point the colonel, sputtering out "I'm sorry's" said, "I wouldn't tell you that now for anything." Unfortunately for him she observed well and even took notes enough to have me easily identify who it was from her description.

That Friday night, (yes much happened on Friday nights), knowing how things were she began with telling me, "I met this Air Guard colonel." She then provided her astute description and asked me who that was. I had no trouble identifying who it was. Once I had told her his name, and she had duly noted that fact as well, she then told us the story of him calling her our mother.

Sometime later my mother, who was drafted in WWII and worked in the radiation labs in Seattle, was asked to speak at a Women's Day celebration at Kulis. It was held in the Operations Theater and this particular colonel was still the commander. I took delight in introducing her to him as 'My Real Mother." He did blush.

MILITARY PART 7—THINGS WRONG

I wasn't going to put a part in about all the things I found wrong with the military but have been told it would be only part of the story if I excluded it.

In my opinion the worst military fiasco happened in Alaska. I have tried very hard to confirm my facts but it appears that everything concerning this time period has been lost to time, or not uploaded to the internet, or purposely squashed. It is rather shameful.

In 1992 our wonderful Alaska Adjutant General (AG), Brigadier General Thomas Carroll Jr., died in a plane crash enroute to Juneau. It is sad that his father Adjutant General (Major General) Thomas Carroll also died in a plane crash at Valdez when our AG was a teenager. BG Carroll was a wonderful AG. I quote from his Anchorage Daily New obituary: "The father, like the son, was a quiet, enormously competent, gentle man a leader whose decency and concern for others concealed his own courage and outstanding military record. There was no vanity in his commitment to service and his life was one of modest honor." He was a good man and a great leader. It is also noted here that the current Adjutant General has been at his post for five years already.

I am not sure why after General Carroll's death they appointed as the new Adjutant General a regular Air Force commander. He may have been stationed in Alaska in the Air Force but he was woefully ignorant of the ways of Alaskans, particularly Native Alaskans. He did great damage in two short years. I was glad to see that the Alaska statutes now read that preference must be given in choosing an AG to Alaska Guard folks and that they also must be a citizen of the state. I firmly believe this was changed because of this disastrous appointment made by Governor Wally Hickel. When Wally Hickel left office, Governor Tony Knowles replaced the AG shortly after taking office. There was a reason it was called Wally World.

The choice of Governor Knowles was an excellent one—he chose Jake Lestenkof, pulling him from retirement for the appointment. General Lestenkof is a Native Alaskan of the Aleut people born in the Pribilof Islands. He had a career in the Alaska Army Guard. The Pribilof Islands are a group of four volcanic islands that are North of, but included in, the Aleutian Islands that extend over 1100 miles from the southwestern corner of the Alaska mainland. General Lestenkof is purportedly the highest ranking military officer of Native heritage. If Alaska looks like an elephants head, the Aleutians are the elephant's trunk.

One of the first actions by the AG appointed upon General Carroll's death was to require a no-notice urinary test of every Alaska Guardsman. Since smoking marijuana in Alaska was decriminalized in 1975, its use was   prevalent and for the most part accepted in Alaska. Marijuana use can show up in a urinary test even 30 days after smoking. I heard that nearly 50% of the rural Army Guardsmen failed. The rural Alaska Army Guard, begun as the Alaska Territorial Guard, or Eskimo Scouts, dated back to WWII and often was a family tradition bridging three generations. Everyone who tested positive was discharged. (Alaska Army Guardsman from one of Don's prints is shown on the right.)

This was a severe blow to family across rural Alaska and resulted in over 100 congressional inquiries being filed. I heard that we set two records: one for the most filed from one state in one period and two that there were more filed from Alaska that period than all other US states combined.

t also resulted in another critical problem—post closings. Apparently if a Guard base or post falls below 50% manned it must be closed. Many of the rural Army Guard posts were two or three people and this made them fall below the 50% manned criteria, creating the most closures at once in their history.

Don and General Lestenkof at the General's retirement ceremony are posed in front of the 5-panel pen and ink original piece they asked Don to do as the gift from the Alaska Air National Guard.

One of the first things General Lestenkof did was to hire the Hightower Group to come to Alaska and investigate this whole crisis. Since I can't seem to find any material on all this in my research I don't know if General Lestenkof was able to reopen any of the posts the previous AG had closed. It was a devastating period for the Alaska Guard.

One of General Lestenkof favorite things during his term as the Adjutant General was working on the Aleutian Island World War II National Monument on Attu Island. When Don agreed to do his retirement present, the General told Don his favorite things to be included in the piece. The two favorites on the far right in the photo (top right) were his Elmendorf AFB fighter ride and that Attu Island memorial. What an honor for Don to be asked to do this by one of the most famous of the Aleut people.

Many people don't know that the only enemy occupation in North America in WWII, was by the Japanese and it was in Alaska. Billy Mitchell said to Congress in 1935 "I believe that in the future, whoever holds Alaska will hold the world. I think it is the most important strategic place in the world." Japanese forces occupied Attu Island in the Aleutian Island chain in 1942 and it was believed they planned to make it an airbase from which attacks could be made on US forces in Alaska and on the west coast of the continental US. It would also give the Japanese a strategic position of Alaska's coast for controlling the sea lanes across the Northern Pacific Ocean. In the 1943 Battle of Attu units of the 7th U.S. Infantry Division, with the help of Canadian reconnaissance and fighter-bomber forces, took back the island.

Photo bottom right from *Orthodox Church in America* article, June 17, 2016 shows General Lestenkof in the turquoise jacket helping unveil a related monument at Saint Nicholas Church in Juneau.

Boris Merculief and General Jake Lestenkof unveil the monument

In WWII, some 800 Aleuts living in the Aleutian and Pribilof Islands were forced to resettle in camps in southeast Alaska. It was estimated that over ten percent of the evacuees perished with this move.

Charlie Siegel in Alaska
Pre-WWII

As I have said, my life is a series of circles and of things coming back around to me. As I write about a man from the Pribilof Islands (General Lestenkof), I think of my mentor, Charlie Siegel. His family was evacuated from the Pribilof Islands in 1942. Before signing up for the military in WWII he helped his family with the forced move to Southeast Alaska. He was a photographer in the Army Air Corps when it changed over to become the U.S. Air Force. He told me he got mumps, measles and chicken pox all within the first years of leaving the Pribilof Islands.

My father was not around much. He didn't live with us after my 7th grade school year. I was in high school when he died a few years later.

On Bainbridge Island, Washington, I had a cousin named Jimmy. He also hung out with Charlie. When Charlie needed a model for an ad he was placing, Jimmy came and got me. I was impossibly shy but Charlie coaxed me into modeling for that first advertisement. He would find interesting places to take Jimmy and I and he became a dear friend and mentor to me when I so desperately needed it. He was the resident Bainbridge Island photographer and his photo lab was my place of refuge and sanctuary. I became his photography model in exchange for lessons in photography from a professional photographer. He was the first of my modeling jobs.

WWII "Self- waiting for Incoming aircraft. Monitoring radio traffic. standing .... of AT-6. Our P-51's were coming home nearly dry! Dead Stick?? Compien, France 1945."

"Fürth 1946 · Self... 'Lookin Cool' Planning big photo mission. ...To Paris - no doubt... Note Helmet by window... great candle holder."

He taught me composition. He taught me about apertures, f-stops and lens filters. He taught me how to mix the chemicals for the developer, stop bath and fixer and to process film. We found innovative things to do during the developing process like shooting photos of my face in a double exposure with photos of fall leaves we had taken.

He mailed me a dozen photos of airplanes he had taken while in the Army Air Corps. They were my connection to him and with the photos above I kept them carefully in my wooden treasure box. It was an old cigar box from my dad. In Germany I told this colonel on Spangdahlem about them. He asked to borrow them to have them duplicated. I asked for them back and he told me they were too valuable to be carried around by some 20 year old airman. He stole them—people can be so mean.

As soon as I got home from school I escaped to Charlie's shop at Lynwood Center.

One time I brought my younger sister with me to see Charlie. We had a sort of secret Abbott language called Iggity. When she used it and said something to me Charlie asked about it. I explained how it worked. When we both needed to laugh he would ask me to say Igloo in Iggity (Iggity-Gliggity Oo). He said it sounded water in a creek. His pet name for me was Bubbly.

I kept in touch with Charlie after I left Bainbridge. We wrote pages long letters to each other from Hawaii and Germany. He encouraged me to continue photography and even photography modeling. He tole me he was very proud when I joined the Air Force. What a difference this man made in my life and I thank you, God, for the gift of his friendship.

(Top Photo) Charlie was the sponsor of our Bainbridge Island Independence Day Parade float. I think it was in 1968. My father came to visit with all his enthusiasm and we entered the festivities.

(Side Photos) Just by the length of my hair you can see over the years I modeled for Charlie.

(Bottom Right Photo) Charlie Siegel in his Lynwood Center Photography Shop on Bainbridge Island.

I would go on to model for Charlie even after high school. Bottom left photo is around 1972 with my Seattle roommate.

When I moved to Hawaii I completed a formal modeling course and even had a professional model portfolio. I only had small modeling jobs because I was too short but I did do a television commercial for Super Printer that aired in Honolulu. The only photo remaining from my modeling portfolio is in the bottom right. I sent a copy from Hawaii to my mom because I was wearing a dress she sewed me. We couldn't afford a high school prom dress so my mother had sewn one for me. It was a Holly Hobbie Doll type dress with puffed long sleeves and a high lace collar. It was sewn of a soft cotton fabric whose pattern was predominately white with lines of small yellow flowers with crisp green leaves. She strategically added lace and I loved that dress and felt beautiful when wearing it.

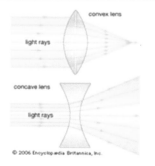

Convex lenses are thicker in their center than at their edges and concave are thinner in the center than at their edges.. Convex bulges and concave is hollowed out. Concave lenses are used for nearsighted glasses; Convex for farsighted. Image from Encyclopedia Brittanica.

My father loved science and science fiction stuff. When he worked at Pt Mugu Naval Station, science fiction author Robert A Heinlein's wife was their departments secretary. On our homestead there were stacks of old science fiction magazines. He often made science experiments into games.

When we lived back East he found this mail order science store. We got 8x10's of the first closeup photos of the moon when NASA's spacecraft took photos of it from space. I was in 5th grade when he bought a box of lenses from them. This was one nice cardboard box with decorative metal on the corners. It was filled with 25 different lenses each in their own small manilla envelope. Some were magnifying lenses, some were convex and some concave. Together with a toilet paper roll, a mirror and some of those lenses he and I made my very first kaleidoscope. I carried that around the world with me in my small treasure box until my boys destroyed it. I still collect them.

When my father's company made a model of the U.S. under sea vehicles for the Chicago Museum I got all the extra HO Gauge model stuff (buildings and scenery pieces). There was a deal in the back of my comic book from which I earned an HO Gauge train and he helped me build a train table. It was 8 feet by 8 feet with a lake and mountains. I learned about modeling with Perma-Scene.

This issue of **Scientific American** magazine, May 1963, was all about Moiré Patterns. My father bought me a set of Moiré Patterns. He was not around and I had no idea what they were so I took it all to Charlie. There was a cardstock thick printed pattern and two acetate, see through, matching patterns for each of the 10 or so patterns. About Moiré Patterns from Wikipedia: "Consider two patterns made of parallel and equidistant lines, e.g., vertical lines. The step of the first pattern is p, the step of the second is $p + \delta p$, with $0 < \delta p < p$. If the lines of the patterns are superimposed at the left of the figure, the shift between the lines increases when going to the right. After a given number of lines, the patterns are opposed: the lines of the second pattern are between the lines of the first pattern. If we look from a far distance, we have the feeling of pale zones when the lines are superimposed (there is white between the lines), and of dark zones when the lines are "opposed" "

When you lay one atop the other (as in one acetate on another or one acetate on the same card pattern) and move it, new and interesting patterns are created. I am tickled to say they are an optical interaction not an optical illusion. We read all the instructions in the book and performed the given experiments that came with the kit. Last we put a negative of a picture of me in the enlarger and while Charlie shot the picture I moved the moiré patterns under the enlarger lens.

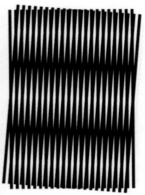

One of our dear friends said that I should never give up the hunt for my stolen Charlie photos. I can't remember the colonel's name but he did not work in maintenance. One possibility is this—they had an emergency situation and needed a Top Secret document typed. No admin on base had higher than Secret. Since my father had a Top Secret they chose me to do the typing needed over several days in the Headquarters. This could have been the event that led me to getting a special assignment to OSI Headquarters. This is my best guess of where I met the colonel. Another possibility is that he could have been an aircrew member that I debriefed, I frankly don't remember.

As we talked he said he was really interested in airplanes. I told him about the WWII aircraft photos Charlie had just sent me and I show them to him. He asked if he could borrow them to get copies made, and I said yes.

Before I left Spangdahlem, I went back to that colonel and asked for my photos back. He told me they were too valuable to be carried around by some 20 year old airman. He stole them in truth. He made it clear that if I, a lowly airman, made an issue about the photos it would not go well for me or my career in the Air Force. *I still want them back.*

Perhaps he is not even alive any longer, after all that was over 43 years ago. Perhaps he still has them, or perhaps he passed them down or gave them to someone else. If you have ever seen a small collection of photos of WWII aircraft, printed in black and white, on heavy duty photo paper, various sizes (with none bigger than 4" x 6") and each would have a description of the aircraft on the back in Charlie's distinctive writing (shown below left) that could be them. Below right are two photos of me at that time when I was stationed in Germany at Spangdahlem Air Base. I was Airman Phoebe Abbott. The black and white photo was from the base newspaper where I was recognized for drawing cartoons of all the aircrew assigned to the 81st Tactical Fighter Squadron. I was temporarily working in the 81st AMB Debriefing Office. If you are that colonel, please give me my precious photos back. The color photo is before we changed to POMO maintenance and I was in the Autopilot/Instruments Shop of 52nd Component Repair Squadron.

My dad was exciting to be around because he always had great ideas. He also had great charisma and would be the life of the party no matter the age of the party attendees.

While living in Virginia they did a model for the Chicago Museum of Technology. I have a cartoon of the operation to the right done by artist and illustrator, Pierre Mion.

Pierre Mion worked with Carl Sagan, Norman Rockwell, Jacques Cousteau, Isaac Asimov, Wernher Von Braun, among others, and was one of the main National Geographic illustrators in the 1950s and 60s.

At any rate around this time my father had his first heart attack, which I don't know if we three younger kids were even told anything but that he was not feeling well. With my mother and just older sister (who would trade off driving with my Mom), we left to spend the summer in Alaska, leaving him in D.C. This was a rough trip driving from Washington D.C., through Canada, to Homer, Alaska (around 5,000 miles) towing a fold up trailer to live in. There were us three youngest kids (I think Meg was 3, Melissa was 10 and I would turn 13 at the end of the summer), and my collie, Lady McBeth. Part way through Canada my dog got big ticks we found bloated with blood. Another time the axle broke on the trailer and took days to get fixed.

After the summer, instead of heading home to Maryland, we moved to Washington State without my dad. Details on what was happening was obviously above my pay grade, so I was in the dark about the what how and whys of this time. We had lived in a 4-bedroom house in a new subdivision in Maryland. We had real store bought clothing and extra shoes. We were upper middle class I would guess.

Now my father was gone, my two oldest siblings were gone, my mother had to get a fulltime job. The best one she could find was working in a model shop at an architectural firm for $2.50 per hour with four kids still in school. I am sure it was a difficult time for her.

Now that you know the definition, I say she was formidable because the first time I lied to her she truly inspired fear in me.

She was the most capable person I knew. She was like her mother. I was always small when I was young. At 5 years old I could pass for a large toddler. My mother taught swimming in California. When I was just crawling, I crawled out of my stroller and jumped in the water. My mom said it scared her to do it but she let me go down three times before dishing me out, hoping this will give me pause. It did not. I was like a fish in the water. I would climb the ladder to the high dive and walk out ready to jump. At about 24 inches tall this commanded attention and I waited for it, then jumped. (The photo below right was taken in California.)

I loved to climb and my brother had a tree house. He had nailed slats on the front to get up in it and just months old, still in diapers, I went right up them. My mother was scared I would fall out of the tree house and yet she wasn't sure the slats would hold her. When she finally got me down she made him take the slats off so I couldn't climb it.

Photo below is me at the top of the flag pole in Homer, Alaska with my sister, Melissa, below, holding the rope out of my way. Not long after conquering the tree house my mother, a girl scout leader, had a meeting. My older sisters and brother were supposed to be watching me but I climbed the flag pole in front of the building the meeting was in.

Some woman ran screaming into the meeting yelling, "There is a baby up the flag pole!"

In Homer I was 5 or 6 years old when climbing the flag pole we used to swing out over the valley. A woman at the nearby motel saw me and demanded my parents get me down before I got hurt. My father casually said, "She'll come down when she is ready." and shut the door.

Yukon Island is in the distance across Kachemak Bay.

My dad was exciting to be around because he always had great ideas. He also had great charisma and would be the life of the party no matter the age of the party attendees.

While living in Virginia they did a model for the Chicago Museum of Technology. I have a cartoon of the operation to the right done by artist and illustrator, Pierre Mion.

Pierre Mion worked with Carl Sagan, Norman Rockwell, Jacques Cousteau, Isaac Asimov, Wernher Von Braun, among others, and was one of the main National Geographic illustrators in the 1950s and 60s.

At any rate around this time my father had his first heart attack, which I don't know if we three younger kids were even told anything but that he was not feeling well. With my mother and just older sister (who would trade off driving with my Mom), we left to spend the summer in Alaska, leaving him in D.C. This was a rough trip driving from Washington D.C., through Canada, to Homer, Alaska (around 5,000 miles) towing a fold up trailer to live in. There were us three youngest kids (I think Meg was 3, Melissa was 10 and I would turn 13 at the end of the summer), and my collie, Lady McBeth. Part way through Canada my dog got big ticks we found bloated with blood. Another time the axle broke on the trailer and took days to get fixed.

After the summer, instead of heading home to Maryland, we moved to Washington State without my dad. Details on what was happening was obviously above my pay grade, so I was in the dark about the what how and whys of this time. We had lived in a 4-bedroom house in a new subdivision in Maryland. We had real store bought clothing and extra shoes. We were upper middle class I would guess.

Now my father was gone, my two oldest siblings were gone, my mother had to get a fulltime job. The best one she could find was working in a model shop at an architectural firm for $2.50 per hour with four kids still in school. I am sure it was a difficult time for her.

More than anything I feel sadness for her having to endure all that while being separated from her one true love. Did she know that my father was in the last few years of his life? Was he on a road to self-destruction and she chose not to stay and watch and that is why they separated? I will never know the answers. From then on we were raised solely by my single mother. They were tight times financially and yet I would benefit from knowing her burden and of seeing her throw back her shoulders back and go on. The bravest of the brave, that was my mother. And she was wise, and kind, and graceful and good.

Because she worked in the labs in Seattle and they could not afford to lose anyone, they drafted her in World War II. (Photo left is her draft notice at $1620 per year salary.) This is where she met my father. Here is the meeting in her own words.

I want to tell a couple stories which took place before we were married. I had ample warning! In the spring of 1942, just a few months after Pearl Harbor, the people of Seattle were very worried. We were really a prime target--Boeing, several huge shipyards, Fort Lewis, Bremerton Navy Base and the Naval Air Station on Lake Washington at Sand Point. We had black-out curtains, search light crews (one in Fos's front yard on Mercer Island) and anti aircraft crews. The young men who had not been drafted were either joining up or in an "essential" war related job. I was working for the Chemical Warfare Services (CWS). They had a lab (actually part of the building) to test the product of a company making activated charcoal for gas masks. Regular activated charcoal has preferential absorption. That is, it prefers the lower gases (tear gas, etc.) usually non-lethal) to the higher, more lethal gases--Mustard, Phosgene, etc. This meant that if a person had been exposed to say Phosgene and it had been satisfactorily removed by the activated charcoal, then had gone through some chloropierin gas (tear gas) which it preferred, it would give up the Phosgene in order to take on the chloropierin. Not good. To alleviate this problem, CWS had developed a liquid they called Whetlorizing solution (a combination of mostly ammonia and copper--very blue and very smelly. Bill and three other young engineers were hired sometime before I was there to get that part of the operation running. On my first day, the major (my boss) asked me to go out with a company man and check the empty weight and paint that weight on each barrel. The company man was Bill and he had a helper to bring the barrels on a hand cart. We got finished and Bill asked if I wanted a ride back to the major, so I hopped on. We went careening down through the plant, turned a corner and there stood Bill's boss and the major. The poor major stammered and could hardly get out "W-W-What are you d-d-doing, Miss Powell?" The next day, bulletin boards carried the message: No Fraternization between Company Employees and Chemical Warfare Service Personnel."

I want to include this other story my Mom wrote about her and my dad.

One more quick story.... Most "essential" companies were working 24 hours a day, seven days a week. I worked swing shift (4 PM to midnight) for a week, then two weeks graveyard (midnight to 8 AM) as I was taking 12 hours a week at the University of Washington. Bill worked on a rotating shift (2 days of each shift each week). He was also at the U of W when he could fit it in working on his graduate degree in wood chemistry. We often met for breakfast. As a result of all this my mother had not met Bill, so he was invited to dinner on a Sunday. The night before something had gotten jammed in an overhead valve in the Whetlorizing system. Before he was through, Bill was dyed blue from head to toe. When he arrived at my house the next morning, he wore a white shirt and tie, sleeves and neck buttoned tight and a very red face and hands. From 1/2" below his collar and 1/2" above his sleeves, he was completely blue. He finally confessed to my mother and showed her what his arms and legs looked like. She laughed and laughed.

We were married in March 1943 and left immediately to drive my 1933 Plymouth coupe to the Bay Area. Bill had been hired by Pan American to train as a flight engineer. We found a place up in the hills between Oakland and Berkeley and I went to work at the radiation lab on the Berkeley campus. At this point, Pan Am was flying out of the naval base at Treasure Island. Bill trained and flew as an assistant engineer on the Boeing Clipper from San Francisco to Hawaii for about six months. He had to join the Navy and was then loaned back to Pan Am--this in case they were captured and so would not be considered spies. He was then sent to Hawaii for six months and flew on PBM's and PB2Y3's (flying boats) from Hawaii to Brisbane, Australia, stopping periodically in the Marshall Islands, Fiji, and New Caledonia. They were primarily flying important parts and personnel. He returned to San Francisco a short time before Gretchen was born in May.

My Mom spent 23 years being a housewife (from 1943 until 1966) so her science education was now worthless. Having shared with my father building that model for the Chicago Museum she found she liked making models and had a great aptitude for it. While there at Naramore, Bain, Brady and Johanson she made many models including one of the King Dome before it was built. I don't have photos of those but do have photos of the ones she built in Alaska when she had her own company, Alice Abbott Models. Bottom 4 photos are the Sullivan Arena in Anchorage, still in operation. Top left a Wasilla, Alaska development in the 1990s. After the oil spill, she built a model of the Valdez super structure used in the court case. Here she jokingly put alcohol in the hand of the man on the bridge.

My Mom's models were used in advertisements, court cases and museum displays. Several are still in the Anchorage City Hall and were until recently in the Anchorage History Museum, but I think only one still remains in there. It is the one of the whole Exxon Valdez and I helped fabricate the generators on the deck of the ship. When she neared deadlines she hired us to help and paid $18 an hour so we were always willing. Top right is Kotzebue Hospital before it was built.

One of the unique characteristics of my Mom was her ability to change her relationships with people. She never placed them permanently in one status. By this I mean, when she was my mother she was in charge and make no mistake about it. She used psychology to bring us up right and as adults to keep us doing the right thing. But when we became adults she changed and never told us what to do, unlike others older than me. She would give advise if asked, she would warn if warranted but she opened the opportunity to be a friend. She was a very dear friend to me and to Don. After I got over my showing off as a teenager, angered at being blamed for things I did not do, which she gracefully apologized for later, we became friends. I took awhile to come to a peace with abuse done to me, certainly none by her, and she helped me get over all that and leave it behind.

I miss her every day. One of the things I am most grateful for is that Don and she became friends before she died. She told me how much she liked and respected Don and how she knew he was just a perfect partner for me… one true loves.

Here is an excerpt from my father's resume titled "Creative Concepts."

   1943-Contributions to high impact plastics
   1945-Experimentation with diboranes and elemental boron c
   1945-bonded wood chip panel board
   1947-constructed 3000°Celsius furnace
   1949-patent application on cermets
   1949-radar reflective ferrite paints
   1950-semiconducting sub-oxides of titanium
   1951-fiberous carbon
   1952-Al_2O_3 flame sprayer for refractory coatings
   1953-digital automatic oil well logging computer
   1954-automatic 200point oil field remote warning system
   1955-high pressure air regulator 3000psi +/- 0.1% accuracy
   1956-gas plasma studies, ionization of N to H spectra
   1957-hot press, 3000°C at 6000psi
   1958-sputtering of thin films of borides for ocean measurement
   1961-super-anisotropic materials for one axis conduction
   1961-saline sensitive films of borides for ocean measurement
   1962-design of expendable airborne bathythermograph
   1963-new concepts in high strength filaments
   U.S. Patent issued on Fibrous Carbon, September 1962.

PHILSOPHIES OF LIFE

RANDOM THOUGHTS

The Christmas party at Raven's Wing School of Art is over and they have all gone home. Today, in celebration of Christmas and before a two-week break, we held a potluck. People did art. People chatted and spoiled the dog. People browsed in the delicious contributions. And at lunch we all shared food and good company. This school is so much more than a classroom or a building. It is a companionship, a fellowship, a friendship. It is a bit of sanity in the craziness of life. It's a no politics, only love, zone. We give hugs.

We had the rush of folks coming. I had quiche to cook and a salmon ball to obviously not do the right way. There was either too much sour cream, or too much cream cheese or not enough salmon… it wasn't solid enough to pat into a ball even with way more pecans than usual. It slumped down immediately into a tall puddle mountain when I put it on the plate. Aarg.

Did I mention that I have a tall aversion toward strong fish smell. I have to be prepared before even opening tuna. We ate a LOT of tuna when I was in high school. Tuna salad, tuna casserole, and even tuna patties which we knew we were lucky to have. Either it was more expensive or they had not yet begun to pack it in water and it was oil saturated. Dish soap was nearly rationed. If you did not wring out that tuna properly, your whole meal would be oily. I have to this day not discovered a tool (other than big thick rubber gloves) that can allow you to easily drain that smelly tuna without storing the smell on your hands for hours afterwards. My imagination, or my good olfactory gifts, allowed me even with rigorous hand scrubbing to still smell the tuna hours later. Ew! In a good store those days you could find tuna for $1 a can and feed a whole family with that one can. When I was in high school my mom had to start over making $2.50 an hour, with four kids still at home – tuna it is! I have a special Irish tuna on toast recipe from my Mother-in-law. Moving on.

My aversion to the fish smell could be from the summer in Seward working on a herring operation when the smell of rotted fish could not be washed off. I think I should file a civil suit because I was complete traumatized by being unable to wash the smell of dead herring off my person. Two showers a day (was all allowed at my mom's house), for two weeks in a row, after which a stranger sniffed me and with a look of disgust asked, "Been fishing?" That is one of those life moments that unfortunately you never forget.

My life moments have been and are today a grand adventure. Sometimes you get stung by the nettles or bitten by a bee on those rare adventures but they are worth it for the delight at the end. Don and I have ventured through the deadly jungle and found the nirvana in the center. It is the end of the search. We have found just what we were looking for. It is a new adventure every day and it is good. We are richly blessed by God.

I am a water baby and have always loved being in the water, any water. In life today I imagine I am a fish swimming gladly gracefully amid the multi colored sea weeds weaving and waving with the flow. I admire the corals and the algae too. I see a friendly turtle with a big grin on his face just a munching away at algae, and I see small fish kissing the coral. As I swim my buddy, my love, my partner swims up beside me and we share a silly grin. We hold fins and glide together. It is a beautiful thing what Don and I have. Sometimes we swim in a whole school, sometimes we swim together, and we also swim alone as we create. The magic is that once we are done creating, and often part way through, we can't wait for the other to see what we have made.

With Don's help I have sloughed off that heavy coat that others forced upon me for much of my life. I have donned a wild warm but light weight purple coat with great fluff that sparkles as you move. Clothed as such I can dance like any fairy. It is an intense moment of freedom when you leap high deciding you will do what you will do without concern for the opinions of others. Of course, I do always consider the opinion of him, my love.

My heart just fills up with love when I watch him spin slowly around looking at our school, at his studio space, at how awesome and perfect it is for us. We feel such great joy sharing it with family, friends, students, and visitors. When you walk in the place smells of wood, raw wood that it is partly built from, antique wood that is in the walls, and carved wood of many flavors. There are eclectic things on the walls that hold interests for many people. There is color and warmth and a feeling of creativity and love.

I have come to know that I cannot always tell when sarcasm is being employed, or a joke is being played. Unlike most humans I see the world differently, it is as if things present to me visually as one pixel at a time. Slowly they evolve fitting together to form the final picture. There are so darn many pixels, too many really to count or track, that in survival at times I just take a snapshot, accepting things for what I see they are. This has resulted in mistakes. It might look like a fish, but if it doesn't smell like one too then it probably is not a fish. In   defense, I could say that I adopted the philosophy that the faster I moved, the quicker I got done, the less of a target I presented. I have the capacity to take out and examine the snapshot later to discover things I had not seen. With maturity I have learned to stop and look closer in the moment, to record more details in my snapshot. While a snapshot can be examined, nothing compares to the sounds, smells, tastes, and view of life happening. I try to really understand situations… what DO I hear, see, smell or taste and most importantly, what do I feel. If only I would listen more often to my feelings, for they are keener than I had thought.

DEEP INNER SILENCE
Deep inner silence exists for me not, Unless in Nod's world I am safely caught
For my mind chatters, bothers me all day, Even when I don't listen to what I have to say.

ADULT TOYS

I worked for Henderson County at one point and one of the supervisors of another branch and I were talking. He mentioned a cool desk sitting toy he has. I told him about one we have that is a small plastic crate that on one side has an eyeball and there is a button to press that makes it begin to yell, "EXCUSE ME, EXCUSE ME, EXCUSE ME… CAN YOU LET ME OUT OF

HERE!" My sister had an original one in which the crate was 2-2 ½ inches square and the crate wobbled down the table as well as yelling. Mine is a key ring remake. I have a number of points to make from this toy.

Number 1: The above story continued by me telling him that I had lots of fun small things in my adult toy box at home. This man looked at me like I was an alien insectoid. Again, I tell you I see the world differently. I went home and told my OTL the story. He threw back his head and laughed… apparently there are a whole line of sex toys that are commonly sold as "adult toys." I went back to that supervisor and explained my mistake. My adult toys are cool little science things, clever speaking animals, several Kaleidoscopes because I really like them, and one engineering marvel I got at the Seattle Science Center that closes to a 5-inch ball but can be opened into a wonder of 12 inches.

I have a toy that was my mothers, and is thereby very precious, because she had the same fascination for life that I have – mine just came later. My mother's fascination with life came to my notice in Germany. She came to visit when my son was born. I was stationed in Germany and with that 5-day old baby we toured Germany together. She pointed out the manmade engineering marvels like bridges with the cables in an upside down 'V' shape. She asked where the poverty was. She asked about the clean streets, the people, the military, the town, the surrounding area, the castles and ruins, the grape harvesters, the sky even. I was completely in awe. I rarely had met so curious a person. You see she had ridden through the many crises in her life and was at peace in her older age. She had a one true love and lived a life with him but he was now nearly 10 years gone. Her children were raised and off. When she came to Germany, she was, I think, 59 years old. She vibrated life. When I took her to the on-base bar some guy tried to pick her up and it tickled her pink. She had a wonderful sense of humor, especially when looking at life. My mom was formidable because she commanded my respect - she was intense, she was capable, and I might even swear that she could read minds. She was also one of the coolest moms a kid could have. I dragged my friends to my mom's house to meet her. She was kind and generous, she was loving and wise, she was my good friend.

Number 2: The reason that they are adult toys goes back to the time that I got my box of precious toys down when we had special visitors and two children, a brother and sister, grabbed for this orange squishy animal toy at the same time. Each got ahold of one end and they would not either let go or give in. As I watched they pulled and stretched that poor thing until with one loud pop, and a shower of some unknown liquid toy filler, it ripped in half. I took that box of toys and I put a sign on it. I had envisioned, "THIS BOX OF TOYS WILL ONLY BE VIEWED OR HANDLED BY RESPONSIBLE, KIND ADULTS!!" I sadly viewed the two limp plastic pieces that were handed over to me. After they left I on a hunt. I had to find the perfect container for my toys. It had to be able to be shut with a lid. I saved things downstairs and found a great one right away. It was a beautiful almost heirloom box. The box I found had no end handles or top handle so how was I to hang a sign because this box WOULD have a keep out sign on it. I had to design something that would not mar the box but would complement. Well, I did. As the time passed designing the tag for the box, I forgot how long a sentence I wanted. I got done with a very classy yet cute 3 x 5 index sized card that was perfect. At that point I looked at the paper where I had with anger written the sentence… "THIS BOX OF TOYS WILL ONLY BE VIEWED OR HANDLED BY RESPONSIBLE, KIND ADULTS!!" That is when I wrote Adult Toys on the small tag.

Number 3: I love toys and Legos are on the top of the heap. If I find an especially cool toy, I want to have it on hand to show and amaze someone who needs a smile in their day. My son has been known to announce, "We don't have time for Show N Tell today, Mom." Cool toys bring out the smile in all of us. I don't like my toys broken, grabbed, smashed, buried or even at times slobbered on. I have a sign about that in my art studio. Toys can be hard to replace (hence the above crate that while it does yell, does not modulate across the table.

Now I am well past the age of 59, but with circumstances our lives have evolved into a great thing. Now I can recognize that I have survived horrible traumas but I have the best partner a person could have. We support and inspire each other. He gives me peace and fire; he gives me comfort, guidance and advice… he gives me wings to fly. We share love unconditional. "…the greatest of these is love." (1Corinthians 13:13). Now I am my mother, I am curious. I am delighted. I am a wondering mind.

Number 4: Too many years of my life I was the person locked in the crate yelling? "EXCUSE ME!" EXCUSE ME!" You could just call me Beckon Call Betty. You might think this is a simple thing, this phrase excuse me but it is not. How many different ways have you heard the words, "EXCUSE ME!" used? I like the image of If you had one of those fabulous frilly skirts like in the original West Side Story, and you stomped up to some one and with great skirt swishing spit out, "EXCUSE **ME!**" Then you sashay right off that stage in perfection. That is one way of looking at it. Another way might be you could put on a thick mafioso accent and sneer, "WELL EXCUSE-A ME!" This attitude can be used while acting as a lady of the night as well and is most effective if you add Big Boy to the end of the phrase. You could pretend to be Fonzie on Happy Days. Saunter over, slump against the wall and give the look of pure disgust while sadly shaking your head in almost disbelief, as you question in distain, "EXCUSE ME???" You could be the shy forest fairy on her first day in town getting lost and softly whisper, trying carefully, shyly to get someone's attention saying, "EXCUSE ME". Or you could be one hornet angry teacher in the front of the class, waving a ruler around wildly! You as a class have been caught being way too rowdy for the premises and are being rudely called back into reality. "EXCUSE ME!" **EXCUSE ME!"** each progressively louder. There is an art to timing witty comments during these moments. I will warn you that teachers, and military basic training instructors don't take kindly to remarks from the peanut gallery during those golden moments. I assume there are many other categories of professionals, heathens and Vikings included, that would take this lack of discipline personally. It can be a dangerous world friend.

A Child
8/14/2012

You birth a child - such a wonder!
Joy claps in like mighty thunder.
This Gift. From Him.
It just fills you to the brim.
You fall right down, upon your knees,
Telling God, "Thank you!" and "Please,
Help me lead this little child
Let us dance together free and wild
Have us laugh and always play
Laughter ringing through the day.
Let me swell up with pride
In this person at my side.
Help me learn and to be wise,
To be all the awe in their eyes."
And God above, He Makes It So.
Your child grows and you know
You kept God's trust and raised him well
Grabbed and rang that victory bell
Delight rings out in youthful voice
For making, for having, "their own choice"
Adulthood beckons, draws them on....
Then Suddenly They Are Gone!!
Grief bedevils...
belittles....
betrays.
Consumed by it you're lost for days.
Frozen, solid, in sure disbelief
No one, no where, provides relief
Succumbed and feeling broken down
Doesn't matter what goes on around
Two will cling and together cry
But separate you will by and by
Alone to contemplate this truly, totally,
awful fate.

"Why, oh Why, God, Couldn't it
Wait?
Just one more minute, one more
smile,
Let me enjoy him so for another while,
I've been faithful, tried to be true,
Listened, accepted guidance from you,
But still for me you chose this path
Can I ask, "Did I incur your wrath?"
"STOP!" He yells, "Have you no faith?
You Listened Not To What I Saithe!
He is here, standing, with me,
He is just as happy as happy can be.
You will get to see him again,
Stay the course and you will win,
but only by listening when I speak,
for I am strong, you are meek.
You don't know my mysteries,
but you will, if you please
Just accept the gift I gave
Be strong! Be brave.
I love you and I love him,
Your child fair tickles my whim,
You raised him well,
I think he's swell!
Go on! Go on! Get Back To Work!
Don't let me see you squirm and shirk.
Your Father knows what's best for you.
Trust in Me - Live it True.
Tomorrow will come way too soon
When we three will stand and sing a
tune."

The End

IT'S A NEW BEGINNING
Oct 7 2016

It's a new beginning, a sprouting of wings you might say.
Like the new dawn, It brings great promise down our way.

We have hope and sure faith that have often saved the day.
They are gifts from Jesus, to whom we lovingly pray.

We are marching bravely on, knowing all will come out right.
We're blessed with enduring, walking on in God's sight.

Unresolved

Aug 16, 2023

The days slip by in silence

Leaving much unresolved.

Is this fate as some say,

Of my lack of being well involved?

ATTITUDE
August 2016
Everything is attitude,
And YOU decide that, Dude!
When things go quite wrong
You can sing a woe-me song.
Or you can learn and soldier on,
And start with gladness every dawn.
When things are hard it could be a test,
I know you want to do your best
And it could turn into a fabulous quest.
So this is to give you a bonus clue
Remember what and how you do
Is **completely** up to you.

CAVORTING CATERPILLARS
Sep 20, 2017
Their movement is so very slow,
It's not something our eyes can know.
But in the fall when the harvest is finally in,
And the days are so sunny that it's almost a sin,
Then every single size and sort
Of caterpillar begins to cavort.
They're bellies are full, needs are met
And to them it's the very best time yet!
So to a music only they can hear
They twitch and dance from head to rear
(the other third holds tight to the ground,
Cause they don't want to go tipping down.)
I saw it in God's technicolor too
It would really, totally, DEE-LIGHT you.
An intricate dance with a secret woven in,
Or a tale of some place they may have been.
Never the same length, never the same day,
But they all perform it the exact same way.
A mystery, a wonder, that I'm working through
And "just lettin' ya know in this here po-em for you."

AWHILE
May 29, 2015
When you frown,
your whole face sags down.
When you wear a cheery
smile
your face is perfect for
awhile.

Dieting
10/04/2012
Its quite a trial, arguing with my butt,
'Cause it's not even stuck in a silly rut...
It's homesteaded. Already cleared the land.
Built a cabin and now its striking up the band.
I have to wipe off that big dimply grin,
Drag it from that rut - it's really settled in!
You say convince it that fat is really bad,
When that's all its wanted or ever had?
It's a classical, learning, symphony.
A battle of huge proportions for me
That are filled with day dreams of pastries and butter
I'm floating in a sea of chocolate... (I shudder...)
.....
It **is** quite a trial but I am on that road
at least my heart is grateful for the lightening load.

DONS SPARKLE
August 2013
The sparkle in your eyes
Promised adventures bold and true,
So I took your hand
And traveled off with you.
We have battled storms that left us tattered and torn,
But we held each other through
Just as we had sworn.
We encountered dragons
And that toll was mighty too...
But somehow we survived
Always together
Me and you.
Oh we've seen such beauty
That it nearly snatched our breath away
We're trying to capture it in art,
Again
Each new day.
Still I see that sparkle
That promises adventures bold and true
And I thank God
That I get to experience
Them with you!

DEEPER LIGHTER TRUTH
September 2017

Below the shiny cover
hidden in the pages inside
can be an excellent adventure
wanting to take you on a ride.
Seek that deep and light filled truth
open that waiting book
you never know what you'll find
if you only take a look.

EVANGALISTIC BABIES
11/19/14
Evangelistic Babies come and tug on your clothes
They remind us our Father sees all and knows
how our actions tell a story too
You choose the actions that you do.

Evangelistic Babies sing with joy that's so large
it grips your heart and really takes change
Jesus touches us through their tiny hearts
that's when the magic really starts.

Evangelistic Babies changes lives and fortunes true
hopefully making better people of me and you
care well for this precious given gift
with it your life will renew and uplift.

FROM THAT SHORE
February 2018

I look for him in the shadows
Mischief sparkling in his eyes,
And yet I see him lifeless
Draped across my thighs.

Where has gone the child
For whom my hopes were so high?
My tears track down my face
As I ponder still I cry.

All the dreams we spoke of
All the hopes we held inside
For my beautiful boy child
On that day they died.

That was his path
Not my choice at all,
He was neither my puppet
My pet, or my doll.

Pride in his shoulders
I saw him meet life
Barely a challenge
Not for him a strife.

Smiling in wonder
That child filled my heart
I responded in awe
God's gift was pure art.

Again I am grieving
I know that I always will
Never will I find
I am not wanting him still.

Yet day by day
I accept the loss more
It has been an arduous swim
From that distant shore.

WORRY WART

May 2011

I'm a fussin' fidget worry wart
Who worries things too long
I can't stop thinking about them
And that's just plain wrong

Fussily the thoughts go round
Then round again in my head
This makes me fidget
In my chair or in my bed

I worry "What will happen?"
I worry "What can I do?"
My mom says all that worrying
Will make a wart come too.

So if you don't want warts
(Like I have everywhere)
Then make your worry status
Free of every care.

WILD THING
November 2017

I am a wild thing

Who does best out of doors,

So that's where I'll be

After my chores.

Winter or summer,

In the beauty of fall

And of course in spring

My most favorite of all.

Hearing the bird sing

Smelling the earth,

As seeds and life

Find rebirth.

Counting the petals

Kissing the wind

Finding adventure

Wherever I've been.

Wonder of wonders

Is all around me

And like all of nature

I must be free!

He Helped Me
Sep 20, 2017

One night when I was at my lowest
And struggled to just go on,
I fired up my imagination
For at least my thoughts were not foregone.

I thought of everything that was uglier
And things ever so much worse,
I lined them up like poetry
Made them rhyme like perfect verse.

Once I had them examined
And labeled each with a name
I found in comparison
My problems had shrunk in shame.

Then my mind felt relieved
As I turned toward His light,
And He hugged me and helped me
Straight through the night.

Life's Stages

My preacher tells us there are stages, that our life's path fulfills.

Beginning as babies learning to walk we have the spills.

Then the years of childhood when we learn our basic skills

A, B, C and times tables, this stage is the drills.

Followed on by the teen years and the challenge of the wills,

This hormone popping stage when we're all seeking thrills.

Now we get a home and a yard with all the frills,

Making this stage in life, the stage of bills.

As our life goes on, we've more aches and more ills,

This old age he tells me is the stage of pills.

Lastly our life force in this world stills.

And as we go to meet Jesus it's the stage of the wills.

Phoebe Blackwell

Oct 16, 2007

LORDY, LORDY

March 18, 2021

I tole the lady bout me an mah wife,

"We're both kinda weird," I said.

Well Lordy, Lordy, ain't we all,

Just what is raight in the head?"

She musta been a full blown professor

Sortin' my philosophizing out that way.

An better than all the rest,

I didn't even have to pay!!

My Heart is Full
Sep 20, 2017

Today is a special day
For 33 years ago today I gave birth
As a mother it changed me
I reevaluated my worth.
Such a delight was my son
So much laughter and life glowed out
I thought he would always
Be there to doubt
And to question
To wonder what something meant
But sadly that's just
Not how it went.
So today I celebrate
His birthday for him
With my love still filling
My heart to the brim.

My favorite dreams
October 14, 2011

The brightness of all flowers
I see them fourteen deep
The sound of Grampa's snoring
Lulling me to sleep.

I'm tasting snowflakes
Landing on my tongue
I am smelling ocean
By wind its waves are flung.

I feel my mama's heart
Cuddled here in her lap
These are my favorite dreams
When I take a nap.

ONE LITTLE SPIDER
October 14, 2011

One little spider hangs from a thread,
Two roly-poly's roll up and play dead.
Three silly centipedes tapping all their toes,
While four lovely lady bugs are sitting on a rose.
Five giddy grasshoppers hopping left and right,
Six flashy fireflies lighting up the night.
Seven silver moth friends sing to the moon,
Eight eager fleas make one itchy racoon.
Nine monarch butterflies travel from afar,
Ten bugs squished flat on the window of a car.
Now I have done my numbers one through ten.
Do you want me to recite them once again?

MAMMAS SWEET TEA
May 2014

Mammas sweet tea
With honey from a bee
chicken fried just right
Fireflies at night
Fall leaves of beauty
Apples crisp and fruity
Folks who love with heart
Views that fair inspire art
That's North Carolina to me
A place I am Blessed to be.

Parenting
July 2015

Being a parent is not easy
and there's ever so much to do
you can only try your best
and have hope you'll make it through.
Then you must send them flying
to taste life on their own
because it is a big mistake
to keep on tending them
after they have grown.

PRAY FOR MY AMERICANS

Pray for my Americans, scattered on cots in a
makeshift dorm
their tragedies' great in the aftermath of the storm.
But they are heroes, my heart is gladdened as I hear
and am moved by their stories, so that I've shed
many a tear.
And then when my heart leapt, when she sang
God's glory out
"Yes!" I am on my feet, joy giving a shout.
Those are my Americans every race and creed and hue
Brave and strong and honorable, they can be so true...
Carrying each other; comforting children in their fear;
Gripping in gladness when they finally find someone dear.
But working together always as only my Americans can
Even pets and children, and every woman and man.
9/1/2017

PEACE OF YUKON ISLAND

June 2014

Day is done

and our tools are finally stowed,

The Bay settles in calmness,

Like when it has just snowed.

The elephant wades happily

Amid the sunset glow

This is the peace of Yukon

That I've come to know.

JOY
Joy is a wonderful feeling
It can be enjoyed by all.
Your heart feels like flying
You shout out a rooster call
Joy is a gift from Jesus
He created it with you in mind
Surely it is the best feeling
That a lucky soul can find.
2018

STATES OF WORRY

I am a born worrier, I am having to stop and trust in God and that is a work in progress.

My mind can conjure up amazing scenarios of destruction. I have assisted in, been party to, or witnessed in astonishment an enormous number of "accidental" home destructions. I thought this was normal in a house hold of many children who play rough. At one point I was from one of the larger families growing up in Homer, Alaska.

Destruction can also be quite effective with just a few children, as in the three sons that I birthed, if their destructive tendencies are well-honed. Just ask my saintly husband. He thinks he is very far from sainthood. But anyone who takes on three highly intelligent, wholly belligerent, charmingly clever, out-of-control boys, in a 3-against-1 living situation and survives it with a friendly smile is in fact a saint.

Did I mention the 29 holes in the walls when he moved in? There were more and bigger after he moved in, but he is a patient man. Did I mention the youngest setting his room on fire the night Don moved in with us? Don had told me he was tough as a kid, "tough as a pine knot," but that my boys beat anything he'd ever seen. I think he said that as we watched my middle, red-headed son, ride a 100-foot falling spruce tree to the ground before our eyes. My oldest rolled my Subaru, airborne then back on to the wheels, denting all six sides, with his middle brother in the car, on the way to take SAT tests. That's the bad news. Good news is that the middle brother, in 7th grade at the time, scored in the top two percentile nationally in math on that exam. Just as his older brother had 4-years before, he qualified for the John Hopkins Talented Youth Program. The youngest was given and IQ Test when he was in 3rd grade. The test giver stated, "I have been testing kids in Alaska for 25 years and that is the brightest child I have ever met. These three against one … sainthood!

Three wild Indians with a mission: Get rid of this man who threatens to bring order to our mayhem. It did not take long for them to discover that household destruction floored my husband in its audacity and set him on his heels for a moment. It became the flavor of the day.

My father-in-law had always felt God had cheated him. He gave him a fine strapping boy a man could be proud of, but danged if that stallion could be broke! He then trusted that if he just waited, God would step in and reward him by giving his son wild uncontrollable children of his own. I'm sure he was bitterly disappointed when the man was blessed with two children that loved and respected their dad and did not go teen crazy and cause him untold heartache. No doubt my father-in-law probably prayed about God dealing him unfairly. Then this poor man entered my world. He would call his dad and relate the latest episode with my boys. His dad would laugh so hard he couldn't get his breath. Actually, his delight might have been spilling over when he told him, "Son, marry this girl so you can delight me with laughter in my old age. I dare you!" Don't dare my husband, or my kids, or me for that matter.

So began the war of the ages. I tried to warn him but he pshawed me. This was when I entered Third Phase Worry Syndrome.

The First Phase Worry Syndrome began when I birthed my first child. No matter how much I had babysat, nothing quite prepared me for the enormity of responsibility involved in being a parent. While that was bad enough my second child was born without a fear factor and there was just no telling what he might attempt. Suddenly I had three boys and was greatly outnumbered. Then I would see my boys dare each other to do something to annoy their abusive father. This usually happened so sneakily, so fast, that I would reach panic level before I could act to prevent their actions.

I could not take that any more so we soon were not married. Second Phase Worry Syndrome set in when I found myself a single mother of three wild boys and languished in heavy debt.

Third Phase was when I became involved with an amazing man that I knew was my destiny. I also knew he had to be able to survive my boys and heck, at that point, I couldn't get a day-long babysitter that would take all three. Three wild Indians on a mission is enough to make anyone worry.

Now years later one has passed, one had four boys of his own and lives in Alaska, and one lives a state away in South Carolina. I no longer have to worry about their day to day actions as they are responsible for their own.

Finally, I have harnessed my tendency to worry. Based on experience, my analysis is that you can only achieve this when you trust God. Things are going to happen, good and bad, that is the journey of life. You must meet these challenges head on. Their purpose is the forming of your character. You can survive if you just let go. Know that God is in control, it may be a mystery now, but one day you will understand. As long as you are on the path, trying your best, He takes all your worries away.

After The Storm

An unenhanced photo I took on a morning walk with our dog Kodiak (Kody) on April 10, 2021.

RAVEN AFFAIRS

RAVEN'S NEST

Feathering your nest is an important part of a bird's life. There must be a place where you can fluff out your feathers and lean back and relax. It must be kept free of cats and hawks. It can be a mobile nest, like the gypsy wagons or the circus cars. I would take one that was lined in silken pillows and shared with Don.

Of course, we would come up for air, … we have to ride atop the train and feel the excitement of the wind rushing by. Adventure comes to us on the prevailing wind and we glide through it with purpose and bravery.

Your nest can be carried on your back in a pack if you are not yet ready to settle. If you are very brave and extra mobile, one perfect pillow to lay your head on at night is all you need. Perhaps all you have time for is to pin and unpin your lost feather up on the wall.

There comes a time in most fowls lives, when settle is what you need to do. You need to just go ahead and build that nest. You can be a world flier, but still have an awesome nest to come home to.

That is what we have, an awesome nest. We also have been blessed with a wonderful, brave and ship-worthy crew of family and friends who are helping us with this home port creation. It is always changing, growing, improving... It is the Raven's Wing establishment and we call it Ravenswood.

We will feather it with gardens flowing down the healthy branches that touch the sky. We will have such learning, sharing, creating and inspirating that it permeates the entire tree. Joy will happen. Laughter will ring out and the notes of it dance like fairies down the branches and at each landing add sparkle to the twigs that border the nest. We will be watching for you.

RAVEN'S TOGETHER. The Ravens in this picture are: Up in the treehouse in progress… Don and Beth are holding a rope around a beam that loops over a branch. Josh is on a ladder on one end of the beam ready to nail it in. Larry is on a ladder at the other end of the beam nailing. Meanwhile, Norma is on the ground with a water cannon squirting Larry as he works. Next to her is Larry's wife Brenda saying, "OMG!"   Art is out on a branch wiring a lamp in. Monique and Bob are putting in parquet wood flooring tiles. Paul and Elias (with the big hammer) are on the deck building a box.   Hanging from the bottom of the deck is a big sign RAVEN'S WOOD SCHOOL OF ART. To the right of the tree trunk is a computer where Chris is working, and Rhonda and Faith are picnicking on the to the right of him. Below the deck on the lovely mossy surface lots is going on. Pat is teaching watercolor painting at one end. Denise is teaching colored pencil at the other end. Betsy, JC, Cornelia, and Gretchen have a brush in one hand and a pencil in the other ready to work. Phoebe is down front center pointing out where the next projects can be done. We are Ravens Together.

RAVEN'S QUILL

In February of 2020 we were stuck apart from everyone. We finally got the school built in 2019, opened our doors, and the pandemic hit. I decided to create a newsletter to cheer everyone up. I called it the Raven's Quill. It was the usual hodge podge for me containing Guild Goodies; Beyond the stick figure showing new students work; Birdasize yoga poses by a sky known yoga instructor; Raven Pearls from the deep (Boanthropy, frostnip, hyperbolic paraboloid, Truel a neologism, Gensis, Hawking and Adams quotes) and the claim that the Three Amigos were conspiring to build again. I didn't hear much of a peep until a month went by. Then the comments came, so in April I published my second Quill. Meanwhile, we built a strawberry patch; removed four truckloads of dirt to straighten the driveway and built a 100-foot long straight wall and called it the strip. We were having so much fun carting rocks around that we continued our wall on down to ring our Japanese maple tree, put in new dirt the length of the strip, moved plants from around the yard to fill it in, and bought and planted five new hydrangea bushes to go with the two we had. Next we flattened the driveway and added rocks, Don loved the tractor time, built a rock garden with a bridge

and grandkid painted stepping stones in the back yard; created a strawberry bed, planted a raspberry and a blueberry patch; sewed a bunch of covid masks; streamed way more television than we should have; used Larry's example and stationed grabber and gloves at the door to avoid human contact; and had a fence put in so Kodiak could run.

As I published the Quill, the topics, style and voice changed.

April 2020 edition maintained the Raven Pearls from the Deep (left); the Raven Tales from the Nest (right); and regular Raven Tales.

I did 10 in 2020 and an even dozen in 2021 and 2022. We are nearing 12 for 2023 which will be 34 editions.

Thoughtful Raven (above); Birdasize (above that); as well as Kid Art and Ink Blots.

In the May 2020 Edition our newly adopted dog, Kodiak, made the front page. Raven Tales from the Nest, Raven Pearls from the Deep, Raven Tales, Birdasize, Guild Goodies, Ink Blots and Kid Art stayed on board. And we added a new skiff to the fleet—Bird Brains.

The June edition had Raven Tales from the Nest; Guild Goodies, Bird Brains, regular Raven Tales, Ink Blots, Kid Art, Birdasize, Raven Pearls from the Deep and a Partridge in a Pear Tree (PIAPT). Not really a PIAPT included but I was feeling like it was getting so repetitious… And we brought aboard Contributions R Us.

July 2020, Edition 5 nothing changed and it was running 9 pages. August 2020 Edition 6 we added "What's Happnin' Round the Olde Homestead." and Last Looks and came in at 16 pages.

This is getting boring, beating a dead horse. Moving on... I have a summary of each of the Quills that you can look at and request a copy.

One of the best additions, in my mind, was Don's suggestion that we have an article called Study of the Masters. It would feature one artist per month and would be an in-depth look at that person from my own, un-art educated point of view. I have enjoyed doing this but as always have strayed from the line adding in Mark Tobey because he was my sister's favorite instructor, doing snow and sun art for one month, doing a whole family one month (Wyeth), and even Laurel Burch a personal favorite of mine but hardly classified as one of "the Masters."

I love adding the artwork and things people are working on and I try to find interesting stories, add an art technique or art topic (after all we are a school of art), and to publish the ever changing schedule of events. I hope people enjoy reading it as much as I enjoy compiling it. I don't ever get more than about 10 comments out of the more than 100 addressees. I am still wondering why that is.

RAVEN'S WING SCHOOL OF ART

Raven's Wing School of Art has become something truly special. Because it is a huge part of our life the story must be included. Logo by Phoebe Blackwell. This is the story of how a small white shed in our back yard has become a wonderful art school that is changing people's lives.

The Raven's Wing School of Art

By

Phoebe A. Blackwell

RENOVATION OF DORIS PLACE HOUSE IN ANCHORAGE

Before Don there were some very bad days. On two occasions I locked myself in a bathroom and painted it. The first was the bathroom between the kids playroom and the VHS storage room. I did this in 1994.

Back Bathroom Middle (or Second Floor)

The rocking chair my mother bought me to rock my babies in ... it was one of the few things really mine.

I actually began the first renovation by myself. I pulled up the bathroom floor of the main, front bathroom on the second floor. Underneath the linoleum was another old thin wood flooring. I worked at it hard for a time, prying up each board. My ex wanted dinner cooked so I went to do that. Meanwhile he worked on the floor by venting rage. He would smash the board near the wall on each side, throw the middle piece into the hall and shove the end pieces back into the wall. I never could get them out. We then put in a 3/4 inch plywood floor over the joists, added linoleum, and when we put in the nice pedestal sink I had bought we found a problem. The floor and wall were so far off level that it required an inch thick board behind the sink to attach it to the wall. This so infuriated my ex he left. I cut the board edges in the shapes of waves and painted the bathroom white. A few days later I locked myself in and painted whales on the walls. At one point this was registered at the Anchorage Women's Shelter as a way "to take back your life a wall at a time." 1994

The Whale
Bathroom

In 1998, Don and I began the real renovation of the house on Doris Place in Anchorage.

The first 'room' we did was the arctic entrance. This was a small 8 foot by 8 foot room at the front of the 2nd floor. It allowed you to come in the door, and shut the outer door (and weather out) before opening the inner door.

We spent an entire week and earned many blisters prying up the tiles in that small 10 x 10 space. They just poured glue down, 1/4 inch thick, and plunked the tiles in the glue.

Don picked out a great oak finishing board to top the wall paper that we pasted half way up the wall. It was like a wain-scotting effect. We add-ed a matching runner at the top.

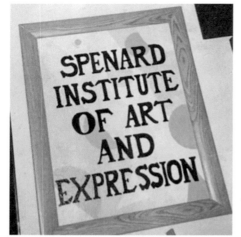

The next room we did was the dining room. Before Don, I had painted the room white. It was no small task after the two older boys had a sharpie marker fight in the room. Sharpie is very difficult to paint over. I finally had to use white out on each and every mark, then paint over that.

Don and I installed cork board on the outer wall to display the artwork the boys were doing in school. I painted 'Spenard Institute of Art and Expression' on the wall, and Don used oak boards to frame it so it looked like a framed painting.

My mom helped us build a long planter on the half wall that was there.

Third floor boys bathroom.

When we pulled up this linoleum floor we found beneath it was pressboard with rat tracks chewed in a maze like pattern. By the toilet you could see all the way pulled up the pressboard we found the tar paper from the roof they built directly on.

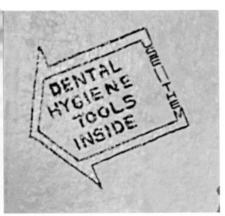

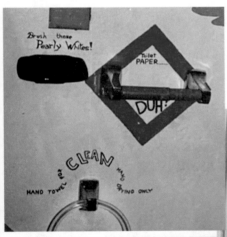

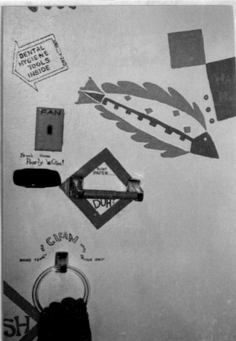

We painted the living room a purple so light it was almost white. I painted the door to the 1st floor (we called it the basement) purple with iris's going down the side and a string of purple polymer beads I made. The circle on the door was my interpretation of the celestial symbols for the day Don and I got together.

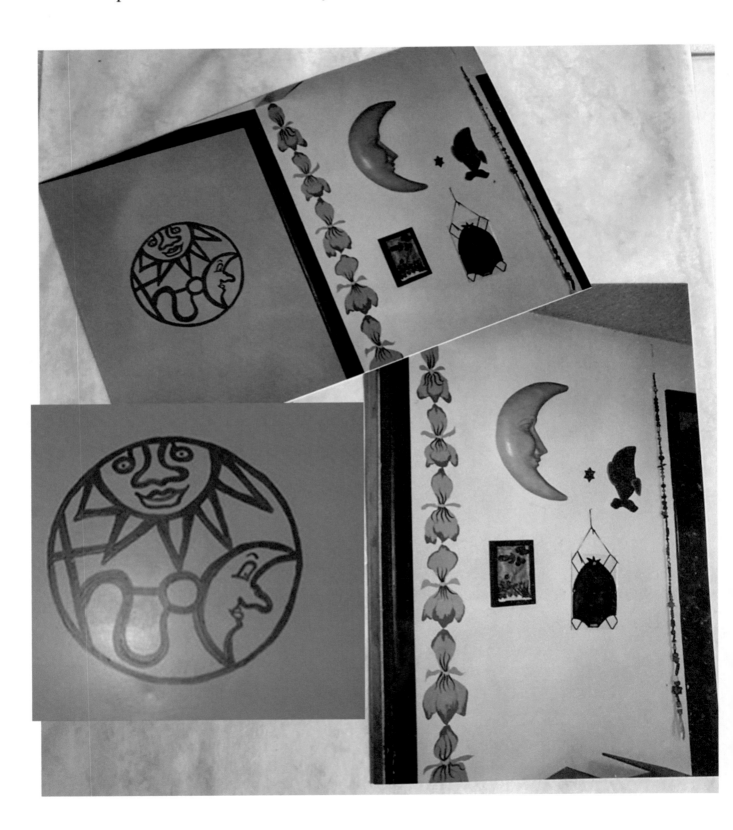

We moved the boys 'playroom' upstairs to the old kitchen area and took that room for our bedroom. We found a wonderful nautical runner and decorated the room to match that. We did not paint over the measure on the wall where the boys height and ages had been marked for years.

My brother-in-law, Vern, said he would help Don replace the kitchen floor. There were waves in the floor and we thought it was from the fire that was once in the house. Where the ceiling was torn open on the first floor (directly below the second floor kitchen), we could see some of the beams were charred.

They pulled up the kitchen floor linoleum, then the wood below, then the wood below that. The brother-in-law took one look, put his tools down and told Don they were done for the day. In true Alaskan style he said he would need to go home and get drunk and think about how this could be fixed. The joists did not go all the way across. One on the left came half or three quarters of the way across the area, then the next joist was all the way across, but the following one came only part way across from the right. That was what was causing the sinking places.

After the floor was fixed and new linoleum put down Don bought a brand new stove and dishwasher. One of the boys sprang the door hinges of the dishwasher the very first week we had it.

It wasn't like they used the dishwasher, they put the door down to stand on it to get something up in the cupboard!

They had learned from my ex to do no 'women's work' and until Don got them trained, lived like pigs. The photo top right was dirty dishes from one trip down to the boys room. We moved the two older boys downstairs first, and when our niece, Beth, came to live with us we put her in a room on the 3rd floor. I painted the wall to welcome her (photo bottom right).

So many things had to be unlearned, like that pink and purple were 'girly colors' no boy would like.

The boys were not pleased with the purple in the living room and rudely told me (waving a hand at the top of the stairs), "The purple stops here!"

From where they drew the line at the top of the stairs I painted the stairs down first a pale baby blue. Then I drew all kinds of characters on the walls, being most intrigued with those of Native American culture. Then using sponges I added dark green and dark blue in a pattern where ever there was not a design.

Before all this was done Don hired an electrician to come to remove the disposal we had cut off and professionally install the dishwasher. The guy was amazed no one was electrocuted when he found the wires my ex had left laying on a 2x4 behind the dishwasher.

We had a different electrical company come and fix the electrical for the house to stop blowing fuses. $3500 later we had a new electrical service. I was kind of worried it would not work out when the guy stuck a screw driver in the box outside and it arched electricity so we saw it inside our bedroom, with the curtains closed, and it welded the fuse box door up and open.

Thank God for Don's fast reflexes as the guy had asked him to hold the door open and he let go when the guy stuck his screw driver in the old fuse space.

In order to begin renovating the third floor we decided to move Chris down with the older boys. There was severe conflict between Nicholas and Chris so we built a wall sectioning off another room for Chris. We installed an all new locking door for his peace of mind. (Nicholas would later take a chisel to break into the room.) The new wall created a hall to his room. I painted "Entering The Home of " at the front of the hall and bricks and ivy down the left side. On the other side we mounted book shelves for his many books. Chris was an avid reader and a special fan of the Harry Potter books which he practically memorized.

Don painted a wonderful flying Harry Potter breaking out of the bricks at the end of the hall which you saw as soon as you entered the hall.

In Chris's bedroom we painted the walls orange, his favorite color at that time. We sewed curtains for all the windows. Then I covered the walls with Pokémon figures. Still to this day Pokémon is one of his favorite characters.

In the bathroom I continued the castle wall brick theme from the hallway and painted more Harry Potter castle type things: Hogwarts class flags, filled specimen jars, Owl Post Service, a castle window, and a sconce with flame.

When we pulled up the carpet on the third floor there were pieces of scrap wood   puzzle fitted together on top of the tar paper roof. They then added three pads and the rug. We had to actually install a wood floor before carpet could be laid.

As we had gone doing rooms we had found that there was not a single straight wall or ceiling in the whole house. We had a professional builder come in and install wall to wall carpeting on the whole second and third floors and part of the first floor. We had an inspection and were told that we needed a third floor egress window, so we also had that professionally installed.

All during the time we were renovating, working full time, and raising three unruly boys, we were also getting our spot on the island cleared and ready.

The first year we had my family mark where they wanted the road to go. We then went down in March 2002 with the boys and our nephew in the winter and cleared a car wide road a half mile through the woods. This gave us access to our site from the most land able beach. In April Don went down and with a crew put the foundation for our cabin in. He had to cut more trees to make a corduroy road through the swampy parts. Spring and fall in Alaska are bogs of mud.

In May not only did we get the house sold but we had our cabin logs delivered on the island and paid the bull dozer driver extra to clean up the road. We now had $10,000 invested just in the road and family comments were made about it being "a scar on the landscape."

On our anniversary, June 9th, we vacated Anchorage, moved to the island, and work on building the cabin began.

It was a dream we had and we seriously put our blood, sweat, and tears into the making of it… but God had other plans.

A corduroy road or log road is a type of road or timber trackway made by placing logs, perpendicular to the direction of the road over a low or swampy area. The result is an improvement over impassable mud or dirt roads, yet rough in the best of conditions and a hazard to horses due to shifting loose logs.   Wikipedia

The original photo (left) of the proverbial saying, 'See no evil, hear no evil, speak no evil' was done in June 1999 during our honeymoon on the island. Don, Phoebe and Paul.

This later became a much loved tradition with out grandkids.

2014

2017

2018

2023

September you come again,
And I yearn for my lost son
In the month he was born.
Another link the woven chain
Since my son was sadly done.
My heart is still forlorn.
Memory travels back to pain
How comfort was none,
Your death like a thorn,
Yet you play in my brain.
I see you wildly run...
Ah September I mourn.

You sparkled and stole my heart
Yet stayed some how a bit apart.
It was more than just your way
Or the way you sassily swayed.
You were here such a short time
Never even to reach your prime.
Gone before you 'en started in
With all that you could have been.
You know I miss you every day
My son who was so wild and fey.

Thoughts of Nicholas September 2nd, 2024

The Quill

I love to research, compile, write and philosophize. I imagine it could be said that I have D of the Q (Diarrhea of the Quill), not a pretty picture, eh?

In 2020 when the Pandemic hit we were disappointed to close the school and miss seeing everyone on a regular basis, but we knew we could not take the chance of spreading Covid more than it   already was.

In February I made the first newsletter for our school to keep everyone in touch. I named it "The Raven's Quill" since we are Raven's Wing Studios and the Raven's Wing School of Art.

This first edition was only 11 pages but had raven stories from Native Americans and quotes and photos of artists at work in all levels.

March I was hospitalized so an issue to did not happen but I was back in form and issued one in April which shrunk to 9 pages. From then on I produced one per month. A few kind people give me feedback and although it goes out to a whole list of people most don't say a thing.

By June I added in 'Contributions R Us' and began putting in photos of artwork and photos people contributed. In December I added in articles about Christmas and the new year (2021) began writing about holidays and their meanings, monthly info from the tree to the gem to the flower of the month.

Most of the Quill's feature some article on doing art, from what kind of wood is best to carve, to what paper is best for what medium. I write to celebrate achievements of our friends and family; I have added in lots of Native American raven tales; and even an article on a Gee Haw Wimmy Doodle (from Larry Fitz).

March 2021 I added in 'Stars for Safety' and did safety articles monthly until October 2022.

There have been spots of Tools of the Trade, Granny Raven's Good Advice, Exercise those Bird Brains, Around the Homestead, Historically Speaking and even Art Challenges (that no one did as far as I know….)

While working on the May 2022 edition I asked Don if there was something he would like to see in the Quill. He responded that he would like me to feature one famous artist per month, so May 2002 saw the addition of "Study of the Masters" beginning with Claude Monet.

By October 2022 I figured I had covered all the safety issues I could think of, and Stars for Safety was dropped. But by now the editions were all past 20 pages long, included whatever eclectic subject popped into my head from animals to climate change to jokes and astronomy.

I have now completed 47 Quills and really enjoy creating them. The front always has the current school schedule, page two announcements, and then photos of artists at work or artwork in progress. I have a summary of all the Quills and when someone is added to the email list I send them this summary so they can write back and ask for earlier editions. Of course there is often my artwork in the different areas.

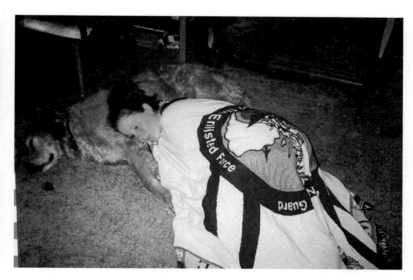

THE UNDER AUNT PHOEBE'S TABLE SERIES

#1 or first generation. Beth (better known as Elizabeth Anne Blackwell) begins the 'Under Aunt Phoebe's Table Series.' In Anchorage nightly we would read aloud to the kids. We went through the Harry Potter books this way. Beth remembers this as some of her favorite childhood memories. She would grab a blanket and either lie under the table or on the dog named Gabe. Later our dog named Kodiak would enjoy sitting on her when she was living with us in 2019. #2 or second generation. Photo bottom left is three of our great nieces (left to right Noelle, Jalon and Faith). The one with the Pink Sleeves on the right hand end is Beth's daughter Faith, the other two are daughter's of Beth's sister, Tiffany. #3 or third generation. Photo bottom right is our great-great nephew. He is Beth's grandson, Findlay Elias.

Three generations laying, playing and crawling under our table are blessings all.

This picture reminds me of so many things. I have to add a few of them here. This photo was taken at our home at 302 Old Courthouse Road NE, Vienna Virginia. I might have mentioned living right up against a gold course. Google maps tells me it is Westwood Country Club.

The ropes were for climbing back up on to the porch from the yard below, the porch poles were 4 inch round steel poles, perfect for sliding down.

My younger sister and I sang in the church children's choir and were dressed for a holiday performance. Behind us you can see a bulldozer. This housing development near Tyson's Corner was just new. While we lived there they began constructing the house next door. Often there was a window left open and we kids would sneak in and play in there after the construction crew had gone home. By the time they were putting in flooring and cabinets we felt like it was our playground. I think there were eight of us: Guy, the boy who lived across the street, and I were both 10 years old; my younger sister was there; his younger brother was there; we had a friend named Sheri, and I think the other three were cousins of Guys that were visiting. We had been playing hide and go seek and had all met in the kitchen when suddenly the front door opened. I whispered "Get in the cabinets" and we all climbed into the nearest kitchen cabinet. Guy and I were under the sink which had a sort of vent in the cabinet door you could see out of.   The realtor was showing the house to prospective buyers, a mom and dad and two kids. We heard them go all through the rooms and quietly, well except for a few quiet giggles, stayed put in our cabinets. Finally they entered the kitchen. By now the kids were getting bored and the boy wandered over and opened a cabinet, only to find a child there. He quickly shut the door and got his sister. He brought her over and opened the cabinet, showed her the child, and shut the door. They crossed to the other side and opened another cabinet and found another child.

We then saw them begin to tug on their dad's arm and we knew the game was about up. We agreed the best exit was out the dining room sliding glass door on to the porch, slide down the porch poles to the ground and run. Guy and I being under the sink discussed this but the others couldn't hear us. When the kid finally got his dad's attention and the adults finally heard that there were kids in the cabinets, Guy yelled "Bail Out" and all eight of us spilled from the cabinets and tried to run. Guy and I did make it out and were in the recreation "rec" room downstairs in our house when the policeman brought my sister home.

Another time in this same house, my mom was having bridge club. She carefully fed us early and told us in no uncertain terms we were to stay in our room, or stay downstairs in the rec room. We were not allowed to come through the living room where the ladies would be. We were in our bedroom but quickly got bored and wished we were in the rec room instead. Since we didn't want to get in trouble by going through the living room we opened our window, unsnapped the screen, and were crawling out so we could run around to the back yard, one floor down, where the door to the rec room was. Just as we were exiting the window a police car drove by and seeing something suspicious shined their flashlight on us and yelled "Hey!" We dropped the screen we were trying to re-hook, ran around the house to the back yard, whipped in the back door and into the rec room. There we stood, holding the door shut with our backs, in the dark, scared and giggling, waiting to see if we were caught.

Photo right:

Front row, left to right:
Sheri, Melissa, Guy's little
brother, and Guy. I am
kneeling behind them.

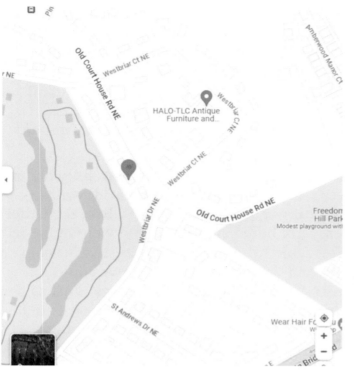

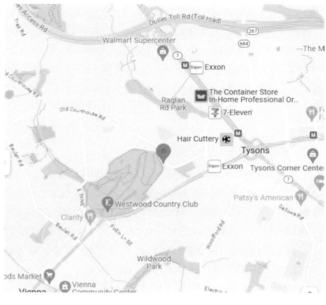

Top are two Google maps, left the red arrow shows where our house was backed up to the golf course. Right shows how close to Tyson's Corner we lived.

Center left is what Google Maps shows the house looks like now.

Bottom left photo is the corner of Old Court House Rd NE and Westbriar Drive NE in Vienna.

When we were young this was a huge drainage system with a square cement enclosure we could crawl into and play in. At the front was a long slot slot to look out at the street. It made the perfect bunker like fort.

Looks like they had to modify it by putting that red metal steel piece in the side walk to allow access but keep the kids out.

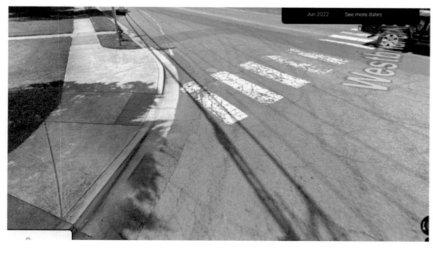

Okay… the Finale!

I now give my self permission to move on to another project, having reached the goal of writing a novel. Thank you to so many people…. Josh first and foremost. He is here every day and our lives are richer, easier and more fun because he is. Then in proper alphabetical order… Art, Beth, Betsy, Bob, Brenda, Bunny, Cornelia, David, Denise, Doc Tate, Elias, Gene, Ginney, Gretchen, JC, John, Larry, Marilyn, Marsha, Monique, Norma, Pat, Paul, Richard, Sherlyn (and Amy if she comes back). They are our friends, our clan, our tribe and our family. We are blessed in them.

Don and I are on a journey. We have enjoyed knowing so many other military buddies, students and friends along the way that there are too many to list but you know who you are. I feel the luckiest person alive to be his chosen mate on this journey. He shouldered my awful baggage way too long. He is the person who taught me how to completely put that baggage down and walk away from it.   Don came upon me and saw a neglected flower upon the side of the trail. He gently up rooted me replanting me in a place of magical love where I feel I have finally bloomed. He is the best of tenders and has supplied fresh, honest light, and the water of love. What a life we have…

Don has been long on a journey. I have studied many fine artists in my writing of the Raven's Quill, our newsletter. The thing that makes them great is the tremendous passion that they throw into their work until it is alive. Don has that imbedded passion...

…Miss Bea was so thrilled to have a small set of Don's prints. In her lovely British accent she told him that she placed them on her dresser where they would be the first view when she woke up in the morning. Each night she would turn out the light, shuffle the order of the prints and without looking place them on the dresser. Each morning they were a delightful surprise she said. I imagine her with her sweet face, tilting her head as she looks over at the little black bear in the tree and says, "Good Morning you sweet dear!"

…Hearing of Kit Frey's grandson loving to just gaze at this creature so alive in Don's print that this toddler believed he could talk to it, and he did. There is the story of the lady from the builder supply down the street who said they created a table for Don's carving   because they liked to talk to him as they passed.

There are so many stories of the positive, lasting effect Don's artwork has had on folks.

And yet, even as we speak of his talent for artwork, I tell you his talent for teaching is perhaps greater. If you could see the look on the face of his Beginning Drawing students when they hold up their amazing final project or the look on another artists face when he analyzes and praises the work they have put their passion into creating. It is his belief in them that gives them the freedom to express themselves freely, the dam is opened and the stream flows merrily.

That is why I believe it is time…. Don's time to be specific.

Feng Ming Chao Yang

Talent succeeds at the proper time.
9/12/2016

If Don would let me I would paint all our walls.

I painted this mini mural (photo above) in 2016, a few years after the kitchen was re-done. It is the Phoenix singing to the rising sun. In Chinese symbolism it means that "Talent succeeds at the proper time" (Feng Ming Chao Yang according to my *Chinese Folk Designs* book where I copied this from). I painted this about Don because I have always believed in his amazing talent and that one day it would be recognized.

I have been delighted to be a recipient of a copy of his very first printed work, and a holder of the most extensive collection of his work there is. I have been angered (one certain gallery in Anchorage and one in Hendersonville) for him at rejection, but recognize that those were small minded, short sighted folks that I now feel sorry for. I have been sad with him when he poured himself into a work and it wasn't recognized or chosen in a juried show.

I have rejoiced with him as he has now begun to achieve recognition and I know this mural saying is coming true. Prayers coming true. He *is* Talent and he is succeeding at the proper time. We remember that God decides what the proper time is, not us, and we are proof positive of His many blessings and fulfilling of promises.

I could and do write on and on about Don, but for the purposes of this book, it needs to have a cut off at some point. (Don complains I write faster than he can proof read - I have so much to say after years of being silent.)

Only now is Don finding the time to just stop worrying about working or production and create exactly as his passion leads him.

The best is coming yet so sit back and watch…

Love, Phoebe

"Behavior Analysis and Judgement."

One last note Phee asked to put in:

I can't be your friend anymore. Your lies hurt me deeply and your actions even more. I misunderstood that your definition of love came with lies, meanness, jealousy and manipulation. These are ugly things that I don't want in my life... so, "Later Dude!"

Regretfully but sincerely,
Phee

It is with great sadness that I add that between the writing time and publishing time, my friend Joyce Teters passed. She will be greatly missed for her love, her huge heart, her wisdom and her friendship by both Don and I.

For two very wise women, my Mom and my amazing Grandmother, I leave you with several of Eleanor Roosevelt's quotes:

"No one can make you feel inferior without your consent." "The giving of love is an education in itself." "Great minds discuss ideas; average minds discuss events; small minds discuss people." "Do what you feel in your heart to be right – for you'll be criticized anyway."

The End

Thanks for listening.

Made in the USA
Columbia, SC
01 October 2024